The American Moment

To Jim and Berna

Men are free when they are in a living homeland, not when they are straying and breaking away. Men are free when they are obeying some deep, inward voice of religious belief. Obeying from within. Men are free when they belong to a living, organic, *believing* community, active in fulfilling some unfulfilled, perhaps unrealised purpose. Not when they are escaping to some wild west. The most unfree souls go west, and shout of freedom. Men are freest when they are most unconscious of freedom. The shout is a rattling of chains, always was.

D. H. Lawrence, *The Spirit of Place*

Yet, America,
Your elvishness,
Your New England uncanniness,
Your western brutal faery quality.
My soul is half-cajoled, half-cajoled.

D. H. Lawrence, *The Evening Land*

The American Moment

American Poetry in the Mid-Century

Geoffrey Thurley

St. Martin's Press   New York

PS
323.5
T48
1978

Printed in Great Britain
Library of Congress Catalog Card Number 77-91071
ISBN 0-312-02884-9
First published in the United States of America in 1978

Note

This book is primarily a study of some American poetry—not *the* American poetry—written after the Second World War. It also argues a thesis, one which is neither pure sociology nor pure historicism, but a mixture of both. I want to make it quite clear now that I do not imagine that I have discussed all the poets active in this period who are worth discussing. A book of this kind which is not a survey or a coverage delimits its field by its own *raison d'être*. Naturally I should be prepared to defend the choice of the poets I have discussed. It would not be honest of me to say that the table of contents which follows represents a purely subjective series of decisions: if a majority of what history judges to be the major American poets of this period are not discussed in this book, then I shall have failed in several important respects. There are so many poets active in America at any given time that it is tempting to adapt to the situation the judgement W. B. Yeats passed on the Cheshire Cheese Club: we may not be quite sure which of them are good and which are bad, we only know there are too many of them. Moreover, the enthusiasm they generate tends to be excessive and indiscriminate. Robert Penn Warren and Allen Tate both wrote some good poetry; but who today would emphasize them in the same way as Cleanth Brooks did in *Modern Poetry and the Tradition*? And what of Randall Jarrell, Karl Shapiro, Delmore Schwartz, Richard Eberhart? I do not say that these are insignificant poets: writers like Schwartz and Shapiro are an important part of the literary life of their time, but they are not great or major poets, and there is a tendency for American poets to be oversold in their lifetime and left in oblivion afterwards.

Nevertheless, although I stand by the priorities expressed in the structure of this book, I regret that its rationale has not allowed me to discuss, for instance, the work of Gary Snyder, John Ashbery, Frank O'Hara and Jonathan Williams. I do not apologize, on the other hand, for not having tried to come up to date. Part of the argument of my final chapter is precisely that it is unhealthy to subject very new work to immediate critical analysis. Not only is the critic bound to lack the necessary perspective and to produce coverage rather than real criticism, but the poetry itself is too readily converted into 'literature'—it loses its dangerous and exciting qualities and thus fails to do its proper cultural work. There is also a danger of vicious feedback: the poet begins to write with the academic analyst in mind. Too short a time-gap between publication and academicization is bad for poetry and for criticism.

Adelaide, 1977   GT

Acknowledgements

The Publisher wishes to thank the following for permission to use copyright material:

Oxford University Press and the Liveright Publishing Corporation for extracts from Hart Crane's 'Chaplinesque', 'Recitative' and 'Sunday Morning Apples' from *The Complete Poems and Selected Letters and Prose*; Corinth Books Inc. for extracts from LeRoi Jones's 'The Turncoat', 'Look For You Yesterday, Here You Come Today', 'Way Out West' and 'For Hettie in her Fifth Month' from *Preface to a Twenty Volume Suicide Note*; Robert Bly and Jonathan Cape Ltd for extracts from Robert Bly's poems 'Taking the Hands', 'Driving Towards the Lac Qui Parle' and 'Where We Must Look for Help' from *Silence in the Snowy Fields* and André Deutsch Ltd and Robert Bly for extracts from Robert Bly's poems 'As the Asian War Begins', 'The Great Society', 'Hatred of Men with Black Hair', 'Written in Dejection near Rome' and 'Looking at New Fallen Snow' from *The Light Around the Body*; Jonathan Cape Ltd and George Braziller Inc., N.Y., for extracts from Charles Simic's 'Summer Morning', 'Marching', 'For the Victims', 'Invention of the Invisible', 'Invention of the Place' and 'Invention of Nothing' from *Dismantling the Silence*; the Estate of Charles Olson and Jonathan Cape Ltd for extracts from 'La Torre', 'Lower Field—Enniscorthy' and 'The Moon is the Number 18' from *Archaeologist of Morning*; John Weiners and Jonathan Cape Ltd for extracts from 'Deepsea', 'What Happened', 'Mermaid's Song' from *Selected Poems* and Cape Goliard Press for an extract from 'My Mother' from *Age of Pentacles*; Holt, Rinehart and Winston, Jonathan Cape Ltd and the Estate of Robert Frost for extracts from 'Tree at my Window' and 'Stopping By Woods on a Snowy Evening' from *The Poetry of Robert Frost*, ed. Edward Connery Lathem, © 1923, 1928, © 1969 by Holt, Rinehart and Winston, © 1951, © 1956 by Robert Frost. Faber & Faber Ltd and Farrar, Straus and Giroux Inc., N.Y., for extracts from John Berryman's '77 Dream Songs', © 1959, 1962, 1963, 1964 by John Berryman, from *Homage to Mistress Broadsheet*, © 1956 by John Berryman, from *His Toy, His Dream, His Rest*, © 1964, 1965, 1966, 1967, 1968 by John Berryman; and for extracts from Robert Lowell's *Life Studies*, © 1967, 1968, 1969, 1970 by Robert Lowell, from *Notebook*, © 1967, 1968, 1969, 1970 by Robert Lowell, and from *For the Union Dead*, © 1956, 1960, 1961, 1962, 1963, 1964 by Robert Lowell; A. D. Peters for an extract from Anne Sexton's 'The Sleeping Beauty' from *Transformations* and International Literary Management for extracts from Anne Sexton's 'Ringing the Bells' and 'You, Doctor Martin' from *Selected Poems* (1964); Oxford University Press for an extract from 'Impalpabilities' from Charles

Tomlinson's *A Peopled Landscape*; Michael McClure for his poems
'Peyote Poem' and 'Canoe: Explication'; Doubleday and Co. Inc. for
extracts from the following Theodore Roethke poems: 'The Auction',
© 1941 by Theodore Roethke, 'Forcing House', © 1946 by Theodore
Roethke, 'Slow Season', © 1939 by Theodore Roethke, 'Big Wind', ©
1947 by The United Chapters of Phi Beta Kappa; 'Moss Gathering' and
'Flower Dump', © 1946 by Editorial Publishers Inc., 'Words for the
Wind', © 1955 by Theodore Roethke, 'The Lost Son', © 1974 by
Theodore Roethke, 'A Field of Light', ©1948 by The Tiger's Eye, 'The
Shape of the Fire', © 1947 by Theodore Roethke and 'Song' from
The Collected Poems of Theodore Roethke, also Faber and Faber Ltd for the
Roethke poems acknowledged above; Faber and Faber Ltd and Harcourt
Brace Jovanovich Inc., N.Y., for Richard Wilbur's poems 'Stop', 'Beasts',
'Still, Citizen Sparrow', 'Castles and Distances', 'Caserta Garden', 'June
Light', 'For Ellen', 'Courtyard Thaw', 'Simile for Her Smile', 'Ceremony',
'A Dutch Courtyard', 'Flumen Tenebrarum' and 'A World Without
Objects is a Sensible Emptiness' from *Advice to a Prophet and Other Poems*,
The Beautiful Changes, Ceremony and Other Poems and *Things of This World*,
also for extracts from 'The Quaker Graveyard at Nantucket', 'As a Plane
Tree by the Water', 'The Drunken Fisherman' from *Lord Weary's Castle*,
© 1946, renewed 1974 by Robert Lowell, and an extract from 'Falling
Asleep Over the *Aeneid*' from *The Mills of the Kavanaughs*, © 1948, renewed
1976 by Robert Lowell; Jonathan Cape Ltd and New Directions Publish-
ing Corp., N.Y., for extracts from Denise Levertov's 'Matins I, II, III,
IV, V, VI, VII', 'Overland to the Islands', 'Six Variations', 'The Spring-
time', and 'Lonely Man' from *The Jacob's Ladder*, © 1957, 1960, 1961, by
Denise Levertov Goodman; Kenneth Rexroth's 'Folding a Shirt' from
The New British Poets, ed. Rexroth, Denise Levertov's 'To the Snake' and
'The Five-Day Rain' from *With Eyes at the Back of Our Heads*, © 1958,
1959 by Denise Levertov Goodman, and Michael McClure's 'For Robert
Greeley' from *Jaguar Skies*, © 1957 by Michael McClure; Little Brown
& Co., the Belknap Press, Harvard University Press and the Trustees
of Amherst College for extracts from Emily Dickinson's poem 'A Narrow
Fellow in the Grass' and 'My Life Closed Twice Before It Closed' from
The Poems of Emily Dickinson, ed. Thomas H. Johnson, © 1951 by the
President and Fellows of Harvard College and Little Brown and Company,
Boston, Mass.; Faber & Faber Ltd and Random House Inc., N.Y., for ex-
tracts from Wallace Stevens's poems 'Sunday Morning', 'Disillusionment of
Ten O'Clock' and 'Woman Looking at a Vase of Flowers' from *The
Collected Poems of Wallace Stevens*, and from 'Farewell Without a Guitar' from
Opus Posthumous, and for lines from W. H. Auden's 'Spain 1937' from
The English Auden and 'Paysage Moralisé' from *Collected Shorter Poems*;
Jonathan Cape and New Directions Inc., N.Y., for extracts from Kenneth
Rexroth's 'A Letter to William Carlos Williams' and 'The Signature of
All Things' from *The Rexroth Reader*; New Directions Publishing Corp.,

viii   *Acknowledgements*

N.Y., for extracts from Gregory Corso's 'Mutation of the Spirit' from *Elegiac Feelings American*, © 1970 by Gregory Corso, Robert Duncan's 'Bending the Bow', 'Such is the Sickness', 'Translation of Nerval's "El Desdichado" ' from *Bending the Bow*, © 1963, 1968 by Robert Duncan, 'Night Scenes' from *Roots and Branches*, © 1964 by Robert Duncan, and 'A Poem Beginning With a Line by Pindar' from *Opening of the Field*, © 1960 by Robert Duncan, and Robert Duncan for lines from 'Mother to Whom I Have Come Home'; extracts from Kenneth Patchen's 'Lowellville Cemetery: Twilight', 'What Splendid Birthdays', 'These Unreturning Destinies', 'Let Us Have Madness', 'The Rites of Darkness', 'All the Bright Foam of Talk' and 'Religion is that I Love You' from *Collected Poems*, © 1936; from William Carlos Williams's 'Every Day' from *Collected Later Poems*, © 1950 by Carlos Williams, and from Hilda Doolittle's 'Garden' and 'Evening' from *Collected Poems of H. D.*, © 1925, 1953 by Norman Holmes Pearson; City Lights for extracts from Allen Ginsberg's 'Lysergic Acid' and 'Kaddish' from *Kaddish and Other Poems*, © 1961 by Allen Ginsberg, and from '*HOWL*', 'In Back of the Real' and 'Sunflower Sutra' from '*HOWL*' *and Other Poems*, © 1956, 1959 by Allen Ginsberg; Faber and Faber Ltd and Mrs Myfanwy Thomas for an extract from 'Old Man and Lad's Love', and 'Adlestrop' from *Collected Poems* by Edward Thomas; Macmillan Inc., N.Y., for extracts from Marianne Moore's 'Marriage', 'To a Steamroller', 'The Fish', 'Nine Nectarines' and 'The Pangolin'; Rapp and Whiting Ltd for extracts from Galway Kinnell's 'The Avenue Bearing the Initial of Christ into the New World', 'Flower Herding on the Mountain' and 'The Supper After the Last'; the Viking Press for D. H. Lawrence's 'Man and Bat' and Philip Whalen for extracts from his poems 'Denunciation or Unfrocked Again', 'Souffle— take IX', 'Souffle—take III', 'Letter to Mme ETS, 2.1.58', 'Homage to Lucretius' and 'Sourdough Mountain Lookout'.

Contents

Part I

Out of Provincialism

Chapter 1

American Poetry
Sketch of a Theory

It is an interesting characteristic of American literature that it invites, and generally receives, critical attention that is either actually or implicitly mythopoeic in bias. D. H. Lawrence's *Studies in Classic American Literature*, for instance, which has exercised a profound influence on subsequent thinking about the subject, begins with a historical theory of *Homo Americanus*. More recent American and English essays on the subject—I think especially of Leslie Fiedler's *Love and Death in the American Novel*, of Tony Tanner's *Reign of Wonder*, of Stephen Spender's *Love–Hate Relations*[1]—have similarly attempted to base their analyses upon a ground-theory of the American soul or the American destiny. Few critics approach American literature directly, as a body of texts which have to take their chance on what they are and say. Often enough, American critics themselves show an underlying uncertainty about the real value of what they discuss. American poems and novels, we are to understand, cannot be approached as for instance English ones can: one has first to accept a mystique of 'Americanness',[2] which somehow waives the normal critical standards. But this defensiveness is also part of the wider cultural phenomenon: it seems impossible to accept America for and in itself. Both American and European writers have consistently sought to interpret America, to make it stand for something else—some ideal, or abstract property, or historical manifestation. From de Tocqueville to Sartre, from Blake to Lawrence, from Baudelaire to Kafka, European writers have been mythologizing America: America is either freedom, or materialism, or opportunity, or dreamland—anything but simply America. And from Melville and Whitman to Fitzgerald and Kerouac, American writers themselves have been reckless myth-makers, sketching image after image of the American soul, and arguably making it more difficult for

---

[1] Leslie Fiedler, *Love and Death in the American Novel* (London 1967); Tony Tanner, *The Reign of Wonder* (Cambridge 1965); Stephen Spender, *Love–Hate Relations* (London 1973).

[2] This is a provincial characteristic, in fact. One witnesses it in Australian literature as well.

America itself to accrete a national self within the mythology.[3] Hence, although Americanness is immediately recognizable, the American himself still seems curiously shadowy, with little real substance or essence, an empty mirror-image of his European forebears: the only tangible thing about Fitzgerald's Gatsby is the dream he tries to live.

At this stage, one becomes aware that the mythopoeic accounts of the American soul are basically sociological: the reason why it seems that one has to mythologize America as one cannot mythologize England or France, for instance, is simply that the Americas were in a way experimental societies, founded by self-exiles already possessed of a fully mature social and political personality. The Americas *were* mirror-images of Europe, as Saxon England, for instance, was never a mirror-image of northern Germany. For the mirror is the consciousness of the colonists, and if no such consciousness exists, there simply is no mirroring. That is, the Germanic tribes who settled in Britain brought with them only the most shadowy race-consciousness: they sacrificed nothing. The Englishmen who settled in North America, on the other hand, brought with them a fully developed national and political consciousness, an identity which they had to set about fracturing in order to justify their own behaviour and to prove themselves. Thus, America was a self-conscious society from the moment of its inception, and it is this self-consciousness which distinguishes the Anglo-Saxon colonists of the seventeenth from those of the seventh century. America could not 'become' itself, as did England or France, by simply growing into itself. America was already, we may say, fully grown at the time it began. We speak loosely of America as a 'young' society, but it is really no younger than England itself. Yet because it was a fragment of England displaced by three thousand miles of water and by the deliberate act of self-exile, the society established by the Puritans handed down to its inheritors two important characteristics; it was an alienated society and it was provincial.

Provincialism is an ambiguous and dangerous notion for a literary critic to use. The Vikings who carved dragons on the ships in which they attacked Roman Britain were not provincial—they were barbarian. America is often thought of as a barbarian society: but it is not barbarian, it is provincial—or it was. This is a fundamental and significant distinction. The provincial is provincial because he is geographically displaced from a culture or civilization whose superiority he acknowledges. The Goths were barbarian to Rome; but the man born of Roman parents in Bath or Aix-en-Provence was provincial to Rome. Americans were never barbarians (unless one regards the Indians as the real Americans), but always provincial. The question I am concerned with in this opening

---

[3] Daniel Boorstin (*The Image* (New York 1972)) has analysed the effect of the mass media on this problem. It is easy to see now that Americans are the victims of their own myths, which the media merely publicize.

chapter—and implicitly in the entire book—is, when and in what ways did American culture cease to be provincial?

There have been different answers to this question among American scholars, varying from 'Never', to the 'American Renaissance' (the mid-nineteenth century) or the decade of Ezra Pound and T. S. Eliot. But before any answer can be offered, it seems necessary first to give a rough indication of the way in which the notion of provincialism is being used. There seem to me to be three broad stages in the evolution of cultural provincialism. First, there is the stage of primary provincialism, in which the provincial society behaves with regard to the parent society rather as Congreve's country bumpkins behaved with regard to London: it gives a crude imitation of its manners. At the second stage the provincial society makes a conscious effort to establish an autonomous culture of its own: in this stage, the provincial society is sure enough of itself to be proud of its own accent, and it is more interested in itself than in the parent society. But at the second stage, which we could call the stage of proud provincialism, the provincial society still, deep down, acknowledges the spiritual and cultural superiority of the parent culture. Only at the third stage does the provincial society acquire its own centre of gravity—a gravitational mass which may well indeed begin to attract the old parent society. In art, the first stage of provincialism is marked by facile copies of metropolitan originals; the second by the emergence of a certain homespun originality, but also by a significant eclecticism, as the more exalted creative spirits look round for adequate instruments; the third by new forms and contents which are not only unique to that society (its provincialism had been in its own way unique) but which compare in depth and wholeness with the best of the parent society.

In the case of American writing (my account must initially be schematic almost to the point of absurdity), one must exclude from the stage of primary provincialism the poetry of Edward Taylor, for instance, who was simply an Englishman who happened to cross the Atlantic at the age of twenty-nine, long after his mind and poetic character were formed. We can say that Taylor would not have written *that* kind of poetry had he stayed in London or Cambridge, but this is not the same as saying he wrote 'American' poetry: the same thing could be said about an Englishman who went to the Hebrides, or into retirement on Dartmoor. First-stage provincialism includes poets like Joel Barlow and dramatists like Royall Tyler who simply made bad copies of English originals. The second stage—the so-called American Renaissance—brought with it an interesting hostility to Mother England that has less to do with the political events of the War of Independence and the Napoleonic Wars than with the natural process of growth. The provincial now tried to convince himself that what had seemed his failings were really his virtues: he was not crude, the parent culture was false; he was not naïve, he was innocent, and so on. Benjamin Franklin had sounded this note of provincial self-righteousness in the eighteenth century, but it took longer to percolate into art, where it had to be translated into form. Melville's absurd attempt in *Pierre* to prove that the American aristocracy is both superior to and more numerous than that of England is really less significant than the kind of novel *Pierre* itself is. An American proud of the achievement of Melville, Poe and Hawthorne might protest at their being called provincial, but provincial they nevertheless were.[4]

The provincialism of the American novel in the nineteenth century takes various forms, and this very variety is a provincial symptom: there is now—the raw provincial imitation of English forms having withered away with time and development—no dominant tradition, and a desperate improvisatory ingenuity replaces real formal control. Poe— with admittedly the 'disability' of an English mother and prolonged boyhood residence in England—wrote stories that take place nowhere, in a fantasy world in which a vaguely English aristocracy idles its time away in German castles. Poe's Tales do not even try to be American, yet he does not imitate English models. He plunders the Romantic poets and the Gothic novelists but what he contrives is desperately his own, and in this wayward novelty lies his provincialism. Fenimore Cooper on the face of it tries terribly hard to be American: what is more American than the white man/red brother mythology of the *Leatherstocking* novels? Yet Cooper's mythology was more impressive to an Englishman like D. H. Lawrence than to an American like Mark Twain. Twain knew that Cooper's novels were as unreal as *Hiawatha*—and in the same sort of way: they took towards the 'Indians' the sort of Romantic attitude that Melville decisively rejected with regard to the Polynesians in *Omoo* and *Typee*. Furthermore, Cooper's 'style' is as elaborately un-American as his subject-matter is unreal, a sometimes successful but usually laborious imitation of Scott. Both style and content go together as strikingly provincial, 'literary' products of a small-town mind.

Indeed, a lack of correspondence between what he actually sees and what he imagines he sees is an often important characteristic of the provincial writer. We do not have to hold a naïvely naturalistic view of the novel to find something wrong with Poe's never-never land and Fenimore Cooper's imaginary Frontier. Lionel Trilling, I think, put his finger on the truth in his essay 'Manners, Morals and the novel'. There was in American life, Trilling argues,

> no sufficiency of means for the display of a society of manners, no opportunity for the novelist to do his job of searching out reality, not enough complication of appearance to make the job interesting.[5]

America was, in other words, simply too jejune and uninteresting a

---

[4] See also Henry James's *The American Scene* (London 1907).
[5] 'Manners, morals and the novel', in *The Liberal Imagination* (London 1952), 213.

society to generate the sort of experience that makes for good novels. The writers of the parent culture (Europe in the wider sense) provided the models for American writers, and it was inevitable that they should produce narratives with the same shape and presumed intentions— mirroring society, analysing motives. Yet there is something of a Franklinesque ingenuity about even *Moby Dick*, for instance—which challenges comparison with the greatest books—that makes it impossible for us to regard it in the same light as *Great Expectations* or *Madame Bovary* or *Fathers and Sons*. And indeed *Moby Dick* is not really a novel at all, but rather a saga, overburdened at times with moralizings and philosophical digressions, a fantastic mix of Old Testament prophecy, whaling manual, marine tall story, Shakespearian soliloquy and Miltonic rhetoric. In this hybrid heterogeneity, *Moby Dick*—though sublime at its best moments— is emphatically provincial, and in a more important and interesting way than either Poe's Tales or Cooper's novels: for *Moby Dick* demonstrates that the first-rate talent in a provincial society resorts to eclecticism in its efforts to consummate its vision, because the society he lives in and the self he has inherited are neither rich nor strong enough to nourish great art. Hawthorne is equally eccentric. *The Scarlet Letter* is a static scenario or oratorio, a mock-up of society in which the characters enter in Puritan dress. It is also, as D. H. Lawrence, observed, a great work:

> It is a marvellous allegory. It is to me one of the greatest allegories in all literature.[6]

But it is not—in a sense that may be inferred from Trilling, and which I would be prepared to argue myself—a novel, and it is provincial. The American novelists of this time fail in that they are unable to relate their moral concerns to the lives they lead themselves or to the lives led by others around them. Melville takes to the high seas—off them he is a prolix bore; Hawthorne resorts to an archaic picturesqueness in order to convey 'eternal' verities through a mechanical and outdated symbolism. The historical critique of Puritanism is really in itself picturesque, and does not refer to social realities of either the seventeenth or the nineteenth century. In this, it partially succeeds: like *Moby Dick* it is a work of curious originality, whose very success derives from its eschewal of its own contemporaneity.

The curious originality—eccentric yet strangely wise—of these works is wholly predictable of major talents working in a still provincial society. Yet the writer who best typifies this second stage of American provincialism is perhaps Mark Twain. There is a tendency among certain high minds in America to overrate *Huckleberry Finn*—to see it on the same plane as Homer, for instance. This is silly, and obscures the real signifi- cance of Twain's proud provincialism: it was surely just because he was

[6] 'Hawthorne and *The Scarlet Letter*', in *Selected Literary Criticism* (London 1956), 363.

so much less great a writer than either Melville or Hawthorne that Twain was able to strike out on his own, into the backwoods, and create in the process the first authentically American idiom in either prose or verse. The vernacular narrative of *Huckleberry Finn* was original in a different way from anything I have so far considered: Melville and Hawthorne were eclectic and—in a specific sense—eccentric, where Twain is original and yet wholly himself, with none of that bookish stiffness that characterizes his greatest contemporaries. The significance of his achievement is, as I say, obscured if we let ourselves be carried away by the indulgent eulogies of certain New England intellectuals: *Huckleberry Finn* is not a Homeric saga, it is not a great work of world literature: it is a more or less wholly successful boyhood story—more of a novel than anything by Melville or Hawthorne in fact—but nevertheless the work of a much less important talent. The paradox is this: in a literature that is still immature, the greatest talents will necessarily produce work that is flawed, eccentric and eclectic, because they are striving to say things which cannot yet be said in the voice of the present society; unified and natural success will be achieved by the secondary talent—the man who knows his limitations and can satisfactorily express himself in the 'idiom of the people'. *Huckleberry Finn is* a better book than *Moby Dick*, more closely organized, more homogeneous in idiom; but it achieves its success precisely in the absence of more 'important' things to say. And this is characteristic of provincial literature.

These considerations help us, I think, to get into focus the real problems presented in American poetry. For to say that a literature is provincial is to say more than that its masterpieces will be flawed, and its successes of secondary weight. It is to say that the society in which that literature is grounded is itself incapable of 'uttering itself' as Jacobean England 'uttered itself' through Shakespeare, Middleton, Webster and Jonson: it is incapable as yet of honouring its own deepest human requirements. It is just this capacity I am concerned with in trying to describe American provincialism in the nineteenth century. A provincial literature, like a provincial society, is one that has not come into itself, one that has not acquired its own centre of gravity. The third stage of provincialism indeed arrives when the society does acquire its own centre of gravity, and the pendulum swings—in our case, from one side of the Atlantic to the other. My concern is with this stage. We have to go below the surface: I am not, that is, concerned with *accent*. W. H. Auden, I think, confused the two things—accent and centre of gravity—in introducing a collection of American poetry:

> One often hears it said that only in this century have the writers of the United States learned to stand on their own feet and be truly American, that, previously, they were slavish imitators of British literature. Applied to the general reading public and academic circles,

this has a certain amount of truth but, so far as the writers themselves are concerned, it is quite false.[7]

('British literature', incidentally, is a new one on me: perhaps only an Englishman long domiciled in America could perpetrate such an atrocity.) The generalization Auden now offers perfectly describes cultural provincialism: 'From Bryant on there is scarcely one American poet whose work, if unsigned, could be mistaken for that of an Englishman.' Of course not: an Englishman could not be provincial in Bryant's or Lanier's way. The provincial is easily recognizable as such; the question that matters is obscured by Auden's somewhat loose phrase, 'truly American'. What is it to be 'truly American'?

Whitman was undoubtedly a great master of rhythm and word-colour, but the very fluency with which he undertook the debate and invocation of Death, or Universal Love—the air of sheer facility in poems like 'Out of the Cradle Endlessly Rocking'—mark him off from his great European contemporaries. Now facility, as I am using the term here, is not just a characteristic of style. Tennyson, for instance, was as facile in one sense as Longfellow; he was frequently facile in the pejorative sense, but his gift for easy euphonies did not prevent him, at moments of maximum stress, from writing like this:

> Dark house, by which once more I stand
> Here in the long unlovely street,
> Doors, where my heart was used to beat
> So quickly, waiting for a hand,
>
> A hand that can be clasp'd no more—
> Behold me, for I cannot sleep,
> And like a guilty thing I creep
> At earliest morning to the door.
>
> He is not here; but far away
> The noise of life begins again,
> And ghastly thro' the drizzling rain
> On the bald street breaks the blank day.
>
> (Tennyson, *In Memoriam* VII)

This is not facile, nor is it merely felicitous, though it testifies to a technical expertise difficult to match anywhere else in Victorian literature (one would have to resort to Heine, I think, for adequate comparison). Tennyson has been stopped in his tracks here, but the technique is at the service of the man: he speaks out of himself, and he speaks for all of us. If we wanted to define a literary classic, or rather to re-attempt the definition in the wake of so many distinguished failures, it seems to me

[7] Introduction to *The Faber Book of Modern American Verse* (London 1956), 9.

that we should have to start by trying to describe the way in which a great poem or novel or play is able to speak about everything in life (the 'human condition') without ever ceasing to be rooted in a particular life. It is a capacity easy enough to recognize even at a distance of half a millennium in Walther von der Vogelweide's 'Elegie'; it is there in Pushkin's 'Remembrance', in Baudelaire's 'Recueillement'; it is there in the *Notturni* of Leopardi, and in Hölderlin's 'Das Liniensleben'. It is there in Tennyson's greatest lyric moments, in 'Break, Break, Break', 'Tears, Idle Tears', and 'Dark House'. In all these examples the defining quality seems to me to be a lambent ordinariness; in speaking about the present impasse, the poet refers to his whole life. And it is a quality that depends upon the poet's being able to speak in some organically connected way for the whole man within him. The note of sublime pathos (of 'divine despair' in Tennyson's phrase) derives from a rootedness in life which only a long history can bring with it; there is a sense of human community in it which is historical as well as local. Baudelaire speaks for all Frenchmen in 'Recueillement', and the Frenchman becomes synonymous with mankind in all contexts.

If we turn from these examples of 'divine despair' to Whitman, it is this wholeness-in-depth, this rootedness of the harmony, this sense of community coexistent with the emotions of the individual man, which is missing. Whitman does not speak for all men, nor to all men, but *at* all men: he is always on the platform. This is why his greatest poem is an elegy for a public figure, not for a friend or lover. There is no doubting the genuineness of the grief in 'When Lilacs Last in the Dooryard Bloomed'. But it seems significant that Whitman should excel in this mode, so that although it does not occur to us to question his sincerity, it cannot help striking us that this kind of emotion—public, even publicized, faintly dramatized—is all that he had to offer. The man's very depths are public. At a point in 'Song of Myself', indeed, Whitman admits that he is addressing a meeting: 'It is time to explain myself: let us stand up.' The quality of classic poetry lies in its ability to universalize the most inward self. The truth is that Whitman had no self to universalize. This is nowhere more evident than in the vacuous generalities of 'Song of Myself', a poem which lies in its very title. 'Song of Myself' is mythopoeic in a way that more or less abandons reality altogether. No poet ever wrote more freely about himself without ever disclosing his real self—except, that is, by accidental glimpses. For 'Song of Myself' contradicts itself, and in its insoluble contradictions lies its flawed authenticity. Nor do I refer to the famous profession of honesty when Whitman declares his intention to contradict himself ('Do I contradict myself? Very well then I contradict myself'). On the contrary, that is the poem's most inauthentic moment—its cleverest insurance policy. I mean rather those near-hysterical crises, when the superman poet gives way to a scared virgin:

On all sides prurient provokers stiffening my limbs,
Straining the udder of my heart for its withheld drip,
Behaving licentious toward me, taking no denial,
Depriving me of my best as for a purpose,
Unbuttoning my clothes and holding me by the bare waist,
Deluding my confusion with the calm of the sunlight and
    pasture fields,
Immodestly sliding the fellow-senses away. . . .

('Song of Myself', 28)

This revelation is certainly honest—more honest, probably, than Whitman was aware. But it is inconsistent with the universal man who strides through the rest of the poem, and these contradictions can't lie cheek by jowl with each other. The man who greets all pain, all suffering, all evil, cannot be the same as the frightened virgin surrounded by 'prurient provokers'. One of them is fibbing. The truth is that Whitman was fractured. He could welcome Death, All Men, Love, the Universe—but when he was touched he squealed: 'O Christ! My fit is mastering me.'

We are not here concerned with the psychology of a single man, but with the limitations of a particular society. Tennyson was a self-contradictory man, as Carlyle saw, a man who left much of himself out of the poetry. But when he was speared by grief he could honour it and show us the whole foundation of the personal life. Nothing is left out here:

Dear as remembered kisses after death,
And sweet as those by hopeless fancy feign'd
On lips that are for others; deep as love,
Deep as first love, and wild with all regret,
O Death in Life, the days that are no more.

('Tears, Idle Tears')

It is this dimension that is lacking from Whitman. Man is rooted in society. Our conception of literature must be very shallow indeed if it does not enforce on us certain correlations between cultural and personal factors. If we place any high valuation on literature it must be because it enables man to understand himself better and to know his own deeper springs. Whitman's shortcomings are the shortcomings of a provincial society. All poetry is a balance of inward intonation and outward form; the forms of verse and language are public, but they become capable of infinite adaptation to the private voice. At the time Whitman was writing in America and Browning in England, English verse had acquired the highest possible degree of naturalness and poise in verse speech. Behind Browning lay Shelley, and behind Shelley lay Wordsworth with his august ease and subtle balance of rhetoric and naturalness. Behind Wordsworth lay the conversational poetry of Cowper and Dyer, as well as the relaxed elegance of Pope and Johnson, who had brought into verse the civilized speech of a great European capital. There are dangers—we shall come across them later—in a too simple-minded dogma of speech-tone in verse, and it is not without significance that American poetics has been as much preoccupied with speech in verse as with tradition. Speech in poetry is always an artifice, but it is an artifice capable of greater or lesser flexibility, greater or lesser emotional compass. The decisive factor in the emergence of the high naturalness of English poetry was the prestige and achievement of the Elizabethan drama, with its infinitely adaptable and refined blank verse. (We can verify this by turning to French literature for comparison: it was not until Hugo's *Hernani*, i.e. after the deaths of the second wave of English Romantic poets, that France began to shake off the tyranny of Corneille's alexandrine.)

What we miss when we return to Whitman after sampling Browning—the air of a man speaking to men, and from within himself, confident that his slightest nuance will be picked up—is not something over which the poet himself could exercise any control, short of crossing the Atlantic at an early age, as Henry James was to do, and immersing himself in the cultural stream of Europe. For although forms and ideas may be transmitted over long distances, the mind of a 'civilization' cannot. This is what made D. H. Lawrence postulate the 'spirit of place',[8] and it is what made American painters cross the Atlantic for a quarter of a century after the masterworks of 'modernist' painting were readily available in America. Whitman lacks the natural civilized speech of Browning, so he had to fabricate his own—a sophisticated pot-pourri of the English Romantic poets and the Old Testament prophets in King James English. It should be emphasized right away that by crossing the Atlantic as his contemporary Whistler did, Whitman would have sacrificed more than he might have gained; my intention here is descriptive, not evaluative. Whitman was possibly a greater poet than either Tennyson or Browning, but his poetry was different from theirs in ways that are only partially indicated in speaking of his greater 'crudity' or 'freedom' (according to whether you are trying to denigrate or exalt him). As a matter of fact he is the reverse of a crude poet, he is subtle and fine in ways that Browning for instance is not; nor is he particularly 'free'. No poetry is free, T. S. Eliot pointed out, for the man who wants to do a good job. The idiom once mastered, Whitman's long line is no easier to sustain than Browning's blank verse or Tennyson's quatrain.

The ways in which Whitman benefited by remaining American are philosophical—concerned with meaning and intention. But to describe his poetry aright involves attention to his emotional register, to the things he could say and the things he could not. For the moment I am interested in the things he could not say because he was American, not because he was Walt Whitman. For his highly eclectic idiom could only be sustained

8 'The spirit of place', in *Studies in Classic American Literature* (London 1923).

by ignoring or avoiding the bedrock states of human consciousness. Whitman writes off whole areas of doubt and conflict by the simple expedient of claiming acquaintance with them all:

> Creeds and schools in abeyance,
> Retiring back a while sufficed at what they are, but never
>   forgotten,
> I harbor for good or bad, I permit to speak at every
>   hazard,
> Nature without check with original energy.

('Song of Myself')

His familiarity with the Absolute is, like Emerson's, unconvincing because too facilely acquired. All this is I think explicable in terms less of the man's personal psychology than of the state of American culture at the time he was writing. He was arguably a greater poet than America had the right to expect at that time, but we must acknowledge his limitations: he could not get the whole man in; he never sounds the whole chord, the depths and heights together, as Wordsworth does at the end of the *Prelude* or in 'Intimations of Immortality', or Keats in the Odes, or Leopardi in the *Canti*.

This could be explained quite simply by saying that there was and could have been no American Browning. Ezra Pound showed his acumen in nothing so much as in his instinctive recognition of Browning as a forbear ('Ich stamm' aus Browning', as he wrote to a German correspondent). To speak the kind of poetic speech Browning spoke, with his civilized intensity and his human passion, is to have knowledge of oneself through long habit of living within a particular social structure, and of seeing oneself reflected in its literary and philosophical products. The inevitable absence of such a familiarity with the self-in-society and the society-in-the-self so characteristic of American literature resulted in the one hand in Whitman's eloquent imitations of intimacy and on the other in the sing-song of Emily Dickinson.

Now it was Dickinson, not Whitman, who served as a focus of aspiration for American poets in the second quarter of this century. There is no doubting the intense brilliance of her mind. If we turn to her from the padded stuffiness of her American contemporaries (and many of her English ones), she seems radiantly alive and 'modern'. Yet once again it seems important to be clear about what she actually achieved, and how it affects us. For if Whitman based his rhetoric on the Old Testament, she based her anti-rhetoric on the Church Hymnal—or on the nursery rhymes of her childhood. One could confirm the general point illustrated here—the inability of American poets in the nineteenth century to create a verse idiom sufficiently flexible and sufficiently rooted in personality to sound the whole human chord—by turning to the sensational jangle of Poe (substituting metre for rhythm and onomatopoeia for music) or to the 'poetic' manner of Bryant or Longfellow. But Dickinson is so much better a poet than these, so much more interesting and vital, that her failure to produce a natural expressive rhythm is the more striking. I say failure, suggesting an abortive attempt. But this is misleading; there was no 'attempt'—there was only the provincial situation and a series of more less successful strategies to meet it. One could not 'improve' on Dickinson's twenty or thirty best poems; but it is, once more, essential to recognize the nature of the achievement represented in them. These sparks of energy, these detonations of sensibility, these clusters of perceptions—do they ever amount to statements about life in which we can lose our own personalities and feel ourselves being expressed and extended? The poet has to persuade us to enter into his voice, to melt into his thoughts, to lose ourselves in speaking (whether aloud or silently) his language. Now Dickinson's sprightly sing-song lacks the power to do this:

> My life closed twice before it closed
> It yet remains to see
> If immortality disclose
> A third event for me.
>
> ('My Life Closed Twice Before It Closed')

At her worst, she is portentous, making her points as a preacher might make them in a sermon. At her best she has no voice at all, she lacks music, simply, and lacking music, lacks also the structural manifestation of music, architecture. It is not accidental that Dickinson's *Collected Poems* is an endless sequence of brief poems: one cannot call them 'lyric', for the essence of the lyric is precisely the musical utterance of the personality. They are rather sheafs of insights—things seen with particularity and love—bound together, often, by a glib theology.

To illustrate by contrast what is meant by her lack of music, I give the following instance of a poem where Dickinson does achieve some measure of music and architecture:

> Grand go the years in the crescent above them;
> Worlds scoop their arcs, and firmaments row,
> Diadems drop and Doges surrender,
> Soundless as dots on a disc of snow.
>
> ('Safe in their Alabaster Chambers')

The inexplicable felicity of the final image here continues the sound-pattern of the preceding three lines, thus obscuring the fact that such sonic support is rare in Dickinson. It is, anyway, the image of a 'small' sound which she has so happily hit off: the general air of 'grandeur' has something playful about it. Dickinson is aping the grand manner, almost like a child putting on a soldier's uniform. I do not dispute a certain success in the attempt; it is the uncharacteristic nature of the attempt I am concerned with. If we compare it with almost any other of her better poems, the difference is clear:

> A narrow fellow in the grass
> Occassionally rides;
> You may have met him—did you not?
> His notice sudden is.
>
> ('A Narrow Fellow in the Grass')

This is the 'real' Dickinson, the one buried under the sound of the other poem, and the real Dickinson is constitutionally prone to botch her rhymes, drop her rhythm and force syntax to jump through hoops of expediency.

Dickinson was a poet of genius, but she never—thank God—tried to produce a 'major' poem.

The poets of the nineteenth century in America fail to speak with that inwardness and flexibility that is the hallmark of fully mature poetry. We see in the various idioms of Poe, Whitman and Dickinson desperate or felicitous strategies designed to fill a vacuum—the poetic equivalents of the novelists' various eclecticisms. John Malcolm Brinnin—in a valiant attempt to describe the course of American poetry—defined the various strategies like this:

> Our poetry was a matter of sentimentality, stodginess, and foolish roistering bravado. Poe had found his inspiration in the fantastic. Whitman had found his inspiration in the future.[9]

The question Brinnin now poses brings us to the threshold of the generation I now wish to discuss myself: 'Why,' he asks, 'may not someone have asked, why would not a poetic programme based on the realities of the present have seemed a logical way out of these doldrums?'[10]

Unfortunately Mr Brinnin goes on to dismiss (in terms I should be pleased to accept) the only poetry of the period under discussion that was based on 'the realities of the present'—the homespun coarse-grained regionalism of Sandburg, Masters and Lindsay. The poetry of the Mid-West poets was, indeed, limited in the way Brinnin says it was, mistaking 'vigour' for 'strength' and lacking 'critical insight'—replacing, as Brinnin says so appositely, 'provincialism polite' with 'provincialism boisterous'. But if Sandburg, for instance, was not concerned with 'the realities of the present', it is hard to know how to attach any meaning to the phrase. The fact is, surely, that 'realism' is an early characteristic of what I have called proud provincialism: the proud provincial—like Mark Twain—scorns to resort to the sort of 'unreal' strategies of Melville or Whitman, just as *they* had scorned to copy slavishly the literary *mores* of England. The 'solution' to the cultural immaturity that forced major talents into

[9] 'Modern American poetry', in *New World Writing* (New York 1954), 230.
[10] Idem.

eclecticism was not, then, realism. Indeed there was not any 'solution' at all, because there was no problem, only the facts of history, society and time.

In fact, Mr Brinnin makes no more of the plea for establishing a poetics based on 'the realities of the present'. Having dismissed those poets who tried to do just this, he turns to French poetry, and argues that American poetry matured when it fell under the influence of Symbolism. That is, in the year 1912, the year of the foundation of *Poetry Chicago* (and the year before the Armory Show in New York). Symbolism, Brinnin argues, catalysed American poetry, so that 'awakening self-consciously and uncertainly to a sense of national culture, we nevertheless realized we had come of age; when we knew that in several fields we could assess and be responsible for a peculiarly American art; when we could see that, after many years of one-way traffic across the Atlantic, the number of creative talents we attracted was greater than the number we drove into exile'.[11] The dangers in the phrase 'a peculiarly American art' have already been touched on: Auden had made the same error as I think Brinnin makes here in speaking of Bryant and others. There is no doubt, for instance, that the painting of many Americans working in America at this period was 'peculiarly American': John Marin, Marsden Hartley, Arthur Dove and Morris Graves, for instance, are 'peculiarly American' in ways that could be analysed formally—in terms of design, texture and pigment—not in terms of subject-matter. Their 'Americanness' therefore is different from the homespun realism of Ben Shahn, Andrew Wyeth or Edward Hopper. But it is no less provincial.

In point of fact, Brinnin's mistake parallels Auden's: where Auden mistook the first period of provincialism for the second, Brinnin mistakes the second for the third: he is identifying the new sophistication of the imagist generation with full cultural autonomy. It is a common feeling among American critics that American poetry did indeed 'come of age', as Brinnin puts it, in the decades that followed the establishment of *Poetry Chicago*. Brinnin himself quotes a practitioner of those years, Conrad Aiken: 'American poetry which begins with Emily Dickinson is so varied, so rich and new, as to compare favourably with any but the greatest spans in the whole history of English literature.'[12] This claim certainly seems inflated now, but it does not seem absurd: and the achievement, or rather the range of abilities represented in the achievement, of these years is such as to suggest at first sight that American poetry had indeed outgrown provincialism. In the case of its two greatest products, indeed, there can be no question of doubt. Neither Ezra Pound nor T. S. Eliot produced poetry in any sense provincial. But their first mature poetry was written in England, and, as we have seen, the conscious intention to join the parent society, the physical immersion in it, transfigures the artist. Eliot and Pound are, as poets, no more American

[11] 'Modern American poetry', 221.
[12] Idem.

than Whistler or Henry James; they are no more American, that is, than El Greco was Cretan. And no less, certainly: the mind that is fertilized is as important as the culture that fertilizes. But I am not concerned here with awarding points in an international culture league: I am concerned only with the nature of American poetry. And for that purpose, the difference between the mind that is fertilized by winds crossing the ocean, and the mind that flies direct to the source—and stays there—is of supreme importance. It is this difference that exists between the poetry of Pound and Eliot and that of their most talented compatriots who remained in America, even when they exiled themselves to Paris for a while.

A clue to its nature is surely found in the critical preoccupations of Pound and Eliot. For if they are Europeans in their poetry, Pound and Eliot are Americans in their criticism. Yvor Winters wrote retrospectively that 'For about fifteen years, Pound was the most influential critic in American letters . . . and when he was replaced it was by his disciple Eliot, who did little save restate his ideas in a more genteel style.'[13] And the main theme of Pound's criticism, as of T. S. Eliot's, is tradition. Eliot in fact specifically argued, in his most influential essay, for precisely the view of cultural insemination I have presented above: 'Tradition and the individual talent' states that 'No poet, no artist of any sort, has his complete meaning alone.'[14] Pound is far more wayward than Eliot: indeed his main critical contention is the hopelessly 'Romantic' one that Europe has lost contact with some Romance purity: it is a Romantic performance we witness in *Make it New,* in *Guide to Kulchur* and *How to Read,* turning China into Cathay and dreaming wistfully of a never-never land of lutes and social harmony. What is more to the point, it is specifically the performance of a provincial—a tourist, and an American one at that. John Malcolm Brinnin once again gives simple expression to this central preoccupation in American culture:

> To be intimate with our history, to have it, so to speak, in our bones and our blood, is a wish that every poet feels with passion.[15]

—every American poet, let us add: the idea of an English poet or a French poet 'wishing' to be intimate with his history! Isn't it enough to be English or French?

Significantly, Brinnin goes on to admit that Hart Crane, the poet under discussion at the point where the quotation occurs, broke under the effort to 'resolve by the power of will what can only be resolved by history.'[16] This seems to me an extraordinarily deep insight into the American predicament—an insight, in fact, which cancels its context. Brinnin has been arguing that with Crane's generation American poetry has fully matured: 'our poets no longer fear foreign influences,' he says

[13] *The Function of Criticism* (Denver 1957), 12.
[14] 'Tradition and the individual talent', in *Selected Essays* (London 1953), 15.
[15] Brinnin, 'Modern American poetry', 233.
[16] Idem.

(writing in 1954), 'but accept them in whatever ways they may serve to modify or expand their ideas or their techniques.'[17] Certainly, Brinnin is right in pointing to the importance of the new French influence on the poets of the period. Pound found imagism ready-made when, a naïvely fluent Pre-Raphaelite, he first crossed the Atlantic; he was the borrower, not the lender, and there was nothing he had to tell the London of F. S. Flint, T. E. Hulme and Ford Madox Ford, who had already decisively rejected both the jingoism of Newbolt and the nightingales-and-roses of the post-Swinburnian school. Imagism had already been 'invented' by Hulme and Flint, free verse had been familiar since Henley and Arnold; French symbolism, through Lionel Johnson and Arthur Symons, had long since had its influence on English writing. Arthur Waley had already shaped the now long-standing awareness of Chinese poetry. But if Ezra Pound really had little to offer London, he had much to offer America, and it is important that at this period Americans—for the first time, arguably—went to Continental Europe rather than to England for their inspiration. The tone and, more important, the ideas of the more advanced American poetry of the 1920s came from Paris, not London. But what was not, in John Malcolm Brinnin's words, to be resolved by the power of the will, was equally not to be resolved by the power of influence. History still had some resolving of its own to do; American poets of the 1920s are sophisticated enough to know that it is in French rather than English poetry that their own immediate interest lies, but they are really only replacing one pap by another.

We can see this in a number of superficial things. Wallace Stevens, for instance, often seems to be speaking French with an American accent. I do not mean the juggling with French words ('le monocle de mon oncle') so much as an approximation towards the refined materialism of painters like Vuillard:

> Complacencies of the peignoir, and late
> Coffee and oranges in a sunny chair,
> And the green freedom of a cockatoo
> Upon a rug mingle to dissipate
> The holy rush of ancient sacrifice.

('Sunday Morning')

Hart Crane's debt to Laforgue is more interesting; it is the structure of attitudes—though curiously gutted of their significance—not mere *bon ton*, that is French in these lines:

> We make our meek adjustments,
> Contented with such random consolations
> As the wind deposits
> In slithered and too ample pockets.

('Chaplinesque')

[17] 'Modern American poetry', 234.

Now openness to relevant influence, like the instinct to know which influence is relevant, is a hallmark of mature literature. Such an interplay had been going on between England and France since Chaucer and Guillaume de Machaut. But the influence and counter-influence that take place between two mature civilizations is different from what obtains between an older culture and one that has hitherto played the role of satellite. Our interest being when America ceased to be a satellite, we can see that it is an important stage in its evolution when it went beyond England for guidance. But if the best American poetry of the 1920s is too poised and refined comfortably to be called provincial, it has still not, I believe, acquired its own centre of gravity. Of this fact, the French influence is only symptomatic. What is really more important is the weight and wholeness of what was achieved. Stevens and Crane are polar opposites between whom we can place e. e. cummings, Marianne Moore and Robert Frost as being the most accomplished poets of the decade. Stevens's *Harmonium* (1923), Frost's *New Hampshire* (1923), cummings's *Tulips and Chimneys* (1923), Moore's *Observations* (1924) and Crane's *White Buildings* (1924) contain work of real brilliance and musicality, witty and penetrating by turns. Yet I wish to argue that there is lacking from them either the full weight of major literature or the wholeness of mind, the orientation simply, to make the 'weight' tell. What is missing can be illustrated, by contrast, with some contemporary English volumes— Lawrence's *Birds, Beasts and Flowers* (1923), Hardy's *Winter Words* (1927), the posthumous poems of Wilfred Owen (*Poems*, 1920), Edward Thomas (*Poems*, 1920), and Isaac Rosenberg (*Poems*, 1922).

To some extent, the difference between the respective sets of poems can be described as I have already described the difference between Whitman and his European contemporaries. What is lacking from American poetry has been described by an exiled American as follows: 'There is in a good deal of American intellectual, artistic production (recent painting may be the challenging exception) a characteristic near-greatness, a strength just below the best.'[18] Nowhere is the truth of George Steiner's dictum more emphatically borne out than in the case of the best American poetry of the 1920s. For is there not a sense that the brilliance, the sheer facility of Stevens's 'Sunday Morning' or Frost's 'Apple Picking' has been acquired at too little cost, that it precludes the more profound and troubling involvement of the personality that makes for great art, involvement that depends, I have argued, on a power of self-identification of which America was as yet incapable? Is not the poise come by too easily, in the absence of that clogging sense of inherited traditions which hung so heavily about English poets at this time, and which justified Pound in his looking elsewhere?

In the case of Wallace Stevens, for instance, it is not merely the French

---

[18] George Steiner, *In Bluebeard's Castle* (London 1971), 86.

accent that alerts one to an air of excessive ease, but the inability of the
poet to sound authentically the deeper chords of human experience:

> We reason of these things, with later reason
> And we make of what we see, what we see clearly
> And have seen, a place dependent on ourselves.
>
> ('Notes Towards a Supreme Fiction')

The tone of this passage—it is wholly typical of Stevens's longer
philosophical disquisitions—seems to me slightly complacent, portentous,
the tone almost of the professional after-dinner speaker; it is in striking
contrast to the brilliance of his 'lesser' pieces—those iridescent variations,
subtle semantic jugglings that succeed, often enough, in confounding the
mind into a new conception of its experience:

> Only here and there, an old sailor,
> Drunk and asleep in his boots,
> Catches tigers
> In red weather.
>
> ('Disillusionment of Ten O'clock')

It is in the swift wit of such pieces, not in those stolid and ultimately
uninformative ruminations on imagination and reality, that the best of
Stevens is to be found. An interesting instance of his better and his worse
manners (as I see them) lying side by side is his late poem 'Farewell
Without a Guitar'. Here Stevens is consciously practising the mythopoeic
mode of major poetry: the poet, and the man in the poet, is making his
exit from the human stage:

> Spring's bright paradise has come to this.
> Now the thousand-leaved green falls to the ground
> Farewell my days,
> The thousand-leaved red
> Comes to this thunder of light
> At its autumnal terminal—

This is a note one has not met earlier: an approximation to the grave
'personal' voice of the kind of poet he had never tried to be. It succeeds
in imparting a certain weight to the utterance (though the spring–
autumn antithesis does not stand up to repeated reading, especially if one
has Crane's 'Pastorale' in the back of one's mind for comparison). The
lines that follow build subtly and strongly on the implications of the
'thunder of light' and the 'autumnal terminal' (with its daring suggestion
of the bus-station, throbbing with engines):

> A Spanish storm,
> A wide, still Aragonese
> In which the horse walks home without a rider,
> Head down.

That 'wide, still Aragonese' is an essay in metaphysical movement superior, in my view, to Hart Crane's much-praised 'adagios of islands'. Yet its subtle skill throws too much weight on the abstract rumination that follows, a pastiche rather than a summation of Stevens's 'philosophical' vein:

> The reflections and repetitions,
> The blows and buffets of fresh senses
> Of the rider that was,
> Are a final construction,
> Like glass and sun, of male reality
> And of that other and her desire.

This is arguably the most concentrated attempt Stevens ever made to relate those somewhat otiose disembodied speculations about the imagination to real human experience—to suffering and aging and dying. It seems to me to fail ultimately. Only Stevens could have conceived and articulated the 'wide still Aragonese': the last lines might come from the pen of one of his lesser imitators. The attempt to realize a personal myth, in the late allusion to the Blue Guitar in the title, seems dangerously close to self-importance. As so often, the American poet's attempt to speak from a personal centre results in rhetoric: 'Farewell, my days' reads like pastiche, pastiche of the classical European elegy. One thinks of Nashe's 'Adieu! Farewell earth's bliss!', of Walther von der Vogelweide's 'Elegie', or of Heine's 'Mein Tag war heiter'.

These are gestures backed up by an assumed, unconscious personal and national identity, absent from Stevens, and we shall come often enough again upon this particular failing in American poetry. To some extent, then, the incapacity of Wallace Stevens to bring 'the whole man' into his verse ('man alive', as Lawrence called him) may be described in the same terms as were used above to describe Whitman. But in addition, there are other historically delimited factors; for the twentieth century differs in certain fundamental ways from the nineteenth, ways that need to be defined in different terms. The term 'existential' has been applied indiscriminately to a great deal of twentieth-century writing. But this ready abuse is itself interesting. There need be no very close philosophical ties between works which share a common existential quality. Philosophically, for instance, there is nothing in common between Samuel Beckett, the acolyte of Occasionalism, and Sartre, the metaphysical enemy of all Idealism. Yet it is not pointless to call Beckett existential. To apply the term to the author of *En Attendant Godot* is to emphasize the quality he shares with Sartre, and with, for instance, the Lawrence of *The Man Who Died*, with the Eliot of *The Waste Land*, with the Hardy of *Winter Words,* with Edward Thomas—a quality best described perhaps as concrete or unmediated. Modern man exists in a particularly denuded state—shorn of values or belief, of social standards, of political imperatives. Our philosophies have fallen back upon the description of perception, and the need to produce a concrete literature commensurate with this situation is deeply characteristic of twentieth-century Europe, whether in its old locale or in the Americas. Man has, we may say, been rejected by his projects, and thrown back on the facts of perception and experience, and on those moments when the real nature of his relations with the concrete world, and of himself against that world, becomes apparent.

It is this concrete content rather than any philosophy of despair that explains and justifies much that has been written off too easily as 'modish' pessimism. The finest twentieth-century art has been characterized by this enforced contact with reality, and it is in this respect that American poetry of the 1920s appears, when compared with its English counterparts, signally deficient. And again, as the example of Wallace Stevens suggests, it is the historical context rather than individual personalities which is responsible for a general air of lightness in the poetry not only of Stevens but of Robert Frost, Marianne Moore and e. e. cummings. (Crane of course cannot be described in this way; I shall turn to him later.) A certain playfulness demarks the best of Frost, for instance, from the best of his friend, Edward Thomas.

Frost surpasses his master, Whittier, so emphatically that it is tempting to see in the distance between the two poets the course of American maturation. Frost's regionalism, far from being limitingly provincial, like Whittier's, is almost metropolitan in its sophistication. Yet the lightness of tone with which Frost handles his metaphyics is just as unmistakably American as Whittier's homely solemnity. This is true obviously of his more glib manifestos:

> Nature had her head about her
> When she put our heads together,
> Yours so much concerned with outer,
> Mine with inner weather.
>
> ('Tree by the Window')

But it seems to me that even at his very best, in his most 'serious' poems, Frost treads lightly:

> The woods are lovely, dark and deep,
> But I have promises to keep,
> And miles to go before I sleep
> And miles to go before I sleep.
>
> ('Stopping by Woods')

Possibly Frost's finest single poem, 'Stopping by Woods' is extraordinary and perfect: it looks straight into oblivion, and its repeated last line is more than a triumph of musicality: it is a wave sent up from the deep. I have spoken of the differences that exist between American and English poetry often enough in terms suggesting value-judgements. But basically, the differences are simply differences of social and historical situation. Sometimes this seems describable only in terms which suggest value-judgements, yet an adequate description should by rights leave out the evaluations. Nothing could be offered in criticism of 'Stopping by Woods': it is one of the human artefacts of which twentieth-century man has reason to be most proud.

It seems more important therefore, not less, to try to define carefully what it is that distinguishes Frost's verse from, say, that of Edward Thomas. It is not so much *level* as *kind* of achievement we are concerned with. I should like to offer, as a touchstone by which to place Frost's 'Stopping by Woods', Edward Thomas's 'Old Man or Lad's Love'. Now Frost was Thomas's mentor; nor, in this case, did the pupil surpass— he had not the time—the skill and poise of the master. But Thomas's finest poetry possesses a quality lacking even from Frost's best; whether we call it weight, seriousness or power does not matter very much: it is a capacity to jar and shock us into a new awareness of the grounding of the human condition in mortality, and to sublimate the shock, without softening it, so that the reader experiences the full weight of the Aristotelian catharsis. In 'Old Man', Thomas winds his way back through insignificant rituals to the 'truth'—the unchanging condition—within and under them:

> I have mislaid the key. I sniff the spray
> And think of nothing; I see and I hear nothing;
> Yet seem, too, to be listening, lying in wait
> For what I would, yet never can, remember:
> No garden appears, no path, no hoar-green bush
> Of Lad's Love or Old Man, no child beside,
> Neither father nor mother, nor any playmate;
> Only an avenue, dark, nameless, without end.
>
> ('Old Man or Lad's Love')

Clearly, the delicacy required to get at this vision of oblivion testifies to sheer technical ability and artistry of the highest order: it represents, in fact, in its preternaturally fine avoidance of the easier solutions consciousness wants to offer, artistic accomplishment of the same order as Frost displays in 'Stopping by Woods'. But Thomas's ability to step back from himself, as Dickens does so skilfully in *David Copperfield,* in order to watch himself experiencing, without for a second losing contact with that even, sober speaking voice, is something we would look for in vain in Robert Frost. The vague, almost sensuous glamour of 'Stopping by Woods', its silky sounds and its so pleasantly intimated temptation to dissolve oneself in darkness—all this laves our minds when we read: it is a lotion, and in this lies its beauty, its Americanness.[19]

We become increasingly aware, in reading through not only Frost but cummings, Stevens and Marianne Moore, of a persisting playfulness, a

[19] See Geoffrey Thurley, *The Ironic Harvest* (London 1973), ch. 2.

lightness of touch and tone, even when serious matters are being broached —in fact, especially so: we cannot help observing that when the poetry loses its playfulness, as in Stevens's 'philosophical' ruminations, and cummings's serious quatrain poems ('my father moved through dooms of love') there is a distinct loss of interest, urgency and wit. Rhythm gives way to metre, poetry becomes 'literature'. This is in no way to deny or 'downgrade' the excellence of much of what these poets achieved. It is possible, in the first place, that this 'playfulness' can even be an aid to clarity; that it is better, in some ways, to be free of the consciousness of mortality so characteristic of English poetry at this period. There is a certain air of 'end-of-the-road' about Thomas Hardy, and Edward Thomas's earnestness becomes almost morbid.

What I am concerned with is the nature of American poetry, and the dimension in which it most comfortably moved. To put it very crudely, there is no sense in saying that in some way American poets were 'failing', or that they could have done better had they adjusted their conception of the task before them. On the contrary, nothing could be 'better' than the best of Frost, for instance. But my argument is, still, that this 'provincialism' (the word begins to wear very thin at this stage) bears with it certain limitations, and these I must stand by. There are those who will resist the case being put here as vigorously and angrily as those who resented T. S. Eliot's argument that Dante was a 'better' (more coherent, more classical) poet than William Blake, not through any personal superiority, but because cultural-historical circumstances favoured Dante.[20]

The general point is borne out, it seems to me, in the present case by the glaring exception to my remarks about American poetry of the 1920s, Hart Crane. For Crane was never less than appallingly earnest, every poem was the Great Poem. He could only be playful in the clumsiest way (as in 'Paraphrase', which should be read as 'wit' but can only be read sombrely). Alone of the American poets of the 1920s, Crane played for the highest stakes. My metaphor, I hasten to add, is, though not fresh, not careless: the Faustian wager is at the heart of all Crane's work, as it is of so much post-Romantic art: the poet trades in his chances of normal happiness, security, psychological well-being, in the hope of culling the Satanic flowers. Rimbaud and Poe were among Crane's own personal gods; but the syndrome is common in twentieth-century writers much less obviously damned than Hart Crane. I think especially of Mann's *Doktor Faustus* (an explicit if somewhat belated dramatization of the whole symbolist predicament), and of James Joyce. Yet T. S. Eliot and W. B. Yeats, on the face of it such respectable, socially responsible men, also made the Faustian pact a central—if not the central—preoccupation of their work. It is when we compare Crane with Yeats and Eliot, not with Rimbaud and Poe, that his limitations emerge most signally. And the

[20] 'William Blake', in *Selected Essays*, 321.

point is, once again, of general significance. I have already cited John Malcolm Brinnin's judgement that Crane 'broke himself' in his efforts to be a great poet. Yet really it was not only Crane who was broken by the effort to make American life yield poetry on the scale of the greatest European poetry (for that is what is involved) but Crane's well-shod contemporaries, those insider-poets who also, in fact, accepted Mephistopheles' wager. The Satanic poet, such as Hart Crane, trades in his peace of mind, his well-being, and reaps certain rewards—the ecstatic and dynamic imagery, which is Crane's unique gift, for instance. But is it enough? Is it worth it? Modern economics has thrust this dilemma into the heart of poetry; it will never be irrelevant. The agonized nature of Crane's poetry testifies to the intense pressure the doubt exerts on the poet, to say nothing of the actual sufferings themselves—the loneliness, the squalor, the insecurity, the hangovers, the guilt.

But Mephistopheles has two temptations in America. The affluent, the secure life can also be accepted in a Faustian spirit: this kind of poet (who may just be a coward, but may not) believes that only to the man free of sordid economic pressures are the real pearls, the real knowledge granted. So just as Hart Crane rejected, or lost through deliberate neglect, the harbourage of his father's cannery business, so Wallace Stevens put off the business of writing poetry in earnest until he had made his worldly position safe. *Harmonium*, his first volume, appeared in 1924, when Stevens was forty. Later, as Vice-President of the Hartford Accident and Indemnity Company, he will continue to produce poetry regularly, but almost as if on vacation, or on Sundays. 'You can't serve two masters,' whispers the bohemian; the 'secure' poet is gnawed by the inverse doubt: 'Suppose I have traded in my integrity for a hollow skill?'

The sociologist of literature is gratified to observe the differences between Stevens's and Crane's poetry: the power, intensity and drama of the damned, insecure poet corresponds to the cool, low-pressure ruminativeness of the other. We should need to consider a host of other factors before attempting to build much on this single instance, but let us admit that the sociologist of literature at least feels confirmed in being saved the embarrassment of having to explain away what would be a crashing exception to the sort of prediction he is professionally obliged to make. But this discussion needs another context, and is tangential to what I wish to say. My concern in this book is with the poets who wrote after the Second World War: I am all too aware that this introduction is both too long in its brevity, and too short in its longwindedness. But I wish to put yet more strain on the reader's goodwill by suggesting, finally, that the difference between Crane and Stevens is of more than sociological interest. For neither poet successfully treated, or even attempted to treat, the human implications of the Faustian theme as it applies to 'everyday life', as Eliot and Yeats did. My inverted commas around 'everyday life' imply a certain embarrassment. Wrongly perhaps, for there is no other kind of life but the everyday variety. Crane aped Rimbaud, in quite different social and historical circumstances: besides, Rimbaud had recanted, in *Une Saison en Enfer*, and the knowledge vouchsafed there is as much to be taken seriously as the findings, the images and insights, of *Illuminations*. The real inheritors of Rimbaud and Baudelaire were not Crane and Lindsay, but Eliot and Yeats. It was they who explored the real implications of the symbolist predicament—how to reconcile the life of the poet with the life of man within capitalist democracy. The American failure to address the question openly and maturely—Crane hurled himself blindly at a wall, Stevens shut himself away behind one—seems to me symptomatic of a literary culture still short of full growth. 'History', to draw once more on Mr Brinnin's words, still had some resolving to do. Eliot, Yeats, Lawrence, Hardy— these poets rest on a sure foundation of character and society, and can let the myriad aspects of experience revolve before them. The American poets contemporary with them are forced either into a lightness that may be serious but lacks real profundity, or into a strained, schismatic hysteria, sublime at moments, but flawed and baseless. The American *poète maudit* wishes to lift himself by his bootstraps, and, like Hart Crane, 'fling himself silently (noisily) into eternity'.

On the example of Crane I rest my case. There was, of course, much excellent poetry written in the 1930s and 1940s, but nothing—I think it would generally be conceded—to equal or surpass the best work done in the 1920s by the poets I have been discussing. If, that is to say, my case is not felt to be established by now, it is certainly not going to be strengthened by the example of poets admitted to be less strong than those I have already discussed. In one respect, indeed, the poets one most naturally thinks of in moving on from the 1920s to the 1930s—those associated with the Fugitive group, the New Criticism, the *Kenyon* and *Southern Reviews*—confirm my case in a perhaps misleadingly emphatic manner. They took their general critical and ideological orientation from England, and strove after a certain intellectualism they thought to be possessed by the metaphysical poets of the seventeenth century. Although the Fugitive association itself occurred in the 1920s (from 1922 to 1925), it was not until the foundation of *The Southern Review* in 1934 that the new metaphysical academicism really became a force not only in the poetry it published, but in the whole critical orientation. And by this time the work of Empson, Richards and Leavis had made a decisive impact: the essentially regionalist slant of the Fugitives had become the New Criticism, which gave a tone to almost a quarter of a century of American poetry. The object of the criticism in *The Southern Review*, as in Ransom's *Kenyon Review*, was 'close reading of the Cambridge variety'.[21] When later, in 1941, Ransom himself attempted a summary of the achievements of the New Criticism, only one of the critics he discussed at length was actually

[21] See J. L. Stewart, *The Burden of Time* (Princeton 1965).

American, Yvor Winters. The others were Richards, Empson and a long since anglicized Eliot.[22]

Yet it was really only the influence of the Cambridge critics which turned the Fugitive poets and critics from a regionalist caucus into a national force. And here we touch on something more interesting than cross-Atlantic influence and counter-influence. For the neo-metaphysical poetry produced in America—by, among many others, Eberhart, Shapiro, Schwartz, Tate, Ransom, Penn Warren and Jarrell—never, I think, equalled the best poetry produced in England in similar sociopolitical circumstances, and under the influence of the same sort of critical impetus. None of the American metaphysicals matched the tough sententiousness of Empson at his best, either as critic or poet. But if Empson was closer to the 'intellectualist' ideal than any poet of the time, it was W. H. Auden who most brilliantly applied the spirit of the new criticism to subject-matter that demanded it—the social and political upheavals in the West at the time of its greatest turbulence. The difference between American and English neo-metaphysical poetry in the intellectualist years could be measured in terms of Auden's personal brilliance: it was, after all, just chance that made Auden English, not American. But the essential politicality not only of Auden himself, but of Spender, Day Lewis and MacNeice, is far more important than Auden's individual talent. Now, of course, in the case of the Fugitives, the name of the group itself suggests that it stemmed from an essentially reactionary background. In 1930 some of the group (Ransom, Tate, Donald Davidson, Laura Riding and Robert Penn Warren) contributed to a publication of which the very title—*I'll Take my Stand*[23]—suggests a mix of John Birch and Billy Graham, if not the Klan itself. It was in fact not a sinister crypto-fascist manifesto, but a well-meaning cry of horror at the encroachment on individualism and a dignified society of capitalist industry. It is wholly in the spirit of anthologies like *Civilization in the United States*.[24] In the light of all this, it can be seen that the New Criticism, and the poetry it encouraged and promoted, had as its basis an essentially reactionary philosophy: it was dead set against the entire machinery of capitalist democracy and therefore prepared to ignore the huge social upheavals of the time, or alternatively to shrug them off as the inevitable concomitants of the materialist progressiveness it deplored. Thus, the quasi-structuralist (or should we say textualist) bias of its critical canon assumes a reactionary cast. When Ransom says that the 'business of the literary critic is exclusively with an aesthetic experience',[25] when Cleanth Brooks, selecting carefully chosen targets (Max Eastman, Langston Hughes), informs us that the political consciousness in poetry disturbs the

[22] J. C. Ransom, *The New Criticism* (Norfolk, Conn. 1941).
[23] *I'll Take My Stand*, ed. J. C. Ransom (New York 1930).
[24] *Civilization in the United States,* ed. H. Stearns (New York 1922).
[25] Ransom, *The New Criticism,* 45.

balance of secondary considerations, and inhibits the emergence of an 'inclusive' poetry,[26] they are supporting an inherently conservative political position.

This is not to say that a leftist stance was mandatory. On the contrary, as any radical would be quick to point out, Auden's politics were anything but orthodox or revolutionary. But the necessary politicality of poetry in our time does not consist in verbalizing ideological orthodoxy. On the contrary, the situation may demand a stance inconsistent with the politically orthodox. It is in terms of the total fact-continuum ('die Totalität' in Lukacs's term)[27] that the artist's politicality is to be defined. The agitprop and sentimental poetry demolished by Brooks in *Modern Poetry and the Tradition* violates 'truth' as much as fascist propaganda. But it is the tendency of Brooks's book, and of the New Criticism as a whole, to imply that any political stance in poetry is anti-artistic, sentimental, militating against an 'inclusive' poetry.

Such a conservatism is in part an element in the Cambridge critics from whom Brooks and the other New Critics stem. A deeply considered rejection of 'democracy' appears not merely in Eliot and Pound, but in every major European poet of their generation, with the single exception of Bertolt Brecht. But these writers fought out their politics in their own sensibility: their 'conservatism' is worth something because it tells us something about the world we inherit and enhances our sense of the values we are in danger of losing. But the New Critics, like the Agrarians, are *merely* fugitive, they turn aside, are apolitical. Nothing illustrates this better than the experience of Robert Penn Warren. Having as a young Agrarian rejected in horror 'a kind of dehumanizing and disintegrative effect on your notion of what an individual person could be',[28] Warren was later, in 1939, to see fascism in action in Rome, and was honest enough to be shocked at how wrong he had been about democracy.

In this naïve agrarian apoliticality (so similar in certain respects to Pound's fascism) the work of the Fugitives and the neo-metaphysical poets as a whole compares unfavourably with the best that Auden, Dylan Thomas, David Gascoyne and others were producing at the same time in England. American intellectual life at this period was of course a chaos of conflicting leftist ideologies, but this reflection only strengthens the general impression of a literary culture still at this stage incapable of synthesizing human experience into mature poetry. With the exception of Rexroth and Patchen, to whom I shall turn in due course, no American poet succeeded in assimilating the political and social turmoil of the

---

[26] Cleanth Brooks, *Modern Poetry and the Tradition* (London 1948).

[27] Lucien Goldmann criticized Malraux's Stalinist novels precisely for following party orthodoxy at the expense of the human totality. See his *Pour une sociologie du roman* (Paris 1964).

[28] In Stewart, *The Burden of Time,* 486.

time into poetry that has stood the passage of time. We find either second-rate agitprop doggerel, or elitist avoidance. There is no American equivalent—and my assumption is that there ought to have been—of those poems—'Doomsday Song', 'Spain 1937', 'Paysage Moralisé', 'A Summer Evening'—in which Auden involves the reader in his own involvement in the political situation. Auden's brilliant reportage may sometimes make us feel that his concern is to mirror the facts. But his real theme is his own ambivalent and ambiguous attitude towards the facts—his complicity in the bourgeois-capitalist, privilege-ridden society of inter-war England—a society he at once despised and loved, deplored and admired, resented and needed. It is, in other words, the poet's role in the historical situation that counts: 'Which side am I supposed to be on?' Auden brilliantly asked. Through trying to work out his ambivalent and ambiguous position, the poet approaches an understanding of 'die Totalität'. To be born into the secure middle class—as the Fugitive poets and the English Pylon poets largely were—does not debar a man from writing well, nor from honouring the political facts of his time. It is the complex intellectual and moral engagement in the social and historical situation which characterizes the best work of the Pylon school; it is what is most clearly lacking from the Fugitives and their successors in America.

Contrary to the propaganda of Pound and others, in fact, the English literary establishment was proving itself more flexible and more intellectually mature than that of America. England, in short, remained culturally dominant throughout the inter-war years, and this in spite of having lost a whole generation of poets—Wilfred Owen, Edward Thomas, Rupert Brooke, Isaac Rosenberg, Charles Sorley—in the First World War (a fact somewhat brutally ignored by Pound). This fact is surely emphasized by the way in which so many young American poets of the late 1930s who were to play important roles in the postwar years—John Berryman, Theodore Roethke, Robert Duncan—still looked naturally to English models to provide rhythmic and stylistic leads.[29]

Americans have been saluting their emergence from cultural provincialism for almost half a century. The truth is, I think, that American culture, and with it American poetry, only truly acquired its own centre of gravity, its own fullness, in the years following the Second World War. Nothing less than a history of America and of American culture is properly required at this point. I have neither the space nor the power to describe, much less to explain, why and how it was that the United

---

[29] See Howard Nemerov (ed.), *Contemporary American Poetry* (Voice of America Forum Lectures, n.d.); Allan Seager, *The Glass House* (New York 1968), 192–3, for Theodore Roethke's admiration for Dylan Thomas; Roethke's debt to Yeats of course needs no comment. See also Robert Duncan's introduction to the 1966 edition of *The Years as Catches* (Berkeley) for this poet's early indebtedness to Edith Sitwell, George Barker and other English poets.

States came into its own only after the Hitler War. Perhaps it was simply that process of history resolving itself, in Brinnin's terms. Perhaps the most obvious 'explanations'—the exhaustion of Europe, the final collapse of the British hegemony, the sheer scale and power of the American economy—are, taken in conjunction, the right ones. Whatever the truth is, the fact remains that the American moment arrives no sooner than the middle 1950s of the twentieth century, the decade in which Jackson Pollock and Barnet Newman took over from Paris the lead in Western painting. In the middle 1950s American poets, having taken perhaps a last weary look at the dreariness of existentialist Paris and austerity England, start to produce poetry and fiction that is wholly and authentically American without being in the slightest degree provincial. And English poets start to learn from America.

This isn't to say that the poets who dominate the period—Duncan, Ginsberg, Lowell, Berryman, Corso—are the best America has produced. Artists do not spring up to order. There is no Whitman, and the general level of performance was probably higher in the 1920s. But this is not the contention. American poetry of the 1950s and 1960s is remarkable not only in that it is autonomous, but in that it is informed, as never before in American history, with a full, natural sense of personality. Poets like Berryman and Ginsberg attempt, at least, to sound the full diapason of human character: they proffer and analyse themselves as men, whole, in a way that Americans had not attempted before. We cannot say, as we read 'HOWL' or the *Dream Songs,* that 'This is great poetry', as we must when we read 'When Lilacs Last in the Dooryard Bloomed'. But we can have no doubt that the whole man is in it.

Of course, things do not change overnight. Many of the old characteristics of American writing remain: the tone of lachrymose self-pity already familiar from O'Neill and Wolfe, the surface-bound facility that keeps good natural observation from amounting to more than that, an excessive reliance on science or pseudo-science instead of a full sense of personal identity, that air of sustaining an act so well described by Stephen Spender[30]—these things persist. But they persist in a different body.

To say that American culture has acquired at last its own centre of gravity, even to admit the probability of a fairly straightforward relationship between this emergence and the fact of the American politico-military hegemony, is by no means to commit oneself to that crude form of literary sociology deriving its explications from straight political and cultural parallelisms. It does not follow that American art or poetry is the 'best' in the English-speaking world merely because America happens to be richer and more powerful than other nations. There *is* an important kind of correlation between history and art, but this is not it. This fallacious form of literary sociology—surely that 'Kitsch-Soziologie' the

[30] Spender, *Love–Hate Relations,* 209–11.

late Theodor Adorno was so scathing about—appears in Stephen Spender's *Love–Hate Relations*, which casts England in the decadent and America in the youthful role in a simplistic sociohistorical scenario. Overawed by the physical size and the economic dynamism of America —by its sheer 'evil' in fact—Spender despairs of any English (and by definition non-American) artistic contribution: apart from 'a studied provincialism', 'exile', and a third alternative I cannot understand, the English, he says, can 'perhaps . . . maintain distance and sanity'.[31]

Spender supports his case with one of the most bizarre parallels that can ever have been made in the area of culture history: the England of 1970, he suggests, is to America as the Ireland of 1900 was to England— that is, capable of great literature that must, however, be somehow off-centre, leaving it to Americans to say what needs to be said about the modern world. Spender's personal gift for self-abasement has elided unprofitably here with the modest self-deprecation common to so many Englishmen of his age and background. It just cannot be said that England is rustic and little, as Spender implies it is: Donald Davie possibly overstates the case for the importance of the English contribution (in his *Thomas Hardy and British Poetry*), but he is closer to the truth than Spender. Ireland was coming to the end of a seven-hundred-year bondage to England in 1900; it was almost wholly agrarian (as it still is), under-populated, and with practically no experience of the Industrial Revolution. England in 1970 had only a generation since dismantled the largest empire in the history of civilization; it was over-populated, over-civilized, over-industrialized, over-democratized. At no point does Spender's weird parallel make contact with reality. But this merely odd comparison is subtended by a far more serious sociological fallacy. If Spender needed an international relationship from the past to throw light on the present relations between England and America, he would have done far better to take that which existed between England and France in the late nineteenth century. The French Spender of 1872 could have been excused for feeling, as the real Spender did in 1972, that France was so backward industrially, so agrarian and rural, that it was useless for her poets and painters to try to compete with those of dynamic, bustling, dirty, evil Albion.—'Look for instance at our painters,' he might have said, 'Pissarro, Monet, Renoir— how rustic their subjects are! "The Seine at Argenteuil"! "The Poppy Field"!' Yet France, as we know, produced the significant, complex, modern and *relevant* (that is what Spender is really talking about) poetry of the late nineteenth century, not England.

The parallel between Victorian England and modern America, which has been made often enough, seems to have received an added dimension over the past fifteen years. Never has America been more powerful, yet never has she been so impotent as she is, behind her rockets and nuclear

[31] Ibid, 245–6.

shields, today; her inability to clinch the Vietnam war was an intensification of a syndrome that was familiar to the Englishmen who had witnessed the embarrassments of the Crimea, Schleswig-Holstein and the Boer War. The relative decline in English literary achievement from the high point of the novel in the 1860s ran parallel to this political and military hypertrophy. This is not to say that one set of events *caused* the other: on the contrary, it is to sound a warning against making the wrong kind of inference. In the 1950s and the middle 1960s, the English poet alive to his time looked instinctively to America. He is unlikely to do so today.

We must then, to say it again, avoid the mistake of equating the American emergence from cultural provincialism with a historically determined artistic supremacy: the American Moment is not the American hegemony. The momentum built up by American poets and novelists in the 1950s and 1960s seems for the moment to have petered out. There is little evidence that American poetry now is remarkable for either its power and intensity, or its ability to integrate the facts of twentieth-century life into work of the highest quality. Only a crude sociology of literature would suppose that it should be so. The Polish intellectual mindful of the achievement of Penderecki, Andrzejewski, Hłasko and Rozewicz does not let the relative agrarianism of his own country lead him to exalt the might of Soviet industry into cultural 'relevance'. He will be disappointed if he does, as disappointed as the Englishman who turns expectantly to the desert of American music, or even to the new aridities of its painting and the increasing preciousness of its poetry.

Part II

Symptoms of Affluence

Chapter 2

Benign Diaspora
The Landscape of Richard Wilbur

The feeling among American poets and critics that recent British poets have tended to be a little dull[1] is matched by the sense among many English readers that American poets are cleverly empty, the facility afforded them precisely by that absence of social responsibility that makes English poets perhaps 'dull'. To be dull is human, to be empty perhaps divine. These are of course only vague impressions: there's nothing dull about Stevie Smith or John Betjeman, and there's nothing either empty or particularly clever about Robert Lowell or Anne Sexton. Nevertheless, playing the game of transatlantic impressions ('the way it looks from here') can have its advantages: in this case, it may help to focus on what might prove to be a fairly radical difference corresponding to respective sets of historical and political factors. At the same time, it might help us to arrive at the conclusion that the difference is illusory in certain respects.

In the case of Richard Wilbur there would seem to be some immediate rewards. In the first place, the tone of Wilbur's verse—its accent—is more English than that of almost any other American poet one could name:

> In grimy winter dusk
> We slowed to a concrete platform;
> The pillars passed more slowly;
> A paper boy leapt up.

('Stop')

Not only the observational technique here (the deliberate assemblage of detail, the clogging of the verb, 'slowed', to maximize concreteness), but even the subject itself recalls the English tradition that begins, let us say, with Edward Thomas's 'Adlestrop', and continues through the Larkin of 'The Whitsun Weddings'. The sense of arrival in the stanza quoted must inevitably suggest Larkin's great poem:

> And as we raced across
> Bright knots of rail

---

[1] See, for instance, Spender, *Love–Hate Relations*, 241.

> Past standing Pullmans, walls of blackened moss
> Came close, and it was nearly done.
>
> ('The Whitsun Weddings')

But Wilbur's poem shares a more specific quality with Edward Thomas's poem 'Adlestrop', in which the poetic possibilities of the particular situation—the unexpected or seemingly pointless mid-journey halt—were first exploited. Here is Thomas's poem in full:

> Yes, I remember Adlestrop—
> The name, because one afternoon
> Of heat the express-train drew up there
> Unwontedly. It was late June.
>
> The steam hissed. Someone cleared his throat.
> No one left and no one came
> On the bare platform. What I saw
> Was Adlestrop—only the name
>
> And willows, willow-herb, and grass,
> And meadowsweet, and haycocks dry,
> Not one whit less still and lonely fair
> Than the high cloudlets in the sky.
>
> And for that minute a blackbird sang
> Close by, and round him, mistier,
> Farther and farther, all the birds
> Of Oxfordshire and Gloucestershire.

This kind of poem happens in the interstices of normal experience: the social man would continue undisturbed inside his weave of projects and possibilities, never quite at one with the world or with himself until or unless some disjointing happening derails him, and for the moment leaves him with no course but to acknowledge himself. To drop on such happenings, or to work studiously to render the mind accident-prone, constitutes, from one point of view at least, the essence of the poetic life, especially in the post-symbolist world. It was something in which English poets following Thomas Hardy proved themselves expert, with their freedom from ideology and their tense speculative silence of waiting. Robert Frost, too—witness 'Stopping by Woods'—explored the potentialities of this philosophical non-exploring, this anti-pioneering, this active vigilance.

In 'Adlestrop' the observations grow around the poet, much as the silence grows around the train, now drowned in its new stillness; the awareness fulfils itself in the poet, for the actual silence and wholeness (always of course there) profit by the train's unexpected halt to declare themselves in the name, Adlestrop. The major philosophical implications of the experience are, first, that we are the victims of our own expecta-

tions and project-making faculties, and grow estranged from ourselves
by ignoring the actuality of the world in which we in fact pass our days,
and then, that this world constitutes in itself a belonging, forming a
territorial reality to which we give names, but which we then evacuate
of their identity, leaving it to the birds to inhabit the desolate names
until accident reminds us of our common lore and inherited kinship.
This has been a major if not *the* major area of preoccupation of English
poetry since Wordsworth. Macha Rosenthal rightly speaks of some of
Ted Hughes's poetry as a 're-casting of Wordsworthian motifs' and also
pays homage to the English poets' 'absorption of intricate detail into the
speaking psyche [revealing] empathy of an extraordinarily responsive
and receptive order'.[2] With a slightly different emphasis, it is what I
have described elsewhere as being characteristic of the English existential
tradition.[3]

With such reflections in mind, and turning to Wilbur's 'Stop' for
comparison, we might be able to assign to the variables posited at the
beginning of this chapter—English dullness, American emptiness—
more precise meanings than is usual. Where one belongs, one has after
all—to put it simply—less freedom to move. 'I belong here' means that
'here' in some sense *owns* me. To feel that one belongs nowhere might
well be the most fundamentally significant characteristic of American art.
And let it be said that the criterion implicitly in use here is less one of
mere length of time spent in a place (though this can't be irrelevant),
than the degree of self-consciousness attained when the race-experience
in the locale commenced. To say it again, it is not merely the fact that the
American sojourn in that continent has occupied four hundred as opposed
to fourteen hundred years that is significant; what counts is that the
earliest American settlers brought with them an already mature and
crystallized sense of national and personal identity—a sense which, of
course, they necessarily set about fracturing. When the Celts invaded and
pervaded Iberia and the British Isles, even when the Danes and Saxons
pillaged Britain where they would eventually settle, we may take it that
the psyche—both individual and collective—they brought with them
across the North Sea was far more easily adaptable to new environments:
nothing was being sacrificed, everything was being appropriated.

Little was abandoned, their gods were portable, they left no *genius loci*.
How far these possibilities can be quantified and used to any helpful
degree, it is difficult to judge. It may be that the Jewish experience
provides an extreme model for the American, and that the forcible
disinheritance of the Jews had consequences roughly analogous to the
effects upon Americans of their self-disinheritance; that the continent
Americans love so much is a kind of benign diaspora. The sting in the
tail is this: the Jew has always been sustained by some hope of a return to

[2] M. Rosenthal, *The New Poets* (New York 1967), 257.
[3] *The Ironic Harvest*, ch. 2.

Palestine; what happens when no such return or restoration is desired? And what happens to the collective memory when it is spatially dispossessed?

It seems unfair to hang such ponderous impalpabilities upon a poem which Richard Wilbur himself might well feel to be less than heavyweight. Yet the contrast between the naturally arising significances of 'Adlestrop' and the more contrived effects of 'Stop' is an important one, I think. The poem of this genre has to happen in a strange continuum—part-language, part-facticity: it cannot be 'invented'. The poem as percept-structure, in which observations loosely belonging together within a witnessed scene or situation are given an appearance of logical cohesion and inter-relatedness, is the common stock of mid-century poetry on both sides of the Atlantic; Wilbur's superficiality is not perhaps specifically American. What he really wanted to do in 'Stop' was simply to make use of a set of good observations. The scene is jotted down—'The glum cold air', 'the broken ice . . . glintless'. . . . The poet then introduces the second premise, or the antithesis:

> The truck was painted blue
> On side, wheels and tongue.

The synthesis/conclusion makes the passengers share 'Queen Persephone's gaze', and the 'grimy winter dusk' become the mythological underworld. It does not, of course: the poem remains a good piece of descriptive writing, in the 'Adlestrop' mode. One could, as I have suggested, find examples of the same sort in English poets. Nevertheless, 'Stop' seems to me typical of Wilbur in a way that could be generalized: its world lacks just that rootedness, the perceptions lack that 'responsiveness and receptivity' which Macha Rosenthal praises in Wilbur's British contemporaries.

There is certainly no denying the wit and sensibility of Wilbur's earlier collections. *The Beautiful Changes* and *Ceremony* are remarkable indeed for more than this wit and sensibility. The best poems in these books have, in addition to wit, a formal fecundity at the service of a quiet exuberance:

> Beasts in their major freedom
> Slumber in peace tonight. The gull on his ledge
> Dreams in the guts of himself the moon-plucked waves below,
> And the sunfish leans on a stone, slept
> By the lyric water. . . .
>
> ('Beasts')

The academic dangers implicit in the use of 'major' rest easily on the swell of the verse. The rhyme-scheme is forceful and adventurous. We are continually surprised as Wilbur finds new formal implications in the placing of end-words and the cutting-edge of syntax: the 'ripped mouse' that 'cries/Concordance', like the sunfish which 'leans by the lyric water', is an image we remember precisely because of the strategy of the poet's cutting. And to speak of strategy here is by no means to suggest a limiting technical proficiency: it is keenness of awareness which is sponsoring these subtle shifts and emphases. The actual shape of the stanza too, with its bulging, its lengthening and its final recession, is more or less continuously at work modulating our response:

> Meantime, at high windows
> Far from thicket and pad-fall, suitors of excellence
> Sigh and turn from their work to construe again the painful
> Beauty of heaven, the lucid moon
> And the risen hunter.
>
> ('Beasts')

Like the earlier stanzas describing 'the werewolf's painful change' (lines that left their mark on Thom Gunn, I think), this stanza is wholly engrossed in its mimesis: the action of the lovers' pantomime follows the growth and contraction of the stanza itself. The relative lameness of the second half of the long third line—nothing is achieved by the 'strategic' placing of 'painful'—only, I think, serves to underline the general mastery.

'Beasts' is one of a number of poems ('Castles and Distances', 'Death of a Toad' and the Traherne pastiche 'A World Without Objects' are others) in which Wilbur finds with an impressive tact the right balance of constraint and imaginative adventurousness: he seems capable of striking out freely within intuitively adopted bounds, strongly yet with grace, in a manner almost at times suggestive of Paul Valéry, whose imprint is everywhere apparent in these volumes. The poem provides also a fascinating instance of the interrelationship between English and American poets. *Things of This World,* from which 'Beasts' comes, appeared in 1956, while Ted Hughes was at Cambridge. The general indebtedness of *The Hawk in the Rain* to the early volumes of Wilbur is pronounced. Certainly, Hughes took the thing further, pushing well beyond Wilbur's civilized perspective into the hinterland of consciousness. Yet the inspiration lay not only in Wilbur's subject-matter, but in his achievement. It is the ingenuity of the versification here which suggests Hughes: the use of verbs like 'construe', 'sponsors', 'cries/Concordance', the odd inertia of 'slept' in stanza one (an active past participle), the 'turning' of the third stanza. 'Beasts' is interesting too for the clear debt to Auden:

> Making such dreams for men
> As told will break their hearts as always, bringing
> Monsters into the city, crows on the public statues,
> Navies fed to the fish in the dark
> Unbridled waters.
>
> ('Beasts')

Like the pedantic note of 'major freedom' in stanza one, the tired know-ingness about suffering of 'as always', and the freely mythologized politicality of the last lines take their tone from the Auden of the 1930s.

Taking no more than the facetiously rhetorical tone from J. C. Ransom, 'Still, Citizen Sparrow' likewise suggests Ted Hughes:

> Still, citizen sparrow, this vulture which you call
> Unnatural, let him but lumber again to air
> Over the rotten office, let him bear
> The carrion ballast up, and at the tall
>
> Tip of the sky lie cruising.

The strategic placing of 'bear' imparts something of the Hughesian scale and tension, as does, later, the verb in the phrase 'He shoulders nature there'. The academic metaphysics—the bird 'mocks mutability'—seems dated enough, fifteen years after Hughes's 'Hawk Roosting', but again, although Hughes strikes through to a more fundamental and more exciting emotion, we must recognize and respect the work Wilbur did in opening up the field. (I have written elsewhere of Hughes's general debt to Lawrence and other English poets, and this must clearly still take precedence. But Wilbur seems also to have played an extraordinarily decisive catalytic role.)

At the risk of seeming to make Hughes a mere pendant to Wilbur, or Wilbur a mere curtain-raiser to Hughes, I will add to this case the most striking evidence of 'Castles and Distances':

> From blackhearted water colder
> Than Cain's blood, and aching with ice, from a gunmetal bay
> Noone would dream of drowning in, rises
> The walrus: head hunched from the oxen shoulder,
> The serious face made for surprises
> Looks with a thick dismay. . . .
>
> ('Castles and Distances')

It is hardly possible now to read these lines without thinking of Hughes's 'Otter'. Even the bulge-structure of the stanzas—beautifully managed by Wilbur—anticipates Hughes's poem. Here one must drop the parallels: the two poems, like the two poets, now take quite different paths. Yet what Hughes 'took from' Wilbur's poem is arguably what it has most rewardingly on offer—the empathy of its opening winter lines, 'Black-hearted water aching with ice, from a gunmetal bay', and, of course, the witty (rather than dynamic) 'doing' of the walrus itself. Now Wilbur isn't committed to his beasts as Hughes is to his. In fact, Wilbur now moves into more literary territory, contrasting the wildness of nature with the order of civilization. It is a poem 'about' civilization, in fact, and in-evitably about the American poet's disinherited state (although this is not

openly acknowledged—it would be a bigger poem if it were, perhaps).
It is not surprising that things English appear in the second stanza, nor
that the disquisitional curve through France and the Middle Ages finally
comes to rest in *The Tempest*. It is certainly a poem that again and again
suggests the stilled pseudo-action of tapestry, rather than real history: it
is perhaps historiographic rather than actually historical in preoccupation.
Again, the versification is mobile and modestly adventurous:

> So strangeness gently steels
> Us, and curiosity kills, keeping us cool to go
> Sail with the hunters unseen to the walrus rock
> And stand behind their slaughter: which of us feels
> The harpoon's hurt, and the huge shock
> When the blood jumps to flow?
>
> ('Castles and Distances')

The cut from the American colloquial 'go' to 'Sail' is notably effective,
but so is the general shift of the narrative line, exhausting momentum
mid-stanza, and renewing itself effortlessly to cross stanza-bounds and
make bigger formal units. This needs more extended quotation:

> Sometimes, as one can see
> Carved at Amboise in a high relief, on the lintel stone
> Of the castle chapel, hunters have strangely come
> To a mild close of the chase, bending the knee
> Instead of the bow, struck sweetly dumb
> To see from the brow bone
>
> Of the hounded stag a cross
> Crown, and the eyes clear with grace. Perfectly still
> Are the cruising dogs as well, their paws aground
> In a white hush of lichen. Beds of moss
> Spread, and the clearing wreathes around
> The dear suspense of will.
>
> But looking higher now
> To the chapel steeple, see among points and spines
> of the updrawn
> Vanishing godbound stone, ringing its sped
> Thrust as a target tatters, a round row
> Of real antlers taken from dead
> Deer. The hunt goes on.
>
> ('Castles and Distances')

Running through the formal network here is the direct influence of
another poet who assumes particular significance in this context, Gerard
Manley Hopkins. Think, for instance, of the break in the last stanza cited,
'dead/Deer'. It was Hopkins who taught poets to do this sort of thing:

the rush of the meaning through the elaborate stanza-mesh, the bristle of alliteration, the stress of Anglo-Saxon words. But what is Wilbur using the idiom to communicate? Is there any more to the 'dead/Deer' enjambment than the flourish of a brilliant technician? If we write the line out straight, without versification, we see what Wilbur has so cleverly achieved: 'a round row of real antlers taken from dead deer'. Well, of course the deer would be dead! But in the subtle play and parry of Wilbur's versification, it doesn't occur to us to question the meaning behind the verse-effect. And we approach here a much more serious questioning of this achievement of a consummate verse-technician: what, after all, does Wilbur have to offer us?

One thing he has to offer has already been touched on in passing: the soft crumbling wealth in this sort of writing:

> Their garden has a silent tall stone-wall
> So overburst with drowsing trees and vines,
> None but a stranger would remark at all
> The barrier within the fractured lines.

> ('Caserta Garden')

The feel of this is peculiarly Wilbur's own, and the theme of the poem, though not strikingly novel, is something he has made his own and enacted in the gentle resistance the imagery puts up to the restrictions of the quatrain:

> How beauties will grow richer walled about!

It is precisely the philosophy an American might be expected to glean from the example of Europe. When it's there—this kind of pressure and resistance, letting us browse on something that will always be just too big to be exhausted—the poem is safe, safe from itself and from criticism. In a sufficient number of poems in the three earliest volumes, Wilbur supplies it:

> Your voice, with clear location on June days,
> Called me—outside the window. You were there,
> Light yet composed, as in the just soft stare
> Of uncontested summer all things raise
> Plainly their seeming into seamless air.

> ('June Light')

Mere celebration? Of course, but the skill of feeling to *know* what is being celebrated—that is what Wilbur's best verse shows forth. These poems possess a quality which resists and gets in behind the bookish wit, which is, as it were, played with:

> And morning's cannonades of brightness come
> To a little utter heaven in your eyes. . . .

> ('For Ellen')

I'd be pleased with that, if I were Ellen. Something so simple—so simply tender—irradiates the phrase 'a little utter heaven', that the academic conceit reveals its playfulness in a genuinely metaphysical spirit, not the brassy pride of Gongora or Marini, but the mature tenderness of the best Herrick and the early Hopkins. In such an appropriateness between tone, technique and subject lies the quality of integrity, and it is a quality Wilbur can sometimes maintain: so long as the human being in him subtends the poet-technician, the father guarantees the tribute to the child. But it is not always so in Wilbur.

There is, surely, no denying the wit—the intelligent touch that can make a poplar a 'Danseuse', and play expertly and lightly on potential assonances such as 'hebetude' and 'habitude'. The doubts arise when Wilbur asks us to accept what these things mean to him. Later, I shall come to raise more serious questions about Wilbur's inward *engagement*, and of his entire development. For the time being, let us look at the internal logic of the poems themselves. The question is, does Wilbur see the things he observes in terms larger than themselves? Does he feel them deeply in their interrelatedness both with his own life and with his own larger philosophical schemata? Or do they merely contribute pleasing experiences in the mid-century metaphysical mode?

In 'Courtyard Thaw', the subject, setting and treatment closely resemble the approach of the earlier Robert Frost. Here is the mingled metaphysical accuracy of Frost's verse:

> (Or showered by a wingbeat, sown
> From windbent branches in arpeggios)
> Let go and took their shinings down
> And brought their brittle season to a close.
>
> ('Courtyard Thaw')

Later we are told that this thaw was a 'false gemmation', and that it was 'puzzling to the heart':

> This spring was neither fierce nor gay;
> This summary autumn fell without a tear:
> No tinkling music-box can play
> The slow, deep-grounded masses of the year.
>
> ('Courtyard Thaw')

The rationale is plain: the flashy brilliance of the scene ('nature stooping to art') puzzles the poet's heart because it suggests spring—with all its ancient prestige and power—but only in a spuriously brilliant, lightweight sort of way. It is bogus, not the real thing. But if we turn from this to, say, Baudelaire's 'Chant d'Automne' where the structure of the emotion is not dissimilar to Wilbur's, we must feel that Wilbur has simply failed to engage himself in the scene, and consequently failed to engage us, his readers. Now the 'logic' of poetry is always more or less rhetorical: it always asserts a relationship between things which only holds good when certain emotional facts are granted. And it is only the tone of the poet's voice, or something he manages to induce into the perceptions—something, that is, which we apprehend as value—that convinces us of the logical relationship upon which the poem depends. In 'Chant d'Automne', Baudelaire wants to say that the falling of the logs in the yard *reminds* him of the coming of winter, and in doing so, of the coming winter in his life. The continuity of feeling-within-imagery that leads us from the falling of the logs to the building of an imaginary scaffold and to the thudding of a battering-ram, which seems in turn like the beating of the heart—the continuity of feeling is the logic of this great poem. In 'A Courtyard Thaw', the phrase which tells us of the 'inner relevance' of the outer events is quite simply uttered in bad faith: 'puzzling to the heart'. No, they were not, we feel quite simply justified in objecting: there was no empathy into the false spring/fall antithesis: it is just a conceit, an idea to tie together some good observations. Ironically, it is an idea Wilbur might have got away with had he not overplayed his hand in the portentous closing line:

> No tinkling music-box can play
> The slow, deep-grounded masses of the year.

The idiom or tradition of idioms in which Wilbur is working here—it reaches back through Frost to Baudelaire—demands that the images dictate and determine the resonances, those depth-charges whose delayed detonations occur only when the full implications of the image-sequence have occurred to us. In 'The Tuft of Flowers', Frost makes the scythe's revelation of a hidden brook immediately 'symbolic' of a certain value, a feeling for the valuable, or the song of the Oven Bird 'in all but words' frame the question, 'what to make of a diminished thing'. The poet metaphysicalizes the real world, converts it, in Frost's own words, into 'inner weather'. This in the end reduces simply to understanding it: in seeing its poetic implications, the poet isolates the phenomenon's true inscape. This thorough absorption in scenes and seasons known so deeply that love has become a habit of the soul is largely absent from Wilbur's poems—not wholly, as we have seen. He can love things and has the real poet's pleasure in being alive in nature. But the depth of engagement is missing: he can be pleased by things, without their ever really becoming part of him.

Wilbur is perhaps closer to certain contemporary British poets—Norman MacCaig, for instance—than to Frost. MacCaig is also a master at the metaphysicalization of the ordinary. In 'Spate in Winter Midnight', for instance, the first stanza gives us what he has in fact to offer—a superb 'description' of the winter stream:

> The streams fall down and through the darkness bear
> Such wild and shaking hair,

Such looks beyond a cool surmise,
Such lamentable uproar from night skies
As turn the owl from honey of blood and make
Great stags stand still to hear the darkness shake.

In the last lines, however, he must make his descriptive hints symbolic, by suggesting that it offers a microcosm of the turning world, complete with still point:

This
Is noise made universe, whose still centre is
Where the cold adder sleeps in his small bed.
Curled neatly round his neat and evil head.

The suggestion that the still point is also the evil serpent of Genesis is backed up by the observational fact that the little snake alone is still and asleep: the fox and stag and the hills—good, natural things—are disturbed and troubled by the thunderous waters. Now this is, it seems to me, evidence of a recurrent mid-century malaise: the poet has nothing to offer but the observational procedures—methods mastered from the earlier generation of late romantic poets—and the attempt to convince us of universality and importance is hollow. It is a phenomenon we could illustrate *ad nauseam*—copiously enough from the works of MacCaig and Wilbur alone. (The two poets are among the best of a very large group.) Richard Wilbur's 'Simile for her Smile', for instance (shades of 'Le Monocle de mon Oncle'), turns out to be no more than a competent 'description' of a weighbridge:

Then horns are hushed, the oilsmoke rarefies,
Above the idling motors one can tell
The packet's smooth approach, the slip,
Slip of the silken river past the sides,
The ringing of clear bells, the dip
And slow cascading of the paddle wheels.

('Simile for her Smile')

This is admittedly an extreme example of a perception being shamelessly put to work. But the weakness is general, even in *The Beautiful Changes* and *Ceremony*. Wilbur really has not *seen* her smile in the workings of the bridge, or the workings of the bridge in the smile: we have a careful descriptive piece which has simply failed to amount to more than the sum of its parts, and the title of the poem becomes a falsehood. The thud of satisfied inference that characterizes the poetry of Edward Thomas and Robert Frost depended upon a structure of expectation in the poet, a mesh of gratifications and tendencies, which could use the natural imagery fed through it and feed back reports. Wilbur, like so many of his contemporaries, simply imitates the technical properties of feeling.

In this context, 'Ceremony' itself assumes special significance. It borrows generously from the early Milton, and its indebtedness is, I think, wittily and fairly acknowledged in usages which become, in the context, allusions. The reference to the *Comus* song in stanza two, for instance, is accompanied by pointedly Miltonic diction—in particular 'cynosure' and 'nymph'. The whole stanza is an excellent example of Wilbur's witty academicism at its best, using assumed cultural contexts to realize itself as style:

> Let her be some Sabrina fresh from stream,
> Lucent as shallows slowed by wading sun,
> Bedded on fern, the flowers' cynosure:
> Then nymph and wood must nod and strive to dream
> That she is airy earth, the trees, undone,
> Must ape her languor natural and pure.

('Ceremony')

If all poetry were like this, the mid-century accounts of the art in terms of symbolization and non-discursive form ('virtual experience' or 'symbolic action') would be unimpeachable:[4] we could, if we were prepared to forget all about Hopkins, and the later Yeats, and the Milton of the Blindness sonnet, enjoy ourselves in the mirror of Wilbur's verse, much as he invites us, voyeuristically, to enjoy his Bazille nymph. Formally, this is an elegant and shapely piece of work, its conclusion being foreshadowed in the opening stanza:

> But ceremony never did conceal,
> Save to the silly eye, which all allows,
> How much we are the woods we wander in.

But we are surely less than satisfied that the mind that has responded so coolly and exquisitely to the art of Bazille ('A striped blouse in a clearing') knows much about 'tigers in the wood'. This is Yeats's territory—one thinks of the Edmund Dulac poem with its assurance of vigilance and the horrible green birds at the edge of a wood. Again, I don't think Wilbur is being square with us. The peculiar logic of poetry demands that the 'I think' *within the limits of the poem* preface something we might plausibly believe—or believe *him* to believe. When Wilbur tells us that

> When with social smile and formal dress
> She teaches leaves to curtsey and quadrille
> I think there most are tigers in the wood,

we must again feel free simply to disbelieve him. Both within the structure of the poem and on the level of personal assurance, this statement seems false—not a pseudo-statement but a lie. It isn't, in the first place, particularly true that 'What's lightest hid is deepest understood'. Between the

---

[4] See, for instance, S. K. Langer, *Feeling and Form* (London 1953), ch. 14, and Kenneth Burke, *Language as Symbolic Action* (Berkeley 1966).

qualification of stanza one, that only the silly eye lets Ceremony conceal 'how much we are the woods we wander in' (whatever that actually means) and the final statement about the tigers in the wood, comes only the decorative Miltonic stanza, with no gesture towards argument or justification. On no level does the poem convince us of its intellectual or moral integrity.

In 'A Dutch Courtyard', the original of the poet's ideation is the Keats of the Grecian Urn ode. As with Milton in the earlier poem, the debt is hardly concealed:

> This girl will never turn,
> Cry what you dare, but smiles
> Tirelessly toward the seated cavalier,
> Who will not proffer you his pot of beer;
> And your most lavish wiles
>
> Can never turn this chair
> To proper use, nor your guile evict
> These tenants.

The depth of the Keats original is disowned by the introduction of the buyer of the De Hooch picture in the last stanza—a reminder that the poem has all along been a witty, social piece. But, still, it is hard to see the point of doing the thing again—so weakly. 'Ho hum,' Wilbur had said in the Bazille poem, 'I am all for wit and wakefulness.' We don't need this declaration to tell us where he comes from—the Brooks of *Modern Poetry and the Tradition*, the Cambridge critics of the 1930s. But it's worth remarking that wakefulness is to be taken very seriously, and that merely trotting out echoes of the anthologies, with due acknowledgement of the borrowings and a generally light tone about things, doesn't constitute a very interesting sort of wakefulness.

Again and again, we find Wilbur failing to buttress his images and observations with sufficiently powerful *raisons d'être*. Performances on the face of it dazzling prove, on close inspection, to have little or no authentic core. Consider, for instance, that beguiling exercise in the idiom of Byron's love lyrics and Schubert's *Lieder*, 'Flumen Tenebrarum'. The speaker in the poem doesn't 'envy the legendary heroes of the night sky their permanence': he would rather have his longing here. This, one would have thought, was sufficient case against the frozen gestures of the constellations, but no. Wilbur now pulls the rug out from under himself by making his 'being content' explained by the fact not that his ephemeral 'lively longing' is worth more than their frigid immortality (shades of the Grecian Urn again), but on the contrary that the immortality is spurious:

> None outlasts the stream, and even these
> Must come to life and die.
>   ('Flumen Tenebrarum')

Why? Why must they come to life, and why bring in the immortal galaxies at all, if the only point was to enhance the enjoyment of the sex and the kissing on the river? You can say that physical love is better than immortal frigidity, or that it ought to be enjoyed now because we'll come to dust anyway. But to use both arguments seems over-compensating, or just confusing two literary traditions, that of the Grecian Urn ode and 'To His Coy Mistress'.

A more troubling instance is the beautiful Traherne pastiche, 'A World Without Objects is a Sensible Emptiness'. What Wilbur really has to offer here is that stilted stride of the camel:

> The tall camels of the spirit
> Steer for their deserts, passing the last groves loud
> With the sawmill shrill of the locust, to the whole
>   honey of the arid
> Sun. They are slow, proud,
>
> And move with a stilted stride
> To the land of sheer horizon, hunting Traherne's
> *Sensible emptiness* there where the brain's lantern-slide
> Revels in vast returns. . . .

I suppose the 'whole honey of the arid/Sun' is the poem's most remarkable moment, but there is no doubting—once again—the skill of the entire achievement. The poem sustains the camel-like gait effortlessly, bumpily smooth, fluently negotiating. But we cannot think of Traherne or Vaughan or Crashaw and not shake our heads at the sheer vacuity—I use the word advisedly—of Wilbur's lovely utterance. It is really no more than an effusion, as of a machine that intakes literary grist and turns it out all mixed up, with no fixed point, none of that solid unshakable core of orientation from which the glorious radiance of the seventeenth-century poets emanates. For what, really, does Wilbur say here? As far as I can make it out, it is this. His spirit hunts 'a land of sheer horizons' (those 'desert landscapes' presumably for which another eminent American, Willard van Orman Quine, has such a self-advertised taste), where apparently 'the brain's lantern-slide/Revels in vast returns.' Later, the poem becomes another quasi-Yeatsian return from the never-never land of the spirit—with its burning emptiness—back to good old *terra firma*, complete with bracken and sunset:

> Back to the trees arrayed
> In bursts of glare, to the halo-dialing run
> Of the country creeks, and the hills's bracken tiaras made
> Gold in the sunken sun.

Then, having committed himself to this, Wilbur adjures his spirit—inexplicably, in so far as I have followed the poem's rationale—to 'watch for the sight of the supernova bursting over the barn'. The spirit's 'right

Oasis', it now appears, is the 'light incarnate'—some messianic appearance, the second coming. As in 'Flumen Tenebrarum' two rationales seem to be in conflict: what is so important about the lovable 'country creeks and the hills' bracken tiaras made/Gold in the sunken sun', if the spirit is then enjoined to ignore it and wait for the second coming? The answer is that no answer is possible, because Wilbur is playing with effects and ideas, and not really thinking.

For the sake of argument I should like finally to return to my point of departure, by comparing Wilbur with one of his English contemporaries, Philip Larkin. Their poetry has strong general resemblances—the same technical conservatism, astuteness of eye, argument by contraposing montages of perception, a pervasive irony. Where Wilbur is slick, Larkin is wry; Wilbur lacks Larkin's social acumen (compare the poverty of observation in a poem like 'Regatta', for instance, with Larkin's—or Fuller's or Betjeman's—social verse). This goes with the territory: American poets have not that kind of touch. But the really radical difference between the two poets concerns the poet's own participation in his *œuvre*. Larkin's work is structured at all times about his own role, his own development as man and therefore as poet, his relations with the society he is set down in, his relations with the rich literary tradition he inherits, with other human animals, with the whole scenario laid down by convention for modern man. There is an accumulation of weight from *The North Ship* to *High Windows* which in a sense transcends any single poem. Richard Wilbur obscures matters by his habit of padding out slender volumes with often not very distinguished translations. (What possessed him or his publishers to include in *Advice to a Prophet* a scene from *Tartuffe* I shall never understand.) But this is subordinate to the main point: there is no sense of personal engagement in Wilbur's verse, none of that structuring myth that links and lifts Larkin's observations, none of that symbolized personal testament that reaches the level of greatness in poems like 'The Whitsun Weddings'. The Blake influence that emerges in later volumes is interesting, and lends a certain gravity to *Advice to a Prophet*. But I think it came too late. Poems like 'Two Voices in a Meadow' and 'A Christmas Hymn' are Blake-pastiche, just as 'A World Without Objects' was Traherne-pastiche. Wilbur has remained a poet without a core.

It would be simplistic to assert that this absence of a creative personality is identifiably American. But one has seen this combination—extreme facility hand in hand with a certain baselessness—frequently enough in American poets to make one pause lengthily before dismissing the idea. Certainly Wilbur seems to represent a specific mid-century quality. Anglophile, academic, but with a metropolitan poise, correct, but with rushes of gaiety and exuberance that tend to come to nothing—Wilbur embodies better than any other of his contemporaries perhaps a style which we might call, simply, Ivy League.

At any rate, the general air of spiritual cleanliness about Wilbur's poetry makes him an excellent foil for a quite different kind of East Coast poet, one whose work it is convenient to refer to in Macha Rosenthal's term 'Confessional'.

Chapter 3

John Berryman
The Struggle Towards Dislocation

We can only say that it appears likely that poets in our civilization, as it exists at present, must be difficult. T. S. Eliot

I

Perhaps the first matter that needs settling in turning to the poetry of John Berryman is the notion of his being an especially difficult poet. Or rather, since there has been a degree of confusion about the verse necessitating an acknowledgement of a certain difficulty, it might conversely be stated that the difficulty has been one primarily of approach, existing in the minds of his readers rather than in the poems. What is significant, and what makes Berryman such an interesting mid-century case, is that he should apparently have sought to create the impression of being a difficult poet, and that his reader-critics (the two classes overlap almost entirely) should have bought what is beginning to seem a fairly blatant dummy. I should say right away what my tone has already made clear, that I do not regard him as a difficult poet. What we have here is, in fact, a fairly common phenomenon in modern culture, and it's by no means the case that the poet caught playing this game of bluff is thereby disqualified from serious consideration. On the contrary, it is the society and its readership that are on trial. Any serious student of the twentieth-century scene will be aware of the sociological and historical factors which have conspired to make certain orders of allusiveness, ellipticality and referential obscurity all but mandatory to the poet needing to define himself in a vastly unpromising cultural situation.

In the poems of Berryman's first volume, *The Dispossessed* (the parody mid-century title, I take it, refers to Eliot via de Nerval, rather than vice versa), an influence that immediately makes sense in the light of these reflections is that of William Empson:

> The fattest nation!—We do not thrive fat
> But facile in the scale with all we rise
> And shift a breakfast, and there is shame in that.
>
> (Berryman, 'The Lightning')

The throw-away tone—implying an impressively casual attitude towards 'major issues—'the air of expecting the reader to keep up easily, the use of the *terza rima* the tendency towards the broken phrase, even details like the use of 'shift' (Empson's 'Aubade', for instance)—everything bespeaks Berryman's awareness of the English poet-critic's subtle cleverness. Yet the Berryman-to-be is present already in lines like these:

> I see the dragon of years is almost done,
> Its claws loosen, its eyes
> Crust now with tears and lust and scale of lies.
>
> ('New Year's Eve')

In general, perhaps, the later poetry seems to have been written by a man who has spent the past twenty years waiting for these lines to come true, or be verified by time. In 'New Year's Eve', people drink too much, make passes at other men's wives, and generally show awareness of the shabby illusions they live by. Certainly, the verse lacks tension—it is as episodic and strung together as the lives of its characters are silly and pointless:

> Intelligentsia milling. In a semi-German
> (Our loss of Latin fractured how far our fate,—
> Disinterested once, linkage once like a sermon)
> I struggle to articulate
> Why it is our promise breaks in pieces early,
> The Muses' visitants come soon, go surly
> With liquor and mirrors away
> In this land wealthy and casual as a holiday.
>
> ('New Year's Eve')

These lines are interesting from several points of view. Berryman says, 'I struggle to articulate': he then proceeds to state the facts he purports to be struggling with quite easily. He says—without any struggle to speak of—what he had it in mind to say. Now, it is important to note what Berryman sees here: a lazy, over-drinking society, dissolving all oppositions and idealisms in whisky—something strangely close to Herbert Marcuse's one-dimensional America. This vision—if that is the word—was to remain with Berryman until the end. Yet it seems significant that Berryman should feel the need to plead complexity, a complexity he doesn't, when he gets down to it, really seem to require.

In fact, these two things go together, and Berryman's academicism could be given a more than usually precise definition: he was academic in vision (*Weltanschauung*) and in the technical preconceptions that went along with the vision. The fundamentally disabused vision finds nothing outside itself that excites attention; it therefore falls back upon acceptance of what it has been accustomed to observe as the facts of social life— self-seekingness, conceit, foolishness, corruption. A sensitive and thinking man—so the *Hamlet*-inspired ideology runs—must necessarily be out of true with this society. At the same time, the poet-academic must support his disalignment with the justification of himself: the struggle to articulate, the validation of role by the claim of superior knowledge, forms an important part of post-symbolist poetics.

We have here then the binding elements of the academic stance: first, a sense of disabusement with that human and social experience which the insensitive bourgeois finds it all too easy to wallow in; second, the belief in the inevitability of a certain 'difficulty' of expression, forced upon the poet by the recalcitrant complexities of experience, which it requires (so the ideology continues) all the academic poet's intelligence to unravel and articulate. Berryman, as the direct descendant from Empson, Auden and the Fugitives, is a classic mid-century instance of the syndrome.

We can, it's true, point to some masters of the past—Cézanne, outstandingly—who have persevered with an apparently innate clumsiness of manner and ended finally by making a virtue of this lack of professional skill (by contrast with Renoir and Monet, for instance) in order to make great art. I should argue myself that this is not the case with Berryman, in spite of the fact that he produced some interesting poetry late in life. For it is not clumsiness that is most obviously on display in *The Dispossessed*—it is fluent enough, though not especially promising; nor was it the 'struggle to articulate' that finally forced Berryman into his *Dream Songs* manner. On the contrary, it seems rather the opposite. Out of the fear of seeming facile in success, of seeming to find it too easy to express what ought to seem all but unsayable, Berryman takes up the challenge Eliot threw down forty years earlier ('Ours is a various and complex age', etc.), and perseveres with a drive not towards clarity—the Cézanne syndrome—but, on the contrary, towards dislocation. Such a view coheres with the *Weltanschauung* encouraged by the mid-century academic milieu: the poet fears that his own 'ordinary' experience is simply not significant enough to warrant expression *as direct as the poet can make it*. It's important to get this straight: I am not saying that poetry is *ever* simple; on the contrary, I am saying that only methods as simple, driven by a hunger for lucidity as absolute, as it is in the power of the given poet to muster, are capable of enfolding all the subtle complexity of the poetic apprehension. To start with an ideal of 'complexity', in poetry as in philosophy, runs counter to the real requirements of things. The academic poet in a sense refrains from embarking upon life until it is too late, in order, precisely, that he may have something definite and specific to regret and deplore. This is why *The Dispossessed* is so much more dispiriting than any of the later so-called 'Confessional' volumes: in them, the gambit, such as it was, has paid off, and the poet's 'struggle to articulate' has something sufficiently digested and formulated to withstand the mangle. In *The Dispossessed* (pretentiously and tendentiously titled as it is), we are forced to witness life through the eyes of a bad academic party-goer, the sort of character to whom one occasionally, if one is not careful, gets shackled, standing with a never empty, never full glass in a corner, to one side, out of things, getting steadily and imperceptibly sodden.

William Empson, by contrast, is instinct with a breezy vigour: he gets around, and we can accept his allusiveness as, in part at least, the interesting efforts of a highly intelligent man to bamboozle us with a skein of references, hints and inferences, that do in fact, on payment of sufficient effort and attention, reward us. When we turn to Berryman's 'tough' poems (as an Australian critic has called them[1]), we experience something quite different, something which in fact does not tax our intelligence or our ingenuity much at all, except in so far as some effort is required to familiarize ourselves with a personal shorthand. Then, Berryman does not emerge as an especially intelligent man, any more than Lowell does: and I do not just mean by contrast with William Empson, but with, say, a contemporary American like Philip Whalen. It is impossible to read half a page of Empson's criticism without feeling that the man is extraordinarily clever—too clever, perhaps, for his own good. This is simply not the case with Berryman.

Some critics have thought otherwise, it is true. Martin Dodsworth prefaces what seems to me the most sensitive account of Berryman yet to appear[2] with an awestruck apologia for an 'awesome' difficulty: 'the kind of difficulty which he exhibits is itself an answer to the difficulties under which he must labour at the present time'.[3] That is the way Leavis used to talk about Empson and Ronald Bottrall—and, I'd have thought, shows Mr Dodsworth taking the Berryman bait hook, line and sinker. It has never been 'easy' being a poet, or at least in fulfilling oneself as a poet (the gift itself being bestowed willy nilly). But the particular difficulties under which many academic poets labour are really illusory, and the source of this illusion is, as ever, the poet's sense of his place in the scheme of things. 'To be conscious,' as T. S. Eliot profoundly observed, 'is not to be in time.' To be in universities is, similarly, not to be 'in society'. The universities are in one sense the conscience of society, or at least the consciousness, and university teachers are removed from the dynamic life of society: they are neutralized in the class-struggle, no matter what contribution—radical or reactionary—their teaching might make to it through their students. And while it is true that there can be no such thing as (for instance) the working-class don, it is really no less true that there can be no such thing as the middle-class don either: to see the universities as either seats of reaction or hotbeds of sedition is simply to misread the facts. The university teacher is a class-eunuch, which

---

[1] James Tulip, 'Berryman's tough songs', *Southern Review* (Adelaide), VI (3) (1973), 257–68.
[2] 'John Berryman: an introduction', in *The Survival of Poetry*, ed. M. Dodsworth (London 1970).
[3] Idem.

explains not only why so few of our great writers have spent their lives in a university, but also why it is that recent university poets show certain self-destructive tendencies.[4] Unable to break out into the class-history mechanism, but unwilling to accept the real nature of his role in the world, the academic poet tends to distort his own natural experience into the shape of what he conceives to be more authentic or problematic experience. Because of his unnaturally privileged position in society, the academic poet fears that his enthusiasms (which must, in the nature of all poetic experience, form the basis of the poetry) will simply not be acceptable out in the 'real' world, the world every poet instinctively and rightly looks to in the act of composition. The universe is, as it were, engaged in work, time and history, and even eternity is only to be understood from the vantage-point of time.

What this really means is that the academic poet's professional 'difficulty' of idiom is a product not so much of his complex understanding of complex subject-matter, as of—to the contrary—his fundamental lack of faith in the significance of that subject-matter. (It should be noted that the syndrome here is different from the related one in which the country-boy poet—Rimbaud, Dylan Thomas—masks insecurity with obscurity: the academic's complexity is sociologically different.) The truly sane, truly aware poet knows that the job to be done is so difficult that nothing but direct and simple address will enable him to frame its subtleties. This does not mean, of course, that the poetry will be simple: on the contrary, things are the other way about. The saying of the things that need to be said is of itself so difficult that it cannot be said in any language but that which comes most naturally to the poet. The true complexity of the poet is a simple articulation of complex things, not a complex presentation of simplicities. Mr Micawber's tremendous periphrases are all designed to communicate the utterly banal—how to get from the Strand to the City Road, for instance; if he had had anything at all complicated to say, his idiom would have collapsed under the strain, and he would necessarily have used language as simple as he could manage—as simple, 'in short', as the facts deserve.[5]

Berryman's 'difficulty'—such as it is—is then in inverse ratio to his belief in himself and in the significance of what he is doing. I have

[4] Stephen Spender (*Love–Hate Relations*, 223) explains this tendency in terms of the campus-poet's isolation.

[5] We touch here on a general condition of twentieth-century intellectual life, of course. Simone de Beauvoir observed of the young Sartre that he was never so happy as when he could not understand what he was writing. Kant, it seems worth noting, does not give this impression: the *Critiques* are difficult because of the subject-matter, which could only be apprehended and marshalled in the mind with the address to simplicity of which the precise, informal prose is the evidence. We can find in the *Being and Nothingness* of Sartre, perhaps, the first major evidence of that absence of inner conviction, so characteristic of French thought, which was finally to lead to the *Tel Quel* conception of the book-as-object—a very nice way of externalizing a total inner vacuum.

maintained that Berryman is not especially difficult, and I maintain it now. The general impression of difficulty—which has communicated itself as a kind of dread even to the experts in the field—nevertheless remains, and, far from being inconsistent with my assertion of an actual simplicity, is fascinatingly involved with it. Berryman, I have suggested, wanted to be thought difficult, and he succeeded. And this is more positive proof of my general thesis about academic poetry than an actual intellectual complexity would be. The point of bringing forward these arguments is to help bring about a different way of approaching and then reading Berryman's poems, one grounded more surely in a proper understanding of the facts.

The essence of this new modus is the belief—already expressed above—that what we have in *Homage to Mistress Bradstreet* and the *Dream Songs* is a straining not towards simplification but away from it. The toughness of *Bradstreet* is the result of a struggle *not* to articulate. The struggle, is on the one hand, to avoid detection, to avoid being made object (one thinks of Sartre's strategy of keeping on the run); and on the other—paradoxically—to make oneself *thing*. That is, the voice wants to be acknowledged as a thing, it wants to reify itself: yet at the same time, the *thought* wants to disguise itself, to hide in the thickets of verbiage, not be caught naked. And the root-cause of the syndrome is a sociological one: the academic does not want to be reified in—*or rather out of*—society.

These reflections place the techniques of *Bradstreet* in an entirely different category from those of Gerard Manley Hopkins, who gave Berryman —beyond question—more than any other poet gave him. For what we see in *The Wreck of the Deutschland*—the technical model for Berryman's poem—is precisely the poet's labour towards a voice, straining to make himself visible to himself and therefore to others. The Hopkins poem, in other words, exists by virtue of an act of communication: *Mistress Bradstreet* exists by virtue of an act of evasion. Berryman performs a ritual, and hopes that he is dropping enough hints to interest the audience beyond the general sacral situation. To a certain extent and in a certain way, this is true of all poets. But it is also true in the nature of things that the pursuit of poetry involves certain structural properties—among them, the poet's self-identification as a human being: to make things clear to himself is to make them clear to others, and writing poetry would have no value or interest whatever without this assumption. Poetry is, as it were, communicational in its essence. But this communicational essence has always been conveyed through certain means—rhythm, song, symbol, image—which the poet has always wanted to keep sacred and upon which he has always laid a particular emphasis. What has happened in the modern world is that socio-technological circumstances have driven poets to identify the sacred means of poetry with the sacral end: the poet has lost sight of the fact that the means—the rhythms, the symbols, the song— were only designed to make possible a particular communication.

To illustrate the point, I should like to take something from *Mistress Bradstreet*, and then something from the *Dream Songs*. My thesis is that, although *Homage to Mistress Bradstreet* is obviously based upon *The Wreck of the Deutschland*, there is an absolute difference between Hopkins's fracturing of ordinary speech in order to communicate certain tensions and meanings in what in effect is a different speech, and Berryman's attempt to patch together a synthetic speech. This is a fundamental difference in intention (and in intension) that can be demonstrated fairly easily by the experiment of reading aloud: Hopkins's poem emerges through vocal performance (though one would never suspect this from the extraordinarily vapid gramophone recordings that have been made) as a great verbal symphony, in which the stammers and nervous starts that so often puzzle the new reader on the page are taken up in the great press towards articulation informing the whole enterprise. *Homage to Mistress Bradstreet*, on the other hand, simply cannot be read aloud; and if the effort to do so is persevered with (it is obviously physically possible, though spiritually rebarbative), the text is revealed for what it is— private, muttering, occasionally spurious, certainly nonvocal. In fact, one interesting byproduct of a close reading of Berryman could be the refutation of the intentionalist-fallacy fallacy: to understand this verse— as any other, in fact—we have to know how to read it, and to know how to read we have to be able to *feel* its intention, to see what it was looking at; and this is something that merely inspecting the surface and interrogating it for semantic interrelations often cannot decide. An act of intuition or empathy akin to mimicry is what is called for in realizing a literary text (using the verb in the sense a musicologist might understand). 'Getting' a poem is like 'getting' a joke, and guessing intentions is often a prerequisite to interpreting signs. (Having 'got' the poem, of course, we can then pretend that we did so by merely inspecting the signs.)

It will be perhaps a good idea at this point to take up an illustration already taken up by another critic. From an article already mentioned, by James Tulip, I take stanzas 24 to 26 of *Bradstreet*:

> Forswearing it otherwise, they starch their minds.
> Folkmoots, & blether, blether. John Cotton rakes
> to the synod of Cambridge.
> Down from my body my legs flow,
> out from it arms wave, on it my head shakes.
> Now Mistress Hutchinson rings forth a call—
> should she? many creep out at a broken wall—
> affirming the Holy Ghost
> dwells in one justified. Factioning passion blinds
>
> all to all her good, all—can she be exiled?
> Bitter sister, victim! I miss you.
> —I miss you, Anne,

day and night weak as a child,
tender & empty, doomed, quick to no tryst.
—I hear you. Be kind, you who leaguer
my image in the mist.
—Be kind you, to one unchained eager far & wild

and if, O my love, my heart is breaking, please
neglect my cries and I will spare you. Deep
in Time's grave, Love's, you lie still.
Lie still.—Now? That happy shape
my forehead had under my most long, rare,
ravendark, hidden, soft bodiless hair
you award me still.
You must not love me, but I do not bid you cease.

Mr Tulip speaks of 'the multiple perspectives, changing modes of address'; and of 'language unfixing itself in its forms and references' as making the 'manner indeed difficult'.[6] But 'the matter', Mr Tulip goes on, as though a distinction of importance is being made, 'especially the final emotion, seems to set itself out in sharp, free and clear relief'.[7] The implication seems to be that the 'difficulty' of the manner somehow makes this final clarity, this standing forth of emotion, possible. But is this so, in fact? What we have, I should argue to the contrary, is something of its essence straightforward—'passionate'. In stanza 24—the one here which might create for a reader otherwise ignorant of the poem the impression of difficulty—there is an excellent example of the stylistic mannerism I have been hinting at above:

Forswearing it otherwise, they starch their minds.

'It' here refers to the starch that comes later in the line: against normal practice, but otherwise not remarkable. 'Folkmoots of blether, blether' is people meeting in council and talking prosily, stodgily; 'John Cotton rakes/To the synod of Cambridge'—not so easy to translate, but again not therefore especially interesting: merely private, an unrealized hint at the authoritarian morality. This sort of writing is characteristic of Berryman: the style is manneristic and idiosyncratic, determined to translate the banal, the sheerly ordinary, into the 'poetic' by means of a crossword-puzzle allusiveness. One gets used to it easily enough, and I am not saying that it is an especially bad habit, though I admit that it tends to irritate me. It is the sort of game a university poet is inclined to amuse himself with. But is it otherwise and more interestingly 'difficult', with all the suggestion in the word of hidden reserves of 'meaning' and gains made from the manner compounding the matter via ellipses and imaginative con-

[6] Tulip, 'Berryman's tough songs', 262
[7] Idem.

flations? The answer to the question is surely dictated by the next lines of the poem:

> Down from my body my legs flow,
> out from it arms wave, on it my head shakes.

The meaning? Mistress Bradstreet has a body as distinct from her soul, and thereto the usual appendages—a head, hands and feet. The verb 'flow' appears to strive for a certain poeticality—is she enjoying her sexuality in a way forbidden by the Puritan taboos? Perhaps. But the next line makes it clear that Berryman wants to introduce a 'theme', or rather an episode, but doesn't know how to,

> Now Mistress Hutchinson rings forth a call—
> should she?

'Rings forth a call'? Meaning simply that Mistress Bradstreet wants to talk about Mistress Hutchinson, and about her own feelings for her: 'should the call be rung forth?'—That is, is the feeling forbidden? The next phrase—'many creep out at a broken wall'—shows by contrast what Berryman's conscious poeticality usually lacks: this 'wall' is genuinely and interestingly symbolic, in that it is more than periphrasis for the breached orthodoxy. Many of Berryman's critics seem to be looking for this kind of usage in places where the poet is being merely periphrastic, that is, where he is going in the opposite direction from the poetic accumulation of meaning, by simply diffusing, watering down the banal. The paradox is that direct speech—I mean what we find, for instance, in Allen Ginsberg, and what would suit Berryman better in most cases—would in fact be far more economical than the endless would-be subtle hints, nudges and periphrases by which Berryman tries to assure us of his depth. Eliot put it well in contrasting one of his symbolic lyrics—'What is the late November doing?'—with the plain discursive speech that seemed to suit the immediate purpose better; 'That was a way of putting it,—not very satisfactory/A periphrastic study in a worn out poetic fashion' (*East Coker*). Much of Berryman's verse—most of it perhaps— is periphrastic in just such a 'worn out poetic fashion'.

In the stanzas under discussion, the point seems underlined by the relatively free dialogue that follows the introduction of Mistress Hutchinson. I take it that this is what Mr Tulip calls 'multiple perspectives' —that is, the introduction of two inset speaking voices, accompanied— presumably—by the unseen presence of the poet. It is possible on critical paper to make this sound complex, I suppose; in reality, a sequential dialogue between two characters in a narrative, clearly separated as they are according to traditional usage, hardly seems to warrant such portentous language. Perhaps the most interesting thing in the passage that follows—it is in stanza 26—is the long series of adjectives used by Mistress Hutchinson to describe her own hair:

> my most long, rare,
> ravendark, hidden, soft bodiless hair . . .

James Tulip observes of these stanzas: 'Conciseness is everywhere.'[8] Reading about Mistress Hutchinson's hair, I should have thought that the last virtue the verse possessed was conciseness. The Dylan Thomas of *Under Milk Wood* seems a relevant influence, though the tone suggests Rossetti. The poetry here, moreover, is more fluent and coherent than elsewhere, and reinforces the impression that in general Berryman did not need to build up his broken, stammering, elliptical yet periphrastic idiom in order to say things that could not be said otherwise. On the contrary, it would seem sounder to argue the opposite, that Berryman used hints and ellipses as a smokescreen for something much less remarkable.

Yet what he thought unworthy of attention was probably in reality much more worthwhile than the meanings he encouraged the critics to quarry out. For with all reservations allowed for, it must be stated that the finest passages of *Homage to Mistress Bradstreet* transmit something exceptional in their time. The general tenor of this chapter so far will have made it clear enough by now that I regard Berryman's reputation as being somewhat inflated. But it seems to me much more important to rescue Berryman from his admirers than to hurl him to his detractors. I have spent some time trying to establish what Berryman was not, and this is important if we are to understand what he was. The 'style' of *Homage of Mistress Bradstreet* is, in general, patched-up—a put-together job of factitious economies masking an actual slackness and dividedness; ponderousness is dressed up in ellipses that are really periphrases, in order to create an air of tautness and strain.

Nevertheless, at its best, Berryman moves us strongly, and without the aid of the irritating idiosyncrasies meant to simulate complexity. He achieves a language that is genuinely 'tense with love', to use a later phrase of his—natural and stylish at once:

> The winters close, Springs open, no child stirs
> Under my withering heart, O seasoned heart
> God grudged his aid.
> All things else soil like a shirt.
> Simon is much away. My executive stales.
> The town came through for the cartway by the pales,
> but my patience is short,
> I revolt from, I am like, these savage foresters.
>
> *(Homage to Mistress Bradstreet)*

How well and strongly the feeling moves through the verse here, when it is allowed to, taking in its stride deep inward rumination and significant external detail, to make a whole pattern of consciousness, in the manner

---

[8] 'Berryman's tough songs', 262.

of the very finest moments of Browning's monologues. 'My executive
stales' perhaps sails close to the wind (it's hard to restrain a smile at the
unconscious intrusion from the twentieth century here). But the voice-
tone overrides the tricky oddities, and indeed redeems them. 'I revolt
from, I am like, these savage foresters': the inserted phrase 'I am like'
could occur precisely in this way, ruminatively. It marks a change of
mind mid-phrase, an adjustment of thought, leading to an important
insight into kinship with the Indians,—

> Whose passionless dicker in the shade, whose glance
> impassive and scant, belie their murderous cries
> when quarry seems to show.

Again, incidentally, conciseness doesn't seem an essential characteristic of
Berryman's manner: the last clause added, 'when quarry seems to show,'
seems superfluous, given demands of strict economy—the sort of lame
banality that disfigures Robert Lowell's best verse from time to time. The
contrast with the belying impassivity has already been sufficiently
established. But requirements of a different sort are—elsewhere
—satisfied abundantly: we've got the illusion of the thinking-
speaking voice, for one thing, and that's what Berryman most needs at
this point:

> Again I must have been wrong, twice.
> Unwell in a new way. Can that begin?
> God brandishes. O love, O I love.

The Browningesque authenticity is helped out here by memories of
Leopold Bloom, perhaps: it is from Joyce that we have learned so to copy
the mind's habits of notation. The first line of the three just quoted is
enough to let us know the theme of what is to follow—pregnancy, and
then the birth itself. Once again, Berryman's oddities come good; 'God
brandishes'—the neutering of the verb is curiously of the essence here,
with the fusion of pain and ecstasy the childbirth is to bring with it.
Berryman might seem to have jeopardized his naturalness, but in being
robbed of an object, 'brandishes' stands forth more abruptly. In the
stanzas that follow, Berryman is right at the quick of the thing, the forced-
out phrases mimetic of the transfiguring pains of labour:

> So squeezed, wince you I scream? I love you & hate
> off with you. Ages! *Useless.* Below my waist
> he has me in Hell's vise.
> Stalling. He let go. Come back: brace
> me somewhere. No. No. Yes! everything down
> hardens I press with horrible joy down
> my back cracks like a wrist
> shame I am void   oh behind it is too late

> Hide me forever O work I thrust I must free
> now I all muscles & bones concentrate
> what is living from dying?

The strange factualness rings true:

> Simon I must leave you so untidy
> Monster you are killing me Be sure
> I'll have you later Women do endure

The phrases are right in their dryness—thrown-out—so that one of Berryman's closest borrowings from his master, italicized, brings him to his crisis:

> I can *can* no longer
> and it passes the wretched trap whelming and I am me
> drencht & powerful, I did it with my body!
> One proud tug greens Heaven. Marvellous,
> Unforbidding Majesty.
> Swell imperious bells. I fly.

It would not be true to say that this is the only good writing in *Homage to Mistress Bradstreet*, but it so far outweighs the rest as to stand on its own high plateau, neither needing (nor getting) support, before or after, much as A. Alvarez presented it fifteen years ago in his anthology, *The New Poetry*. Call it 'Childbirth' or whatever, and it stands as one of the few poems from postwar America that might be great. The rest is literature. The attempt to make significant the poet's narrator-role (by James Tulip, for one[9]) seems misplaced: the poet's fond farewell to the seventeenth-century poetess at the end of the poem, like his imaginary meeting with her earlier, is almost sentimental. There is none of that powerful presence of the poet which makes *The Wreck of the Deutschland* an act of personal spiritual exploration, as well as an elegy for the dead nuns. Berryman's feeling about the seventeenth century seems merely nostalgic.

It is enough to say that at its best the poem sustains the illusion of the interior monologue with intensity, and with something of Browning's flexibility:

> Veiled my eyes, attending. How can it be I?
> Moist, with parted lips, I listen, wicked.
> I shake in the morning, & retch.
> I brook on myself naked.
> A fading world I dust, with fingers new.
>
> (*Homage to Mistress Bradstreet*)

The reader will forgive me (or perhaps he will not) for taking these liberties with Berryman's verse: I change Berryman's word-order and

---

[9] 'Berryman's tough songs', 262.

leave out his emphatic 'do' in the fourth line quoted to show that his mannerisms are more often than not merely idiosyncratic and unfunctional, clogging rather than facilitating expression. Unfortunately the majority of critical commentary on Berryman's poem has accepted the importance of Berryman's tricks and concentrated on the elucidation of what are frequently mere shorthand references, affectations, academic quirks and whims, rather than poetic necessities. Certainly, the total effect of the poem is not one of complexity.

II

By the time Berryman wrote the *Dream Songs* he had as it were dug himself into something approaching a stable personal style. Inside the twitchy mannerisms of *Bradstreet* something powerful had been present, but intermittently, overladen by strictly academic preoccupations: Berryman academicizes Hopkins, imitating the externals of his style with little of the internal stress, the labour-passage being the exception that proves the rule. But there is significance in the choice of master, more so than in the earlier hero-worship of Yeats to which Berryman confessed.

A concern with the poetics of Hopkins in the 1930s and 1940s was generally disturbing—as witness the attempts to bend the bow made by Day Lewis and Auden in England, and by Lowell in America. But a concern with what Hopkins used the stylistic innovations to body forth, a concern, that is, with his content, was a different matter. A significantly large body of mid-century American poets (Berryman himself, Wilbur, Lowell, Barbara Howes, Vassar Miller) have acknowledged the influence and example of Hopkins.[10] It is a significant influence not just because Hopkins was an attractive and exciting technical innovator, though the new approach to the exploitation of the 'thews and sinews' of the language such as we see in *Homage to Mistress Bradstreet* certainly derives from him. What is much more important is that Hopkins opened up new territory in the poetic exploration of the more basic spiritual and intellectual condition of modern man, the bedrock situations such as are examined also in the philosophical works of Nietzsche and Kierkegaard, and indeed constitute the ground of *Existenz philosophie* as a whole. Hopkins established an archaeology of the human personality as none of his contemporaries did. The *Terrible* Sonnets are in many ways the central tablet of the twentieth-century poetic tradition in English. In England, I have pointed out elsewhere,[11] the problems were different: a more deeply rooted tradition of voice and inflection—unbroken since *Beowulf* both in society and in literature—made for a stable base for exploration. In America, on the other hand, we see in the mid-century preoccupation

[10] In Nemerov (ed.), *Contemporary American Poetry*.
[11] *The Ironic Harvest*, ch. 2.

with Hopkins sure evidence of the need for a foundation to the national psyche such as Whitman had not provided. Thrown back upon the individual personality, American poets looked to Hopkins, I think, for guidance in the analysis and the presentation of the naked self. But Hopkins had behind him not only the long history of England with its steadily accreted 'national character', but also the strength of Roman Catholic doctrine. Poems like 'Carrion Comfort' show that Hopkins could structure his despair and shape his abandonment according to the laws of the Church. Just as mystics gain in stature and strength from taking their place within a regulated theology, so great religious analysts like Pascal, Kierkegaard and Hopkins are given the wherewithal to plumb the infinitely cheerless by an invisible yet enabling instrument of religious orthodoxy. The so-called Confessional poets of America were attempting for the first time in American literary history to found an analytics of the self, such as Hopkins, Clare, Hardy, Edward Thomas and Lawrence had long since established in England. In the absence both of the inherited national self of the English, and of the support and clarification of the Church, the Americans fell back upon Freud—with more or less disastrous results.

The role Freudianism has played in mid-century American society is too wide a subject for the present context. Suffice it to say that two factors seem especially relevant to its understanding: first, the spiritual rootlessness of America (its 'Jewishness') which has already been touched on;[12] second, the affluence necessary to maintain psychoanalysis as a way of life. Psychoanalysis, particularly in the United States, is a way of life which proffers not so much the hope of cure as the promise of companionship for the duration. In America as nowhere else, psychoanalysis has become part of the national lore: the couch, the analyst, the complex have entered into national humour, as they have not in any other country.

The Confessional poets of the late 1950s and early 1960s do not always play around with the content of Freud's doctrines. But the general tenor of their work bespeaks an inward orientation not towards God or Christ or Man, but towards Dr Freud—the friendly understanding analyst, who can be wheedled and abused at will. In particular, they have in common the conception of the self as passive: the Confessional poets alternately flagellate and flaunt, punish and cosset themselves. They see themselves as victims and heroes—sufferers through their sensitivity, heroic in their suffering. This has produced a particular tone—or range of tones— nervous and hard-boiled, whisky-slugging and withdrawn, sullen and self-pitying. Often, the poet plays dumb insolence, treating the reader as analyst, and making him uncertain about the way he is going to turn next.

[12] See p. 37 above.

This is all, of course, fairly predictable behaviour for the mid-twentieth-century American bourgeois, over-moneyed and under-motivated. The poet may confer a role upon himself—rather than choose to fill a role—by joining in the usual chorus of dissent, abusing the Pentagon, the Vietnam war, and so on. But this is usually felt to be hollow: he is aware—although he often writes as if *we* were not—of the anomalous nature of this well-heeled bourgeois attacking the social structure that guarantees his position in the world. And so he does what the man really embedded in the work-machine cannot do—he induces upon himself a nervous breakdown. In the poetry of the Confessional poets, the nervous breakdown is at the heart of things. Associated with the nervous breakdown of course is suicide, and suicide, as the guarantor of integrity and the procurer of authenticity, is the true identifying preoccupation of the school.[13]

It is in fact not so easy to commit suicide: most suicide attempts fail not because it is hard to stop the mechanism working (a pin-prick reaches the jugular), but because the organism revolts against it. The resistance comes from varying depths. Most suicide attempts plainly come from the upper reaches of the range, so that a window is accidentally-on-purpose left open, or the timing is guaranteed to bring intervention before it's too late, and so on. Sylvia Plath never wrote more falsely than when she observed of 'dying' that it was something she did 'rather well': she only mastered it once.

The harmonics of suicide are, however, not my subject here. I am concerned with the quality of poetry sponsored by the cult, and by the social-historical conditions underlying it. What I think we can conclude is this. The true end of Confessional poetry ought to be the analysis of 'reality'—the real relations between the self and the world of its experience.[14] Now the social context of the phenomenon made, in fact, for quite another product: the Freudian preconceptions of the school encouraged a false reification of the self. It was not the 'real' self that was under analysis but the conventionalized Freudian fiction, object and victim, as passive to analysis as to reflection, structured in certain predictable ways—ways which precisely precluded the activity of the active self, the organizing, reflective experiencer. So that the real crunch was always avoided: the tragic clash, the collision of self with itself, of self with 'reality', with God—this was replaced by the session with the analyst, who fills the empty self with spurious content (with a father you hate, a mother you love). The self, we may say, is made of two elements, or rather it has two ways of functioning. It can be subject and object, passive and active; it is capable not only of perception and remembrance, but of apperception and self-awareness. The process of the self becoming visible to itself is what, I submit, we witness in great tragic art—in, for

[13] See A. Alvarez, *The Savage God* (London 1972).
[14] M. Rosenthal, *The New Poets*.

instance, the later sonnets of Hopkins. This self-in-collision-with-reality is emphatically *not* what we see in the poetry of the American Confessionals. Here, the observer 'sits so sly', and cossets himself, casting himself into all sorts of roles, some guaranteed to aggrandize, some to justify, others to punish himself:

> Henry hates the world. What the world to Henry
> did will not bear thought.
> Feeling no pain,
> Henry stabbed his arm and wrote a letter
> explaining how bad it had been
> in this world.
>
> (*Dream Songs*, 74)

Now of course 'Henry' is Berryman's name for himself, and it affords him a certain useful latitude of tone, almost as if he wants to keep those old ironic options open to disappear behind when under probe. One can respect and understand his wish to make himself objective to himself. But the rejection of the first personal pronoun does not by any means guarantee an infallible objectivity towards oneself. One can strike attitudes, be ironical, justify oneself, quite as easily by using an imaginary name for oneself, as one can when speaking more ordinarily through the first person. (Witness the tone of Grass's *The Tin Drum*, for instance.) Henry in Berryman's cycle is alternately approved, ridiculed, commiserated with, pitied, wept over. The net result—what we must try to establish, after all—is, I think, self-vindication: Berryman maximizes pathos, at the same time as he conveys an impression—through using the persona—of complete mastery.

Song 26 gives us an important clue, I think:

> Fell Henry back into the original crime: art, rime. . . .

This is a tone familiar to us from Pound's *Mauberley*: 'For three years, out of key with his time, /He strove to resuscitate the dead art/Of poetry.' It is something we get used to in reading through the *Songs*:

> —Henry is tired of the winter,
> & haircuts, & a squeamish comfy ruin-prone proud national
>   mind & Spring (in the city so called).
> Henry likes Fall.
> Hé would be prepared to líve in a world of Fáll
> forever, impenitent Henry.
>
> (*Dream Songs*, 77)

The Song ends with Henry 'stript down to move on'. And the Songs that follow are the so-called posthumous Songs. From this point in the collection a stronger fluency sets in. The high point of *Mistress Bradstreet* is never attained again, but the tricksy, private shorthand interferes less with what the poet wants to say. It is still possible to sweat over some moments, but increased familiarity with the text makes it obvious that Berryman's 'moments of truth' signal themselves in clear language, a concern to get something said, and that therefore the puzzling mutterings may safely be left as of interest to the scholar only, with no real interest for the reader of poetry. They are failed communication, simply. The shorthand itself is not at all difficult: 'Cawdor uneasy', for instance, is an unhelpful Shakespearian allusion that doesn't in fact add to the mood; the reader who has worked his way as far as Song 52 will fill out the phrase 'when most he' with the rest of the sentence—'needed help.' It may well be true that Berryman falls into these irritating mannerisms when poetically at a weak moment: self-pity gets in the way of poetry's clairvoyance.

The level is not in general sustained throughout the cycle; and in fact, the air of control suggested in the song format with the three similar stanzas is pretty spurious. The academic programme, in fact, is a set of bars for Berryman's teeth. A good conversation piece like Song 55 ('Peter's not friendly') badly needed the intelligent informality of a Philip Whalen to fulfil itself. The technical timidity goes of course with the general tone and content: Song 42 tells us where Berryman's at:

> We dream of honour and we get along.

It is all rather dispiriting, a latter-day stoicism which does not seem calculated to make the most of human intelligence. Turn to the early Ginsberg, to Kenneth Patchen, to Gregory Corso, and Berryman seems stale and confined.

But if there is a certain self-pity at the heart of the *Dream Songs* there is no question but that, by the end of the sequence, Berryman has developed an idiom that is authentically his own, and which is used to say things that matter about his experience—a very representative one:

> The lovely friends, and friends the friends of friends,
> pursuing insights to their journey's ends
> subtle and steadfast:
> the wind blows hard from our past into our future
> and we are that wind, except that the wind's nature
> was not to last.
>
> (*Dream Songs*, 82)

There seems a touch of Byron's *Childe Harold* manner here—the same sense of freshness coming through jadedness, of feeling, momentarily at least, the excitement and the significance of the voyage. And this of course is what the *Dream Songs* are about: the journey of the poetic life that grows out of and merges back into the human life. Hence the legitimate concern with the masters, with Swift in particular:

> Your high figures float
> again across my mind and all your past
> fills my walled garden with your honey breath
> wherein I move, a mote.
>
> *(Dream Songs, 312)*

Berryman has moved through and beyond his idiom here, or rather his idiom has transcended itself. The verse moves powerfully and freely, as it does in the beautiful Spenserian allegory, 'Behind me twice her necessary knight':

> Hard lies the road behind, hard that ahead
> but we are armed & armoured & we trust
> entirely in one another.
> We have beaten down the foulest of them, lust,
> and we pace on in peace, like sister & brother
> doing that to which we were bred.
>
> *(Dream Songs, 315)*

Is it a weakness or a strength that the idiom is pastiche, that so much of the *Dream Songs* gets its content and attitudes from the great masters? It might be a twentieth-century condition. It might be a symptom of that baselessness which has already been diagnosed in American culture, or that characteristically American tendency towards consistent self-enactment noted by Spender.[15] Berryman worked fairly hard at creating a legend, and he makes it hard for us to separate the poetry from the myth. At any rate Berryman at his father's grave parodies the heroes of Shakespeare and Kyd:

> When will indifference come, I moan & rave
> I'd like to scrabble till I got tight down
> away down under the grass
> and ax the casket open ha to see
> just how he's taking it, which he sought so hard
> we'll tear apart
> the mouldering grave clothes ha & then Henry
> will heft the ax once more, his final card
> and fell it on the start.
>
> *(Dream Songs, 384)*

There is a force, an intensity in this which puts to shame the reticence of many of Berryman's gifted English contemporaries. (One would like to know, for instance, what sort of poetry Empson might have written over the past thirty years.) But ultimately there is an inevitability about Berryman's despair—it was there in essence in the 'New Year's Eve' poem written twenty-five years earlier—which suggests an explanation

15 *Love–Hate Relations,* 208–11.

more fundamental than that offered by Spender (the 'absurdity and grandeur' of the campus-poet system). For the Confessional poets were beaten before the start, and although there is a fullness and authenticity in their rhetoric new in American writing, one's final impression is of a fictive self cast in a drama scripted by psychoanalysis, a role which seemed to confer upon the poet some sort of meaning in a life felt to be meaningless.

Chapter 4

The Poetry of Breakdown
Robert Lowell and Anne Sexton

It has become customary to use the adjective 'academic' in a pejorative sense. But although there is a range of poetic vices that can fairly be referred to by the word, there is also a way in which it can be used descriptively, with no value judgement implied. Poetry of the 1930s, 1940s and 1950s, in America and in England, is often academic in that it derives in important respects from academic criticism, in particular from the Cambridge critics and their American followers, the so-called New Critics. This poetry—which can be called neo-metaphysical—places an especial emphasis upon certain orders of verbal complexity; it is prepared to use the conceit, as the Romantic poets were not; it harks back, characteristically, not to the Romantics indeed but to the Metaphysicals. I have given my opinion of the poetry of this 'school' in America,[1] as being on the whole less interesting and less truly 'complex' than the poetry of the English neo-metaphysicals. Berryman owed much of his bias towards obscurity to the New Critical emphasis on complexity. But there was another respect in which the academicism of this kind of poetry hampered the emergence of that very fullness it was designed to facilitate. This was a certain eschewal of, almost a contempt for, the personal voice, and the free treatment of directly personal subject-matter. This is something better illustrated in the poetry of Lowell than in that of Berryman. For although now regarded as a Confessional poet, on the strength of poetry written later in life, Lowell initially established his reputation with the sort of 'impersonal' poetry designed to please the academic ear.

Perhaps the best instance of the purely academic judgement of Lowell is to be found in Alvarez's Preface to his anthology *The New Poetry*.[2] What poetry must have, Alvarez argues—what Lowell and Berryman have—is 'a new seriousness. I would define this seriousness simply as the poet's ability and willingness to face the full range of his experience with his full intelligence; not to take any of the easy exits of either the conventional response or choking incoherence'[3]. Now this concern for

---

[1] See p. 29 above.
[2] A. Alvarez, *The New Poetry* (Harmondsworth 1962).
[3] Ibid., 24.

'intelligence' is easily identifiable. What we have here is that neo-metaphysical academicism where to use 'the full range of his experience with his full intelligence' means to subject the emotion to 'secondary consideration' (Brooks) or 'ironical contemplation' (Richards). Participation of the intelligence means being sensible and ironical about one's experience. There is nothing new (even for its time) in this, and nothing intrinsically interesting. What is interesting is that Alvarez should have written like this five years after the publication of Ginsberg's '*HOWL*,' and that 'choking incoherence' should appear as the enemy. Something like a polarization is evident here. Alvarez praises Lowell and Berryman for having

> assimilated the lesson of Eliot and the critical 'thirties; they assumed that a poet, to earn his title, had to be very skilful, very original, and very intelligent.[4]

How, one might ask, does a poet set out to be 'very original' and 'very intelligent'? These are dangerous virtues to cultivate deliberately, as we have seen in the case of Berryman; as dangerous, at least, as the Georgian virtues of beauty and poeticality. But this is fair indication not only of the way Lowell was being read in the 1960s (he has had a rough ride since), but of the way he probably read himself. His provenance out of the old New Criticism undoubtedly explains the air of strenuously literary toughness so characteristic of his earlier verse, which creates a wall of Lowell, and deals the reader body-blows:

> This is the end of the whaleroad and the whale
> Who spewed Nantucket bones on the thrashed swell
> And stirred the troubled waters to whirlpools
> To send the Pequod packing off to Hell:
> This is the end of them, three-quarters fools,
> Snatching at straws to sail
> Seaward and seaward on the turntail whale,
> Spouting out blood and water as it rolls,
> Sick as a dog to these Atlantic shoals. . . .
>
> ('The Quaker Graveyard in Nantucket')

Now this is poetry as the author of *Modern Poetry and the Tradition* understood it: here are the ironical jibes ('turntail whale') and the studiously non-poetic colloquialisms ('packing off to hell') that prove the poet tough-minded and flexibly ironical. Mr Alvarez thinks so: Lowell and Berryman were 'able to write poetry of immense skill and intelligence which coped openly with the quick of their experience'.[5] This is plainly Eliot's praise of the Metaphysicals as having their senses at their fingertips, but one may well wonder what on earth Alvarez is doing applying

4 Idem,
5 Idem.

it to Robert Lowell. First, as regards the 'immense' skill: look at the first four lines of the extract just cited. The first line is more or less prose, the second and third establish no rhythm—

> Who spewed Nantucket bones on the thrashed swell
> And stirred the troubled waters to whirlpools . . .

To 'stir' 'troubled waters' to 'whirlpools'! A schoolboy could manage better than that. But of course one is not meant to probe that closely: one is intended to be carried away in the excitement, part-Melville, part-Yeats, part-Hopkins, of a literary exercise. Whatever virtues there are in this verse, 'intelligence' is not among them, as can be seen easily enough from the occasional successes:

> To Cape Cod
> Guns, cradled on the tide,
> Blast the eel-grass about a water-clock
> Of bilge and backwash, roil the salt and sand
> Lashing the earth's scaffold, rock
> Our warships in the hand
> Of the great God, where time's contrition blues
> Whatever it was these Quaker sailors lost
> In the mad scramble of their lives.
>
> ('The Quaker Graveyard in Nantucket')

The ineptitude of the last clause (from 'Where time's contrition blues)' reveals how unthinking Lowell becomes once the rhythmic impulse is spent—unthinking, and therefore leaning automatically on the literary past ('Time's contrition' sounds all right but means little that is not banal). Up to this point, the effect is extraordinary, unique, though evidently learnt at the Yeatsian well. A strange rhythmic elevation, immensely powerful, of sheer strain imparted, at length succeeds in lifting the self-conscious Anglo-Saxon verbiage off the ground. The verbs do the work— 'blast', 'roil', 'rock'—and they are magnificently placed. This isn't Yeats, but Lowell, and the fact comes clear in the peculiar inventiveness— inventiveness that has slipped the eclectic halter: 'blast the eel-grass about a water-clock' is something, for instance, which only Lowell would have seen. The whole paragraph in fact creates a fantasy under-sea world which Lowell has earlier in the poem been treating with such literary solemnity. This fantasy is the true inventiveness that makes poetry out of attitudes. 'As a Plane Tree by the Water'—anthologized by Matthiesson in his *Oxford Book*, but omitted by Lowell from the *Selected Poems*—achieves a similar effect:

> The flies, the flies, the flies of Babylon
> Buzz in my ear-drums while the devil's long
> Dirge of the people detonates the hour
> For floating cities where his golden tongue

Enchants the masons of the Babel Tower
To raise tomorrow's city to the sun
That never sets upon these hell-fire streets
Of Boston, where the sunlight is a sword
Striking at the withholder of the Lord:
Flies, flies are on the plane tree, on the streets.

('As a Plane Tree by the Water')

It is the suggestion in the noun 'ear-drums' that starts the whole thing: the characteristically Yeatsian adjective-noun split ('long Dirge)' sustains the impulse until the 'detonation' finally releases the 'floating cities'. To place the adjective at the end of the line is to produce an automatic aesthetic effect: we expect the completion of the sense (the following noun), and yet are held in mid-air. Lowell's entire technique is based upon this and other related phenomena. Nowhere does he exploit the device better than here, where the sheer length of the end-word 'long' extends us to the maximum while the sound of 'Dirge' sets the depth-charge that finally detonates. This explosion in the second (and middle) stanza of the poem is the poem's own *raison d'être*. The first and third stanzas are mostly Yeats pastiche:

Flies strike the miraculous waters of the iced
Atlantic and the eyes of Bernadette
Who saw Our Lady standing in the cave
At Massabielle, saw her so squarely that
Her vision put out reason's eyes.

Lowell does not make the literary reverberations ('And all the streets/To our Atlantic wall are singing: "Sing,/Sing for the resurrection of the King"') seem important enough to him, and the intention behind the symbolism—the flies, the tree and the water—remains obscure and confused. Confusion of purpose and surface seems of the essence, in fact. Much the same is true of 'The Drunken Fisherman', which also nurses a time-bomb within itself:

Is there no way to cast my hook
Out of this dynamited brook?

We don't ask why the brook is dynamited not so much because it isn't that sort of poem (the poem is chock-full of the wrong kind of realism) as because the power behind the explosion is so potent. The powerfully rhymed tetrameters enact the meaning the whole poem gesticulates about—gesticulates so wildly as to make it seem that its purpose is to disguise the real meaning of the whole. The poem is about age and aging, but Lowell seems deliberately to eschew clarity. The drive behind the poem is Dionysiac, yet the surface is all 'technique'—in the most limiting sense of the term. It is almost as if the detonations in these poems represent the deeper creative drive in the poet, a drive which is being continually dammed up by the irrelevant yet somehow essential metrical procedures.

If Lowell had made these deep forces of his yield coherent structures, there would be no hesitation in allowing the major status so often claimed for him. But the fact is, I think, that he does not. These poems—among the poet's most impressive—mingle his major virtues and vices: they are eclectic to the point of stultification, and the technique expended so laboriously in them more often than not defeats its own ends. If the general prosodic method suggests Yeats, the incoherent religiosity that turns Byzantium into Babylon comes from Hart Crane: 'To raise tomorrow's city to the sun' is straight out of Crane's *White Buildings* volume—

> . . . darkness like an ape's face falls away
> And gradually white buildings answer day.
>
> (H. Crane, 'Recitative')

Otherwise, the dominant influence on the earlier Lowell is that of Allen Tate, a poet from whom Lowell himself has admitted to having learned more than from Crane. Tate's influence is suggested, for instance, in the refrain of 'As a Plane Tree by the Water'. Lowell's flies return with something of the portentous regularity of those plunging leaves in Tate's 'Ode to the Confederate Dead'. A still closer approximation to the Tate manner is 'The Quaker Graveyard in Nantucket'. Both poems consciously attempt the grand manner. It is the final section of Lowell's poem that most strikingly suggests Tate's. In Tate we read:

> In the riven troughs the splayed leaves
> Pile up, of nature the casual sacrament
> To the seasonal eternity of death.
>
> ('Ode to the Confederate Dead')

In Lowell:

> The empty winds are creaking and the oak
> Splatters and splatters on the cenotaph.
>
> ('The Quaker Graveyard in Nantucket')

The great commonplace (the autumn leaves as symbolic of death) is being hitched to a deliberately 'solemn' public stance in both poems: both poets exploit to the full the appropriately ceremonial diction— 'sacrament' and 'cenotaph', for instance. In both poems, finally, an effect of ponderous banality supplants the classic relevance so consciously striven for. Both poets seem to have been haunted by the memory of Lowell's ancestor, J. R. Lowell:

> She cometh, cometh to-day;
> Hark! hear ye not her tread,
> Sending a thrill through your clay,

Under the soil there, ye dead,
Her champions and chosen men?
Do ye not hear, as she comes,
The bay of the deep-mouthed guns?
The gathering buzz of the drums?

('Ode Read at the Concord Centennial')

But James Russell Lowell was a Victorian insider, a pillar of the establishment, and carries off the manner; Robert Lowell is a divided liberal of the twentieth century, and does not.

The Tate manner persists in Lowell's later volume, *For the Union Dead*. But Lowell succeeds here, I think, as nowhere else, in balancing his rhyme-stanza style, based as it is upon effort and prosodic 'work', with a more characteristically mid-century naturalness of observation and idiom. In the best poems here the pained tone of the East Coast Confessionals— neurotic, over-intense—is brought to an almost visionary pitch:

A father's no shield
for his child.
We are like a lot of wild
spiders crying together,
but without tears.

('Fall 1961')

Here is that intense self-pity so familiar in twentieth-century writing in America (O'Neill, Wolfe, Tennessee Williams); it seems to spring from something deeply rooted in the American psyche. Yet Lowell has found an unforgettable image which owes its life to an unhinged certitude. A somnambulist's step crosses the break from 'wild' to 'spiders'; the rhyme-pattern—from 'shield' to 'child', and 'child' to 'wild'—is, as elsewhere in the poem, strong, yet unemphasized. Lowell has found a useful stanza here. It, or some variant of it, is used in several other poems of the same volume, ordered yet flexible, allowing the poet to organize sound with less inhibition than had been customary in him, yet enabling him to capitalize upon strong end-rhymes. The placing of the rhyme is free, yet always half-expected: we don't quite know where it will come, yet are satisfied when it does:

Back and forth!
Back and forth, back and forth.—
my one point of rest
is the orange and black
oriole's swinging nest!

('Fall 1961')

Now this 'freedom' means that Lowell has dropped the Grand Manner: no longer does he strive after the Yeats–Crane scale bravely attempted and partially achieved in 'As a Plane Tree by the Water' and 'The Quaker

Graveyard in Nantucket'. He is accordingly able to take in his stride more telling detail than he had before:

> Now the midwinter grind
> is on me, New York
> drills through my nerves,
> as I walk
> the chewed-up streets.

('Middle Age')

Lowell succeeds here in riding the line between the natural and the strained: the rhyme (*York/walk*) is far more intelligently adapted to the needs of the stanza than had often been the case in the earlier verse. And if he would never attain the witty precision of Philip Larkin, or the relaxed relevance of Frank O'Hara's 'I do this, I do that' poems, he did not perhaps really need to. The poet who concentrates too much on getting all the observations in—as we saw with Wilbur—pays a price in verse-tension. Lowell's verse, if often pretentious and stiff, does not, at its best, sacrifice the implicit life and dignity of the stanza to mere observation. In 'Middle Age', for instance, an easy ride of sound carriers the whole poem along: two assonances—the long 'au', 'Talk, York (dinosaur)', and the long 'i', 'grind, alive, I, climbed'—sustain momentum throughout, without the poet's having to force his voice into the rather callow heroics of 'The Quaker Graveyard in Nantucket'.

Thus, although the poems of this volume lack—even at their best— the vibrancy and taut spring of 'The Drunken Fisherman', they possess a new solidity that rests upon a new environmental awareness. Not always, of course. The details are often inert: the poet's natural introversion of temperament (these are the 'Confessions of an Introvert') militates against an easy traffic with the external world, and makes his painstaking efforts to 'get with' his surroundings often glum and dull. It is for this reason, perhaps, that his greatest successes come when he vaults free of the actual to penetrate to the 'more truly real'. An indication of how far his finest writing depends upon an annulment of the objectively real is the outstanding success of the two fine 'falling asleep' poems which help us to gauge how far Lowell travelled between *Poems* 1938–1949 and *For the Union Dead* (1965).

Much has been made of 'Falling Asleep over the *Aeneid*', yet good as it is at its best, it seems to me inferior to its companion-piece in the later volume, 'The Severed Head'. Both poems prey successfully upon that symbol-rich field of consciousness between sleep and waking, when the immediate objects surrounding the poet pass naturally into an internal realm. Lowell might claim to be an expert on this very profitable form of poetic privateering. His mind here bears imagery freely, released from the self-conscious intentness upon being a Major Poet that mars so much of his work. Enlarged beyond the natural just far enough to demand alarmed interest, things—the common properties of the room in which the poet has spent so many hours that he has come by his acquaintance with them slowly, and as it were without noticing them—assume dream proportions and significances that run parallel to his deeper preoccupations. The superiority of the later of these two poems over the earlier lies in part in the new freedom of technique we have observed in 'Fall 1961'.

'Falling Asleep over the *Aeneid*' might be retitled 'Falling Asleep over the *Cantos*'. Certainly no verse could be better calculated to make us value afresh the lissom economy of Pound's 'free' verse than these ponderous couplets of Lowell's:

> The sun is blue and scarlet on my page,
> And *yuck-a, yuck-a, yuck-a, yuck-a,* rage
> The yellow-hammers mating. Yellow fire
> Blankets the captives dancing on their pyre,
> And the scorched lictor screams and drops his rod.
> Trojans are singing to their drunken God,
> Ares. Their helmets catch on fire. Their files
> Clank by the body of my comrade—miles
> Of filings! Now the scythe-wheeled chariot rolls
> Before their lances long as vaulting poles, . . .

And so on; a riot of all the prosodic vices exposed by Pound—rhyme begetting line, exigence dictating matter, instead of controlling it. The verse proceeds by a series of jerks and luggings, as the rhyme-words demand satisfaction: 'miles/Of filings'! And what has been gained by calling the lances as 'long as vaulting poles'? This is the sort of factual detail that might be of interest in a lecture about the weaponry of the Homeric days, but which in a poem is inert and clogging. And no matter how many twentieth-century devices Lowell employs to diversify the couplet-enjambment, hanging a word or phrase ('Ares', or 'Of filings') onto the next line, changing sentence in mid-line to give the fourth quarter of a couplet the chance of a new life with the couplet to come, and so on— the result is almost invariably to emphasize its factitiousness. In reading the poem one learns to hate the iambic torture so thankfully and properly shed by Pound and his followers: we do not merely dread the thump of the final rhyme-syllable, we mentally italicize the final word of every line, as a bodily muscle might come to flinch at the regular fall of a weight it can only just bear:

> Our cost
> Is nothing to the lovers, whoring Mars
> And Venus, father's lover. Now his car's
> Plumage is ready, and my marshals fetch
> His squire, Acoetes, white with age, to hitch
> Aethon, the hero's charger, and its ears

> Prick, and it steps and steps, and stately tears
> Lather its teeth; and then the harlots bring
> The hero's charms and baton—but the King,
> Vain-glorious Turnus, carried off the rest.
> 'I was myself, but Ares thought it best . . .'

And so on. I have found it hard to end the quotation here, not because of any sinuous continuity of meaning or relevance, but on the contrary because of Lowell's habit of pushing in new matter to help out the rhyming. As anyone who has composed heroic couplets knows, the real test of expertise in the idiom is to contain the meaning within the couplet, so that the tight corner left at the final quarter of the second line is adequately and relevantly filled with substance related to the sound of the preceding line. It is likely that Lowell's consistent breaking-up of the couplet—which conflicts with, rather than diversifies, the idiom—derives from technical incapacity rather than from any twentieth-century distaste for excessive formalism: after all, such a distaste could have prompted abandonment of the idiom altogether.

One way of explaining what Lowell is trying to do with all this high-powered 'technique' is to call it music: it is the *music* Lowell is interested in, the sound and the rhythm considered not as functional elements towards full expression but for themselves alone. The sense ('and stately tears/Lather its teeth') must take its chance. Now my examples from 'Falling Asleep over the *Aeneid*', like those earlier from 'As a Plane Tree by the Water', show well enough that Lowell has never had the power or the technique to carry off the grand manner: what Milton sustains over twelve books of *Paradise Lost* and Yeats over whole cycles of lyrics, is more than Lowell can manage for a few lines. Yet at his best, he achieves something that sets him apart from and, I think, above the other New England Confessionals, Berryman and Sexton. His musicality does indicate a concern for something simply 'higher' than truth—the small 't' factual variety, that is—something higher than his own passing states of mind. That is why he is at his best when not dragged down into mere self-pity—when the mental agony is felt to contribute to something greater. And here it seems important to emphasize that to the music of the musical poet, the *content* ('To justify the ways of God to Man', for instance) is of the greatest importance: the music serves, as it makes, the 'content'; but that content is apt to be other than the sum of the specifics indicated in the sense. It is to Lowell's credit that he can make us feel this from time to time.

The question of content or purpose must dominate any consideration of the superiority of 'The Severed Head', yet the way in which the changing inward attitudes are reflected in the technique is most impressive. The later poem shows at once a far greater ease of movement and a far more genuinely personal content. As far as sound is concerned, 'The

Severed Head' has fewer examples of another of Lowell's peculiar vices—
a tendency to get snarled up in his own sonic net, to 'rhyme' one couplet
with the previous, for instance, so that we lose the impact of the rhyme
altogether. (One sequence reads 'bronze, ones, thumb, drum, tongue,
slung'.) This confirms the suspicion that what confronts us is not an
occasional lapse of ear but a tendency to get lost, stranded farther and
farther away from the sense—yet at the same time farther *into* an independent meaning. Perhaps the most alarming example in the poem is the
following:

> I groan a little. Who am I? 'and why'?
> It asks, a boy's face, though its arrow-eye
> Is working from its socket. 'Brother try
> O child of Aphrodite, try to die.
> To die is life.'

('Falling Asleep over the Aeneid')

As if the quadruple rhyme were not bad enough, Lowell has to thrust in
four internal rhyme-words ('child—Aphrodite—try—die'); *and yet the
badness comes somehow good.*

For, there is no denying the crowded energy of the performance, the
exciting spillage of 'classical' scenes which survives the faulty technique.
Figure follows figure, incident crowds on incident; there seems hardly
enough space to get it all in:

> The careless yellow hair that seemed to burn
> Beforehand, Left foot, right foot—as they turn
> More pyres are rising: armoured horses, bronze,
> And gagged Italians, who must file by ones
> Across the bitter river, when my thumb
> Tightens into their wind-pipes. The beaks drum;

We don't quite know what is going on, but there is an authentic dream-
quality here (the confused memories of the reading crowding through the
old man's sleep, of course), and this dream-like intensity is what matters,
I think, not the classical paraphernalia. Herein lies the difference from
Pound: for Pound the personal importance of the classical or mythological
images is precisely their classical and mythological character, so that he
can 'do' the Acoetus myth, or the return of Odysseus, with greater ease
and confidence than Lowell, for whom the actual episode—for instance
the funeral of Pallas—has little intrinsic significance. The first part of
Lowell's dream-vision is dominated by the choking-bird imagery, which
seems to be angling for a kind of Frazerian profundity, but works more
through its strange irrationality than through any anthropological
meanings it might touch on. There is more of Tennyson here than Lowell
probably knew, incidentally: *The Idylls of the King* are hocus-pocus raised
to the level of art, where Lowell's poem is art reduced to the level of

hocus-pocus. Yet the narrative arc that rises through the piled-up scenes has an excitement that eventually transcends the actual content:

> At the end of Time
> He sets his spear, as my descendants climb
> The knees of Father Time, his beard of scalps
> His scythe, the arc of steel that crowns the Alps.

Here speaks the true poet in Lowell, the simple yet great-minded visionary, odd, yet authentic in his oddity, as he is in the underwater gunfire in 'The Quaker Graveyard'. The transition from the height of this vision to the old man's awakening has been beautifully prepared for by the gradually ascending trajectory of the poem:

> 'Pallas!' I raise my arm
> And shout, 'Brother, eternal health. Farewell
> Forever.' Church is over, and its bell
> Frightens the yellowhammers as I wake
> And watch the white caps wrinkle up the lake.

(The last lines reveal how much the heroic couplet can still achieve when handled along its own grain.) But Lowell hasn't finished yet. To have his hero waken into the present in which he began (the yellowhammers serving as connecting sound) would be standard practice. But Lowell's old man wakens into a second 'vision': his great aunt, who died eighty years ago, stands by 'our parlour sabre', admonishing the old man (as a boy of eight) to wake up and get off to church. Then only does he say, 'It all comes back': under the dream-vision set off by the Vergil has been running the forgotten episode of his Uncle Charles's funeral, at which a modern Aeneas (Ulysses S. Grant) stands 'frowning at his coffin', much as Vergil's hero honoured the Italian Prince Pallas in the poem. The thud of the cognition is profound.

And yet it is a performance. What has it all amounted to? The final lines are inconclusive:

> It is I , I hold
> His sword to keep from falling, for the dust
> On the stuffed bird is breathless, for the bust
> Of young Augustus weighs on Vergil's shelf.
> It scowls into my glasses at itself.

The final mirror-image is surely banal in its attempt to provide a formal resting-place for the whole. Lowell has given notice of this inconclusiveness by prefacing the whole poem with the sort of explanatory scene-setting that an actress (Ruth Draper, for instance) might use to launch a rendition, mime or dramatic monologue: 'An old man in Concord forgets to go to morning service.' The brilliant connection, Aeneas being Ulysses S. Grant, doesn't in the end mean more than itself.

There is no need to hold in view some self-expressive, therapeutic conception of poetry to find Lowell's poem finally lacking in real interest. 'Why did he write it?' is merely a rhetorical question we ask to indicate a certain sort of unsatisfactoriness. Yet in describing the superiority of 'The Severed Head' over 'Falling Asleep over the *Aeneid*' it doesn't seem to me that this sort of approach can be denied. 'The Severed Head' *is* more obviously relevant to Lowell's own life, more an exploration of his own experience, more pressingly important to him simply. It is also, as I have stated earlier, technically superior. As in the short stanza poems in the volume, Lowell gives himself more room to manœuvre by adopting a looser rhyme-scheme, or at least a scheme which feels looser. (Again, any poet knows that there seems to be more time to get the rhyme-word if you have three lines, not two, to work in.)

> Shoes off and necktie, hunting the desired
> butterfly here and there without success,
> I let nostalgia drown me. I was tired
> of pencilling the darker passages,
> and let my ponderous Bible strike the floor.
>
> ('The Severed Head')

The last line here has that thump we learned to dread in 'Falling Asleep', but it is mimetic of the book hitting the floor, and the break-up of the third line is quite different from anything in the earlier poem: it is authentically natural and derived from the situation. What follows in general is equally easy, yet, strangely enough, more intense: the Vergil/old man sort of scenario is dropped, and the objects surrounding the poet are subjected to more eerie dream-transmutations:

> My house was changing to a lost address,
> the nameplate fell like a horse-shoe from the door,
> where someone, hitting nails into a board,
> had set his scaffolding. I heard him pour
> mortar to seal the outlets, as I snored,
> watching the knobbed, brown wooden chandelier,
> slicing the silence on a single cord.

There is an alarming persistence of the long 'o' rhyme (it spans eight lines, from 'floor' in l.5, to 'cord' in l.13), but there is nothing in 'Falling Asleep over the *Aeneid*' to equal the uncanny effect of the strategically placed verb 'pour' in this passage, which somehow rescues the entire sequence. The chandelier grows into a nightmare organism, the spectre waits for it to claw for his jugular; and then the second character of the poem appears,

> a man came toward me with a manuscript,
> scratching in last revisions with a pen

> that left no markings on the page, yet dripped
> a red ink dribble on us, as he pressed
> the little strip of plastic tubing clipped
> to feed it from his heart. His hand caressed
> my hand a moment, settled like a toad,
> lay clammy, comfortable, helpless, and at rest,
> although his veins seemed pulsing to explode.

Where does this come from? The weird clarity of this vision persists, and the ghastly figure resolves itself more emphatically into an *alter ego* of the poet:[6] 'the bouillon of his eye ... the same colour as his frayed moustache,/too brown, too bushy, lifted from an age/when people wore moustaches.'

The *alter ego* then tears up the manuscript, weeps and asks himself 'if I exist.' A sheet of glass has suddenly fallen, introducing the aquarium image Lowell rather ineptly plays with in 'For the Union Dead'. Then—most sinister moment in a most sinister poem—the visitor takes out a rusty pen-knife and carves out of paper a malignant image of the poet's former wife,

> Square head, square feet, square hands, square breasts, square back.

He then vanishes, leaving the poet reading the Bible 'until the page turned black'. The episode which has underlain this dream is now revealed (how much more tellingly than in the *Aeneid* poem, when it is given in a stage direction), as the horrible one of Jael 'hammering and hammering his nail/through Sisera's idolatrous, nailed head'. The poem ends with Lowell's own wife's folded dress underneath his head, as if he had in fact killed her.

This is, to my mind, by far the finest poem in *For the Union Dead*, and one of the very finest Lowell has ever written. To turn from it to the title poem is again to be reminded of the frequency with which this highly gifted poet has been prepared of late to go against the true grain of his feeling. Here is the familiar iambic torture, but slumping now into journalistic prose:

> One morning last March,
> I pressed against the new barbed and galvanized

> fence on the Boston Common. Behind their cage,
> yellow dinosaur steamshovels were grunting
> as they cropped up tons of mush and grass
> to gouge their underworld garage.

The job of relating this turgid prose (the level of mediocre TV docu-

---

[6] The verse here reminds me of Alexander Blok's *Dvoinik*, though Lowell can hardly have known it.

mentary) to the poet's past—that past we get so sick of Lowell's referring to in his books—is done halfheartedly and inconclusively. The fish image carries little weight, and I cannot myself see what Lowell is trying to do with it. Worst of all is the metrical uncertainty, sliding from the bookishly 'literary' ('to gouge their underworld garage') to the merely slovenly, the inert prose of this: 'he has an angry wren-like vigilance,/a greyhound's gentle tautness'.

The failure of *Life Studies*, which preceded *For the Union Dead*, had already indicated the direction Lowell was prepared to take. These are the most Confessional of Lowell's poems to date, and the actual settings and routines suggest the poetry of Anne Sexton and others. But the ordeal of the breakdown seems here to have robbed Lowell of the force and rhythmic power that from time to time had lifted his earlier verse. Lacking the wry awareness of a Larkin, and the sharp objectivity of an Auden, Lowell does not succeed in registering the personalities and events outside his own ego with sufficiently telling detail to make the observations interesting. What we have is the sad prospect of a gifted introvert trying laboriously to acquire extroverted precision. We learn that his grandfather

> found
> his grandchild's fogbound solitudes
> sweeter than human society.
>
> ('Dunbarton')

'Stanley' in the mental home is

> sunk in his sixties
> once a Harvard all-American fullback
> (if such were possible)
> still hoarding the build of a boy in his twenties,
> as he soaks, a ramrod
> with the muscles of a seal
> in his long tub,
> vaguely urinous from the Victorian plumbing.
>
> ('Waking in the Blue')

Later, he is 'more cut off from words than a seal'. None of these details succeeds in capturing the life-study here: the reader familiar with Philip Larkin's later work, or the earlier work of John Wieners, will demand more of poetry than this prosy notation. Lowell had succeeded from time to time in sustaining the grand manner, and in exploring the world of his own semiconsciousness. Realistic observation and 'self-awareness' did not suit him at all.

Apparently feeling that his eclecticism and his fondness for the archaic grand manner had made him an anachronism in the world of Ginsberg's 'HOWL' and Berryman's *Dream Songs*, Lowell has allowed his laboured style gradually to disintegrate over the past ten years: if it was factitious, that style, it had at least its own consistency. It *was* a style, a coherent and internally consistent organization of sound and stress, with a characteristic range of inflections and usages which amounted to a man. *Notebooks* (1971), which followed *For the Union Dead*, has given up the ghost entirely: in an apparent attempt to 'get with it', Lowell has lost his own voice altogether, and with it, his creative personality:

> For time is summer, an autumn, a winter, a spring,
> another summer. I began working sometime in June 1967
> and finished in June 1970. My plot rolls with the
> seasons, but one year is confused with another.
>
> (*Notebooks*)

This is not 'responsive' modern prosody (as the arch placing of the article in the third line is presumably meant to suggest). It is not 'free' verse, because it is not verse at all. Jonathan Raban thinks that it 'looks sideways to the twentieth century novel.'[7] A nice way of saying that it is prosaic, one would think. The backbone of Lowell's imagination seems to have snapped, the whole sense of imaginative validity has gone. So that instead of proudly eschewing narrative and the anecdotally 'real', as following his great master, Yeats, he formerly had, he now fumbles after a contemporary naturalism:

> Reading this book to four or five that night
> at Cuernavaca, till the lines glowered and glowed
> and my friend, Monsignor Illich, ascetic donkey,
> braying 'Will you die when the book is done?'
>
> (*Notebooks*)

The result is a mixture of mediocre snapshots ('The slush-ice of the east water of the Hudson is rose-heather this New Year sunset'), inert reminiscences, and occasional asseverations of the old rhythmic Yeatsian:

> No honeycomb is built without a bee
> adding circle to circle, cell to cell,
> the wax and honey of a mausoleum—
> the round dome proves its maker is alive. . . .

The sonnet structure of the whole sequence was, presumably, suggested by the quasi-classical form of Berryman's *Dream Songs*: in Lowell's case it seems little more than a gimmick, seemingly intended to give the disorganized jottings something of a classic scale of reference. This is surely the old Romantic agony enacting itself yet again in the wrestle with words, talent and destiny heroically persevered in by Yeats and Crane. But Yeats and Crane persisted with their differing styles, and never lost sight of the end of the struggle, even when they could not have said

[7] *The Society of the Poem* (London 1972).

what it was. Lowell seems to have lost all sense of the importance of the quest; his style has fallen to pieces. He lacks the strength not only to keep up the heroic manner, but to come clean when the heart has gone out of it: he lacks, all but completely, the necessary frankness and, yes, the intelligence, to make his confessions interesting. A truculent note is continually invading the 'sincerity':

> This year runs out in the movies, it must be written
> in bad straightforward unscanning sentences—
> mine were downtrodden, branded on the backs of carbons,
> lines, words, letters nailed to letters, words, lines,
> the typescript looked like a Rosetta stone.

—an intimation of the poet's awareness of his old rhythmic vices, with a regret that he ever abandoned them at all. There is something disagreeable in the tone he adopts towards the new age he has tried to ingratiate himself with, something self-congratulatory, consorting ill with the confessional purpose, which makes the verse alternately stilted and limp. *History*, I submit, continues the process of deterioration initiated in *Life Studies*. Lowell had attempted to maintain in currency the metrical values of Yeats. Not only his techniques—the over-buttressed stanzas, the heavy dependence on the rhyme-words and the occasional strategic enjambment —but his attitudes, his emotional content, had been dictated by the requirements of an outworn poetics. Like a number of poets of his age— Berryman, Roethke, Sexton—Lowell has tried to preserve the Romantic agony as proof of significance and sensibility. The form this Romantic agony took in his case is of some sociological interest: what we have in the poetry of Lowell, as in the fiction of Saul Bellow, is the cultivation of the nervous breakdown. In *Herzog*, Bellow offers us his awareness of his own lack of purpose in the absence of any more positive motivation. The sense that nothing means anything assumes the status of an ideology: pain is offered as a proof of integrity. *Herzog* is the final running-to-seed of the novel of introspection, just as *Notebooks* is the final petering-out of the old Romantic agony. These are the art forms of affluence in their terminal stages: energy and rhythm have died out, at the same time as the naked self is cushioned from an actuality grown too harsh—or simply too strange, perhaps, and feared more than it need be. A staggered, materially guaranteed version of the Romantic agony ('I suffer, therefore I exist') takes the strain of the artistic venture. The ends of thought and experience have been decided beforehand, and the facts that come the poet's way are tailored to fit it.

Whatever reservations we have to make in assessing Lowell, there remains a corpus of heavy achievement that remains unequalled by any of his American contemporaries. If asked to name the greatest of modern American poets, the American equivalent of André Gide would have to answer, 'Robert Lowell, hélas!'

The late Anne Sexton is certainly the least 'musical' of the poets usually called 'Confessional'. It is even more difficult with her poetry than with that of Lowell and Berryman to resist the inference that its *raison d'être* was the nervous breakdown, and that the breakdown itself—anticipated, endured, got over—provided structure not only for the individual poems and sequences, but for the *œuvre* itself. This is not to deny the authenticity of the 'pain', much less to take a cynical attitude towards it. In saying these things, indeed, I am not concerned with the individual citizen Anne Sexton at all, or with her 'case-history': I am concerned only with a voice and an experiental structure manifested through poetic symbols and rhythms. There is a relationship between the ultimate direction of Robert Lowell's verse, for instance, and its psychological content: the neurosis can be analysed, at least in part, into formal and technical coefficients. The cultivation, we might say, of the neurosis in Lowell's case is related to the sense of a poetic destiny of which the earlier verse had always shown him to be aware. As such, the neurosis, wearily confessed to— 'Everyone is tired of my turmoil'—is read in terms of a greater context: Lowell's sense of himself as a poet (as a major poet) turned towards neurosis, we might say, in its pursuit of itself. In Berryman, we have seen that the poet's sense of his personal destiny early hardened as something ineradicably concerned with a distress, a disruption of mind, that somehow proved him poet.

In both cases, neurosis, though embraced in some sense voluntarily, forms part of a broader conception of the poet's existence. As such, the nervous breakdown (or suicide, the ultimate nervous breakdown) can be read in terms of a transcending vocation, as well as of a sociological condition. The sociological context of course is important: it cannot be accepted as 'natural' or inevitable that at a given stage of its history, the better minds in a society 'decided to go mad'. Mental illness is not confined to advanced capitalist societies, but the nervous breakdown, I submit, is a phenomenon of capitalist society in its present historical and social condition. Not only does it require money to sustain it, it thrives— more significantly—on the emptiness that exists when a sense of pressure deriving from the more basic human needs is removed, and when a sense of historical purpose implicit in the political behaviour of the society fades. Suicide, like the nervous breakdown, tends to be neutralized by the rise of greater basic need—the threat of war, for instance, or dramatic economic depression.

Anne Sexton's poetry, unlike that of Lowell and Berryman, is strictly confined in its formal implications to the facts of neurosis, sickness and death. That is, these things are not given any other status or significance than their own actuality. Of course it might be argued that they *have* no other significance than in themselves. But, *in themselves*: things are not, if I may adapt Sartre, merely *in-themselves*, they are also *for-themselves*. That is, the act of writing poetry—the fact and decision of being-a-poet—

is different in kind from the facts of being born, falling in love and dying. We might, at the risk of over-simplification, say that Anne Sexton's poetry is limited by and to its subject-matter. This would not be entirely true: she is, it is clear from the most cursory reading, an accomplished poet. The verse is at the opposite pole from mere effusion, self-expression (which might perhaps have been predicted from a facile reading of the account I have just offered). And yet her poetry fails consistently, I think, to go beyond its elected subject-matter: it tells us a lot about the way Anne Sexton feels about things, yet little about the way we might feel about them ourselves. The real paradox of poetry is that the more true to its own subject-matter (its subjectivity) it is, the more 'universal' it is. We touch here on a fundamental fact about poetry, and many fallacies abound in this territory. What Yeats attributed to the poetry of Wilfred Owen[8]—a limitation to the passive suffering of war and the pity of war—I am myself attributing (some would say equally shamefully) to that of Anne Sexton. Yet there does seem to me all the difference in the world between the two cases: Owen experienced the 'tragic' dimension of things within a few months. What most men (Yeats was among them) experience in a middle age of slow adaptation, Owen experienced brutally in months, telescoped. Neither the sensibility nor the poetic technique of the man cracked under the pressure—the most inhuman, it could be argued, that civilized man has ever had to endure: Owen gave us—in 'Strange Meeting', 'The Offensive', 'Futility', 'Dulce et Decorum Est', and 'Exposure'—a handful of the indisputably great poems of the twentieth century. In Anne Sexton's accounts of attempted suicide, of madness, of a major operation, we are conscious of no attempt at 'transcending' the experience, no sense even that an unwelcome experience has come across the path of the poet (which is what we have, intensified to the last degree, in the war poems of Owen and Sassoon). Sexton cleaves to the humiliation, for instance, of being shaved, cleared out, objectified, handled, dehumanized and pitied in the course of preparation for an operation, almost as if it were her *karma*, waiting for her since her birth. 'The Operation' is true to the experiences, we feel: the verse moves well, the stanzas plumpen and narrow as they should. It is impossible to say that Sexton is 'enjoying' or relishing the things the poem reports as happening to her. She is manifestly sincere. Yet the alternatives are not merely those of enjoying the suffering or of being shocked by it. This would present us with a falsely clean dichotomy. Nowhere in the *Selected Poems* can we find evidence for the thesis that at some level Sexton was enjoying her suffering. And yet one misses altogether the note of deep shock, anger, bewilderment which informs the poems of Owen. And it seems to me reasonable to compare the equally intolerable situations. There is, I suggest, a level at which the intolerable and the real coalesce, and at which the ache of enduring the repulsive issues in a white joy of understanding. This light of illumination

---

[8] W. B. Yeats (ed.), *The Oxford Book of Modern Verse*, introduction, xxxiv.

is akin to the crisis Pirandello described as lying at the heart of his drama. Although there is nothing false or willed about Anne Sexton's accounts of her sufferings, her poetry lacks the dimension of transcendence—what Eliot called 'surprise'. There is more than a suspicion that the experience of the operation or even the madhouse is, if not willed, at least acceded to: she accepts her sickness. It turns her into a 'shorn lamb', her bed becomes an 'aluminium crib'. She accepts being made a child, an object, a passive thing. In the same way she accepts her status as 'mad woman':

> we are the circle of the crazy ladies
> who sit in the lounge of the mental house
> and smile at the smiling woman . . .
>
> ('Ringing the Bells')

Is it that someone who experiences her madness like this cannot really *be* mad, and yet is determined to play mad, to accept the role that is like a solution? I hesitate before these facile-sounding generalizations, and yet again and again the verse makes me return to them:

> we stand in broken
> lines and wait while they unlock
> the door and count us at the frozen gate
> of dinner.
>
> ('You, Doctor Martin')

She speaks here with the voice of one of Solzhenitsyn's prisoners. Yet Solzhenitsyn's characters *are* prisoners, and their gates really *are* frozen: Solzhenitsyn's men would not be there if they were not held there. Thus there is a tension between the sense of freedom and the actual captivity. It is perhaps the feeling in Anne Sexton's writing that she would have nothing to offer if she were not 'mad' or 'depressed' that makes her poetry, though honest on the human level, at the deep level of art, inauthentic, flat, one-dimensional. For her, there is no world outside the madhouse, outside the neurosis: and thus the important tension of the Solzhenitsyn novel (the source of its interest for us) is absent. Her voice in these poems has a curious quality of dumb insolence, as if she were determined to play upon the sane man's uncertainty. She offers us almost too predictably the imagery of paranoia, of *Pierrot Lunaire*:

> It was the strangled cold of November
> even the stars were stopped in the sky
> and that moon too bright
> forking through the bars to stick me
> with a singing in the head.

It is as if she needs her visitors, the human company, in order to be able to reject them; alternatively, she needs real loneliness in order to be able to blame people.

Transformations was a logically irrational development for the author of *Selected Poems*. It seems on most levels a technical advance on the earlier work: the verse is free (sometimes to the point of being prose) yet economical; the fairy tales are well told, and there are many piercing insights. Each tale is given a vaguely Freudian rationale: 'Rapunzel' is about the love between the older and the younger woman, for instance; 'Snow White' about the sinister attractiveness of the Virgin; 'Cinderella' about economic wish-fulfilment; and so on. A characteristic feature (roughly parallel perhaps to the studied slanginess of the later Lowell) is the pillaging of the advertising and entertainment industries for imagery. The verse is clotted with Ace bandages and Bab-o and Coca Cola and Duz and Chuck Wagon dog food. We find Al Jolson, Houdini, Dior, the Boston Symphony—the whole gamut of mid-century America—giving a light, flip tone to the sardonic stance otherwise adopted. The witty commentary in fact often takes precedence over the sardonic rationale: these transformations are often enough mere doings-over of the tales, copy for a particularly elegant New York edition of Grimm to go along with a set of Charles Addams drawings. In this light it seems thoroughly characteristic of mid-century East Coast America: the clink of ice-cubes accompanies the disabused adult's bed-time stories.

And finally the spell enacted in the telling of the fairy tale fails to work. *The dream won't end.* In 'The Sleeping Beauty', which ends the selection, Grimm gives way finally to Dr Freud, fairy tale to sick joke:

> She married the prince
> and all went well
> except for the fear—
> the fear of sleep.
>
> Briar Rose
> was an insomniac.
>
> ('The Sleeping Beauty')

Sexton's Briar Rose had woken up, upon being kissed, with an all-American 'Daddy! Daddy!' And it is with her Daddy that Sexton's book ends:

> It's not the prince at all
> but my father
> drunkenly bent over my bed
> circling the abyss-like dark
> my father thick upon me
> like some sleeping jelly-fish.
>
> ('The Sleeping Beauty')

It is difficult to escape the conclusion that this rationale has been forced upon Sexton by psychoanalysis, that the world-view has been formed excessively by the peculiarly exasperating doctrines of Freud or of his

American diluters. Anne Sexton still regards herself as a victim, and nothing but a victim. As a victim she expects to be humoured, but not to have to take responsibility for herself. She seems not to have succeeded in locating any centre of self. These are the fairy stories 'interpreted' according to psychoanalysis, not in order to illuminate or to deepen our understanding, but merely to convince us that they are all horrible, and where not horrible (as at the spell-breaking), phoney. It is the common tone of most literature over-exposed to psychoanalysis, from Salinger to Albee. Finally, one's sense of Anne Sexton's creative personality is not that it is too much itself to achieve transcendence, but on the contrary, too little.

Chapter 5

Theodore Roethke
Lost Son

Theodore Roethke is another instance of the American poet whose work it has now become difficult to read free of the mythology and sympathy surrounding the life of the man. To some extent, as in the case of John Berryman, this is because of technico-cultural facts of a sort we have to learn to live with: we simply know too much about the campus-poet, with his over-advertised affairs, benders and madnesses. The poet has always characteristically projected himself in personal myth, and lived a personal myth in himself; but the 'media' (the horrible McLuhanism is appropriate here) today ensure that the poet participates in his own 'legend'—not, be it noted, in the myth itself, but the legend—that is, the half-truth and illusion that congregate about the myth. The various images it is so easy for the poet to get of himself assume roles in the poet's own personal drama. The media have accelerated the process of self-consciousness beyond what many men can handle, and it may be that poets will be forced into a new cult of anonymity.[1]

Roethke illustrates to perfection this frightening trend in American life—it amounts to a publicization of the private, and has already affected politics.[2] But he illustrates as well another aspect of American writing in the mid-century, one already noted above: the tendency to regard oneself as passive, to reify oneself in accordance with a vague but nonetheless decisive Freudianism, as the suffering and junior player in a drama in which the father is cast as the villain/hero. We see this in O'Neill, in Tennessee Williams, and even, to some extent, in Arthur Miller.

The social context in which it was written is not the only reason why Roethke's poetry seems to exist in a ground-mist of vague sympathy for the man which has somehow less to do with poetry than with biography.

---

[1] I think this has already happened in the case of Ted Hughes, an impressive example of a man tough enough to resist the role foisted on him by critical acclaim. Such a role may conflict with a poet's own inward bent.

[2] See Daniel Boorstin's *The Image* for this point. The cult of *Newsweek* newspeak, also, has made American politicians and businessmen excessively reliant on a progressively less organic, less functional argot: the clichés and cute idioms have gradually crowded out that pungency which used to be an agreeable feature of American slang.

The poetry itself cries out for sympathy, the poems generate an emotional miasma which true candour would cancel. Thus, Roethke's poetry—for this reader, at least—has a tendency to turn out to be smaller than it had once seemed, exactly like a building or a hill of which a light mist had given an exaggerated impression. To demonstrate the point it seems especially important to concentrate on the words on the page, more so than usual in fact: since the words one is looking at so often gesture towards 'extraneous' subject-matter, suggesting that we take into account material which our critical sense tells us ought to be ignored. This is not true of his finest pieces—of 'The Visit', say, or 'The Song'. But the peculiar kind of success represented in these poems is related in certain crucial ways to the sympathy-begging rhetoric characteristic of so much of Roethke's less successful work. To get any very clear picture of his achievement, in fact, it seems impossible to avoid looking at the strictly non-poetic elements of his failures: we can't always avoid making extrapolations seemingly irrelevant to critical judgement. We have to deal with the shadowy sub-Freudian spectres in order to come to full acquaintance with the poetic personality.

There is little or nothing that need detain us in Roethke's first collection. It is difficult to agree with Ralph Mills that *Open House* (1941) is 'by any standards . . . a remarkable first collection of poetry.'[3] I should say myself that it was remarkable for two things only: first, in the way that it shows forth a major weakness never to be overcome by the poet, and secondly in that, paradoxically, it gives us no brief to expect from its author anything as interesting as what Roethke achieved as early as *The Lost Son*, which appeared only seven years after *Open House*.

The weakness—to take it first—is a disposition to let rhythm pull the poem along after it, in accordance with the sound of the anthologies:

> Once on returning home, purse-proud and pale,
> I found my choice possessions on the lawn.
> One customer was whipping up a sale.
> I did not move to claim what was my own.
>
> ('The Auction')

This is the kind of music—studied, academic, pre-ordained—Roethke was to make, intermittently, until the end of his life. His line shortened at its best, and at its worst expanded loosely. Yet this orderly academic tread—what we see in some poems which have become celebrated, 'The Dance', for instance—remained Roethke's staple idiom.

Ultimately, the reservations it seems to me we must make about Roethke seem justified by this rhythmic academicism alone: Roethke never perhaps—or only rarely—eluded the confines of a Yeatsian conception of the poet as maker: and to strive to be a maker, in poetry, is almost certain to make the striver a faker.

[3] Ralph J. Mills, Jnr, *Theodore Roethke* (Minnesota 1963).

By common critical consent, Roethke 'found himself' in *The Lost Son*.[4]
Yet perhaps 'found himself' is the wrong phrase to have used. The
second collection is so much better than its predecessor because in it—to
the contrary—Roethke started looking for himself.

There is, first, the significant arrival of first-hand material. In place of
the pedantries of the first book we find the scenes among which the poet
passed his childhood noted with a new sharpness:

> Vines tougher than wrists
> And rubbery shoots,
> Scums, mildews, smuts along stems,
> Great cannas or delicate eyeless tips—
> All pulse with the knocking pipes
> That drip and sweat . . .
>
> ('Forcing House')

There is here an obvious—and obviously significant—advance on the
Frost-ish manner of the earlier pieces:

> The haze of harvest drifts along the field
> Until clear eyes put on the look of sleep.
>
> ('Slow Seasons')

All the poems of one complete section of *The Lost Son,* in fact, evoke the
dense crowded greenhouses of Roethke's childhood. In general, perhaps,
description is their medium. It is wholly right that this material should
choke the poet's pages, but it is easy to feel in reading 'Big Wind',
'Carnations' or even 'Child on Top of a Greenhouse', that the concreta
are at the beck of metaphysics picked up from books. 'Child on Top of a
Greenhouse' leaves us wondering why everyone was 'pointing up and
shouting' at the end. And 'Big Wind' seems, in the last analysis, to be
much ado about relatively little. The anecdotal content of the latter poem
('We stayed all night/Stuffing the holes with burlap') preponderates over
the ship-conceit the poem really has significantly to offer:

> She sailed into the calm morning
> Carrying her full cargo of roses.
>
> ('Big Wind')

A second look at Ted Hughes's 'Wind' ('This house has been out at sea
all night') is, I think, enough to point up the laboriousness of Roethke's
initially impressive but ultimately rather creaky performance. What he has
seen and felt with the poet's eye is the lovely ship of roses, and its sailing
into light. But the conceit really has to compete with a mass of narrative
and descriptive detail, which, far from lending it support, puts it in the
shade: Roethke has, in other words, 'set it up'—or sent it to the wall.

[4] Stanley Kunitz thought it 'the great book'. See his 'Theodore Roethke',
New York Review of Books 1 (17 October 1963), 22.

In 'Moss-Gathering', on the other hand, we find evidence of a different sort of uncertainty in the poet: Roethke takes an excessive and, to me, somewhat offensive care to inform us of the emotion aroused in him by the activity referred to in the title and 'described' in the body of the poem. He does not, in other words, make us feel what he felt— he tells us what he felt, and implicitly invites us to praise him for his tenderness:

> And afterwards I always felt mean, jogging back
>   over the logging road,
> As if I had broken the natural order of things in
>   that swampland,
> Disturbed some rhythm, old and of vast importance,
> By pulling off flesh from the living planet.
> As if I had committed against the whole scheme of
>   life a desecration.
>
>   ('Moss-Gathering')

—By picking up bits of moss? Oh, come now! The flabby portentousness is something that fills Roethke's later volumes ('Journey to the Interior' is an example), and it is tied in with the felt need to inform us of the emotion. Roethke wants us to applaud his sensitivity, and the absence of any more interesting purpose in the imagery leaves that imagery merely descriptive.

What is perhaps most interesting about these poems in *The Lost Son* is the conception they embody of poetry as compost:

> Cannas shiny as slag,
> Slug-soft stems
> Whole beds of bloom pitched on a pile,
> Carnations, verbenas, cosmos,
> Molds, weeds, dead leaves . . . .
>
>   ('Flower Dump')

What makes Roethke's dump interesting for us is that single tulip blossoming on top:

> One swaggering head
> Over the dying, the newly dead.

This is pedantic ('the dying, the newly dead'), but it connotes a poetic fact: it is the thing Roethke *saw* here that has poetry, not the somewhat laboured treatment he subjects it to. These descriptive compost pieces with their slagged and rotting matter are the first really individual poems Roethke wrote, and they advertise a deeper preoccupation, one that was to run throughout Roethke's later poetry, the notion of himself as his own compost. 'Myself is what I wear,' he wrote later.

At a good moment he was to say that

> Mad as the wind I wear
> Myself as I should be . . .
>
> ('Words for the Wind')

Again and again he was to give voice to the strangely comic despair of the flesh, reminding one of Cyril Connolly's joke, that every fat man has a thin man trapped inside him trying to get out. And when Roethke wrote—despairingly—of 'the angel within me', he meant, surely, the spirit imprisoned not by the sins of the flesh but by the excess of the flesh. 'There's no joy in soft bones,' Roethke wrote at one point. Most significant of all perhaps are his observations 'My meat eats me' and 'this fat can't laugh.'

Along with these sad insights goes the interesting series of introjections Roethke was to make into 'minimal' creatures, those 'numb nudgers in cold dimensions'—toads, snails, crabs, rats:

> Snail, snail, glister me forward
> Bird, soft-sigh me home.
> Worm, be with me.
> This is my hard time.
>
> ('The Lost Son')

At this point in the poem (which is by general agreement a central one in Roethke's development) one feels acutely aware of the difficulty mentioned at the beginning of this chapter, that in trying to bring out the inner skeleton of Roethke's work, one seems driven to talk about the personal life of the man. It seems impossible to avoid this anomaly here, since in describing the first, one is perforce referring to the second. It is perhaps this open-endedness of the verse—the poem opens out onto the inchoate and unarticulated terrain of the life behind it—that makes it impossible to go along with some of the more enthusiastic evaluations of the poet.

In passing from the greenhouse-and-compost poems of *The Lost Son* to the title poem itself, we are aware at once of a new mastery:

> At Woodlawn I heard the dead cry;
> I was lulled by the slamming of iron,
> A slow drip over stones,
> Toads brooding wells.
> All the leaves stuck out their tongues.
> I shook the softening chalk of my bones.
>
> ('The Lost Son')

Later he says that he

> Fished in an old wound,
> The soft pond of repose;
> Nothing nibbled my line,
> Not even the minnows came.

The genre is not new in itself, or in itself especially remarkable: the backward trip to childhood in search of the poet's identity—there is something suspect in this recourse to procedures which Wordsworth, some 150 years before,[5] inaugurated with such impressive authenticity and power. This script is, we feel, already written. There is no denying Roethke's touch here, though. Here is that poetry of stillness and deft silence he was later—in 'The Visit'—to bring to a high pitch of achievement:

> The way to the boiler was dark,
> Dark all the way,
> Over slippery cinders
> Through the long greenhouse
>
> The roses kept breathing in the dark.
> They had many mouths to breathe with.
> My knees made little winds underneath
> Where the weeds slept.

('The Lost Son')

Once again we are reminded of the curious relationship between Roethke's anguish in his physical existence and the substance of the poetry itself: not only in the bear-music he adapted with cumbersome grace from the rhythms of Yeats, but in the very essence of his perception—in the marrow of his soft bones—Roethke's bulk lends to his poetry, good and bad alike, a consistent character.

There is no doubting the immediate source of Roethke's quest in 'The Lost Son'. Ralph Mills cites the final stanzas of the sequence, and observes that 'We can hardly fail to notice here a recollection of T. S. Eliot's *Four Quartets,* a series of poems which parallel Roethke's in some respects.'[6] Mr Mills thinks that the difference between the two sets of poems is largely that between the Anglo-Catholic poet's need of order and the American Protestant poet's approach 'which bases itself on personal knowledge and evidence, on the lone individual's apprehension of the transcendent'.[7]

But Eliot's poem is—supremely—based firmly on 'personal knowledge and evidence', and the only knowledge of the transcendent we can have is that of the lone individual, as Eliot's constant reference to the dark night of the soul in the experience of the Christian mystics attests. The difference between 'Burnt Norton' and 'The Lost Son' is not the difference between the sturdy individual experiencing the transcendent alone and the hierophantic Anglo-Catholic leaning upon dogma, as Mr Mills's explanation suggests. The important question concerns the quality of the

[5] We can of course return to Vaughan and then to Cowper. But it was Wordsworth who crystallized the idiom for the modern poet.

[6] *Theodore Roethke,* 28.

[7] Ibid., 28–9.

experience. Roethke's questions in 'The Lost Son' mimic the form of Eliot's, but they do not, as Eliot's do, succeed in raising the matter of the infinite. They remain quizzical, often whimsical:

> Tell me
> Which is the way I take
> Out of what door do I go
> Where and to whom?

And later,

> The shape of a rat?
> It's bigger than that . . .
>
> Is it soft like a mouse?
> Can it wrinkle like a mole?
>
> Could it come in the house
> On the tips of its toes?
>
> ('The Lost Son')

There is more than a touch of A. A. Milne and Walter de la Mare to these interrogations: clearly Roethke wishes to evoke profundity by questioning the ordinary. But the form of Eliot's questions is imitated from the outside, with none of that closeness to experienced uncertainty which reveals the proximity of the numinous and the immanent. Eliot's great poem interrogates memory in order to adumbrate the contours of the transcendent: our ordinary experience, the poem tells us, is simply the other side of a reality which has always been there. Thus, the shapes of reality and of the transcendent are identical, but inverted.

Significantly, Roethke slides—in 'The Pit', section 2 of 'The Lost Son' —into Eliot's *Waste Land* manner: 'Where do the roots go' ('What are the roots that clutch'). The weakness of Roethke's verse here testifies to an ancient truth of literary criticism: that poetry can hold fast only to the truths the poet knows. Roethke's poetry here, as always, succeeds only in touching those experiences within his ken. This experienced reality is, to put it baldly, simply more confined, both as to breadth and as to depth, than that of Eliot. Roethke's rather diminutive scale is, presumably, what the teasing, quizzical questions are intended to disguise. Eliot reveals his stature when he answers his own disturbing questions with his own profound answer:

> I will show you fear in a handful of dust.
>
> (*The Waste Land*)

Roethke on the other hand falls into a flip 'enigmatic' manner when something in the nature of a statement, a position, seems required by the context:

> Who stunned the dirt into noise?
> Ask the mole, he knows.
> I feel the slime of a wet nest.
> Beware Mother Mildew.
> Nibble again, fish nerves.
>
> ('The Lost Son')

This is surely *faux-naïf* rather than prophetic, a studied approximation to the tone of Christopher Smart, suggesting meanings which are not there. Roethke took more than a title from Smart ('Where knock is open wide'); he took, or tried to take, the air of familiarity with occult knowledge capable of setting the trivial and banal down side by side with the queerly and inexplicably significant. There is an important area of preoccupation here which aligns Roethke with many of his American contemporaries. For the nutty-yet-serious tone of much of 'The Lost Son' can make the reader think of Saul Bellow's Moses Herzog:

> I have married my hand to perpetual agitation
> I run to the whistle of money.
>
> ('The Lost Son')

Now Bellow is closer to the American Breakdown (so-called Confessional) school than any other novelist. And there is something padded about Herzog's agony, something half-willed about it, as if to experience, or rather to express, pain were to have established integrity and identity. The writer, as it were, lets himself go mad because he cannot otherwise feel that his existence means anything.

To draw attention to the parallels between 'The Lost Son' and the poetry of Eliot, then, is only to emphasize Roethke's limitations and their wholly representative nature. 'Was I too glib about eternal things?' Roethke himself was to ask later. The answer is, yes, when those eternal things lay beyond his reach. In poetry it is never easy to say when the ephemeral has been made eternal, or conversely, when an image or memory-trace is too slight to be made an eternal symbol. The whole of post-Romantic poetics is built upon the Wordsworthian premise that the true subject of poetry is the process whereby the simple and transient become the complex and eternal. A thing simply experienced becomes, in the process of being apprehended, part of an indefinitely complex continuum of experience, a continuum embracing, in the case of the great poet, not less than everything. In Roethke, we have a clear example of the poet who is clear and subtle on 'minimal' experiences, and vague and rather crude when these minimal experiences are related to 'ultimate things'.

The 'minimal' experiences in 'The Lost Son' are the poem's real subject-matter—the 'slow drip over stones', the toads 'brooding wells', the 'soft pond of repose'. Roethke feels his way back, with an extraordinary deft tact, into the world of his childhood. Only Roethke, we feel, experienced these things this way:

> Sat in an empty house
> Watching shadows crawl
> Scratching.
> There was one fly.
>
> ('The Lost Son')

It is a world of absolute silence and absolute aloneness, the realm of those 'numb nudgers in cold dimensions' with which the poet displays much extraordinary sympathy. The advance represented in these passages of 'The Lost Son' can be seen easily by comparing them with the denser 'compost' poetry of the first part of the book. Roethke was not comfortable in that rather self-consciously extroverted realism: even 'Frau Baumann, Frau Schmidt, and Frau Schwartz'—which remains one of Roethke's most memorable pieces—moves uneasily between a slagged realism and a more stilted, literary idiom—

> They teased out the seed the cold kept asleep

—and 'Child on Top of a Greenhouse' seems now a curiously joyless poem, in spite of Roethke's laboured attempts to convey the exhilaration central to the experience remembered: it reads now like an episode from 'Struwelpeter' rather than one from *The Prelude*. (What *were* they pointing at? The poem is teutonically heavy with guilt: the wise old psychoanalyst would know, we feel.)

A transition to the mature manner of 'The Lost Son' is made in the beautiful lyric 'The Waking'. It is worth noting perhaps that hardly anyone else was writing like this in 1950:

> Far in the wood
> A nestling sight.
> The dew loosened
> Its morning smells.
>
> ('The Waking')

With the exception of Geoffrey Hill, it is hardly possible, I think, to point to another poet of the time writing quatrains so well. 'The Waking' itself, nevertheless, partakes too much of the official Romantic ideology to belong with Roethke's best achievements:

> My ears knew
> An early joy.
>
> And all the waters
> Of all the streams
> Sang in my veins
> That summer day.
>
> ('The Waking')

Poetry will always, probably, be concerned with this 'early joy', and with the celebration of it. Yet when Wordsworth tells us that his heart leaps up when he beholds a rainbow in the sky, we believe him and accept without question the point and the sincerity of the assurance. Perhaps this is because of the curiously deliberate, cautious way in which Wordsworth recalls next that it was so when he was a boy, and then hopes that it will be so when he is old. The marvellous lyric—two stanzas, embracing three tenses in its tight arc—is in the nature of a superstitious 'touch-wood' ritual. Roethke's poem lacks this kind of complexity. The remembered experience is somehow annulled in the elegant yet laboured retailing of it. 'Another joy-in-nature effusion' is likely to be our response —a response not likely to be repeated in the presence of Dylan Thomas's poems about South Wales, which I think inspired Roethke here.

No, this kind of fervent celebration—the simple experience becoming in the telling of infinite interest for us—is not for Roethke. And, in general, whenever he assures us directly of what he has experienced, he fails to convince us of his integrity.

> And I walked, I walked through the light air;
> I moved with the morning.
>
> ('A Field of Light')

There is something superfluous about such utterances, just as there is something impotent when Roethke exclaims

> To have the whole air!
> The light, the full sun . . .
>
> ('The Shape of Fire')

These lines are strictly academic: that is, their content—which embraces their tone and their attitude, of course—is in some sense prescribed by the tradition. And this tradition which, properly speaking, exists to elucidate the impact of experience upon sensibility, and should be present behind the poet's shoulder, is itself offered within the particular content. The academicism here is something Roethke shares with Wallace Stevens: the metaphysics of the Romantic poets and philosophers are being played with, not used. There is no attempt to go beyond them. Thus, although there is no doubt that Roethke did experience that 'early joy', and therefore that the statement

> My ears knew
> An early joy

is biographically true and 'sincere', the utterance is poetically quite dead. We must bear in mind that when we praise a poet for 'authenticity' or for 'sincerity' or for being in earnest—for meaning what he says—we are, strictly speaking, only making a value judgement about an aesthetic fact: it is the achievement in the poem we are praising, not the poet's 'honesty' or his capacity to experience. No good poetry can be written without either honesty (both in the ordinary human sense and in some obscure 'poetic' sense) or a capacity for powerful and joyous experience. These are necessary but not sufficient conditions, along with the ability to use the language, and other more routine mechanical skills. Just as when we say that a poem or sonata will *last,* we are really making a statement about the quality of the art, not about the future, so, when we praise honesty or authenticity in a poem, we are (strictly speaking) referring not to the poet's personal character—much as this is attested in the poem— but to the nature of the poetic achievement.

'The Waking' is—I submit—although personally sincere, aesthetically bogus. At a higher level of comprehension, the personally authentic can become—in the absence of that peculiar effort of the will and intellect demanded of the poet—artistically *in*authentic.

Roethke is particularly interesting from this point of view. He is a confusion of self-flogging sincerity and quite blatant and factitious artistic fakery. The higher he strove, the worse he wrote: the bigger the scale attempted, the more resounding the tinkle of his bathos. 'The Lost Son', for instance, succeeds in opening up the world peculiar to Roethke: a world of curious and at times sinister aloneness and silence, in which the slightest sounds become ominously audible. It fails when Roethke attempts to relate the remembered boyhood experiences to an exalted plane of religious significance:

> Was it light?
> Was it light within?

('The Lost Son')

We are justified, I think, in answering Roethke's rhetorical questions with 'The hell it was!'

Much the same is true of 'The Shape of the Fire'. The first section is almost completely successful in the new vein initiated in 'The Lost Son'. The subtle, enigmatic images are so lightly touched on as to be all but imperceptible:

> Water recedes to the crying of spiders.
> An old scow bumps over black rocks,
> A cracked pod calls.

And later,

> Shale loosens. Marl reaches into the field.
> Small birds pan over water.

Or,

> A low mouth laps water.

('The Shape of the Fire')

Now this highly distinguished writing is in fact interspersed with some fairly portentous questionings:

> Will the sea give the wind suck?

The rationale of the whole—which is to say its larger structuring—is again revealed as the neo-Wordsworthian self-justification by love of the natural:

> Weeds, weeds, how I love you.

There is also over the whole passage an ominously 'nutty' tone, again anticipatory of the later Bellow ('These flowers are all fangs'), which shades into an approximation to the tone of the Shakespearian hero under duress:

> Wake me, witch, we'll do the dance of the rotten sticks and
> Farewell, farewell, fond worm.
>
> ('The Shape of the Fire')

There is something indefinably American about this passage: it is the tone, very nearly, of O'Neill and Wolfe, themselves yearners after the great rhetoric of Shakespeare. It is what we find in the later Berryman.

Nevertheless, Roethke is well on the way to his own voice here. We could give no better idea of the tightening process to which Roethke was submitting his own sensibility and style than to compare 'The Shape of the Fire' with 'The Visitant' (included in *The Waking* of 1953). At the end of another somewhat purposeless childhood reminiscence, Roethke hits on one of those subtleties peculiarly his own:

> The wind sharpened itself on a rock.

Then, 'a voice' sings, and what it sings is this:

> Pleasure ground
> Has no sound,
> Easily maddens
> The uneasy man.
>
> Who, careless, slips
> In coiling ooze,
> Is trapped to the lips
> Leaves more than shoes.
>
> Must pull off clothes
> To jerk like a frog
> On belly and nose
> From the sucking bog.
>
> ('The Shape of the Fire')

It is no accidental similarity of diction and situation which unites these uncomfortably lyrical quatrains with the opening stanzas of 'The Visitant':

> A cloud moved close. The bulk of the wind shifted.
> A tree swayed over water.
> A voice said
> Stay. Stay by the slip-ooze.

('The Visitant')

Going back to the earlier lyric, we must find ourselves less satisfied than we might initially have been with its loose lyricism. It had striven for an air of tightness, but was full of puzzling oddities that mimed enigmaticism: 'Coiling ooze'? And its entire grammatical form—it is an extended hypothesis—in the end makes it inconclusive, neither acceptably general, nor pregnantly aphoristic. The 'coiling ooze' on which the 'weary man' might 'slip' is now, in the later poem, tightened into a single superb phrase: we can feel no doubt that the 'slip-ooze' was what Roethke himself was on, nor that he has provided us here with an authentic metaphor for the human condition. The form of the poem is now that of the factual statement: yet the very factuality derives from the full absorption of the recollected natural imagery into a contemplation of the present—and, yes, about the eternal—what doesn't change. The facts have become wholly metaphorical. Again, the sinister experience is anticipated by an ominous quietude—'A cloud moved close. The bulk of the wind shifted.' This is a dimension from which the usually heard things —footsteps, the larger physical movements—have been bracketed out, so that only the very slightest movements are audible. We think of Poe's Roderick Usher, and can hardly resist the conclusion that this is a poetry of psychoneurosis: at the bottom of the experience is the crab, that 'quiet breather'. The 'mountain's downy girl', who comes and leaves the poet in the beautiful second section of the poem, draws from Roethke some of his subtlest and most relaxed music. But it is surely significant that she should come to him in a dream, and leave him complaining, 'Where is she now, the mountain's downy girl.' The bright day has no answer: this was a girl that never existed in bedroom or bathroom, for she is Pre-Raphaelite, troll—wish-fulfilment fantasy. The poem ends as it began with nature silent and unresponsive, yet somehow menacing:

> A wind stirred in a web of appleworm.
> The tree, the close willow, swayed.

('The Visitant')

Roethke's is a poetry of aloneness, terminal aloneness, one would think, of a neurotic intensity and completeness. He never succeeded in the Wolfean vein of large, generous realism: the love poems of *Words for the Wind* are generally below his best, literary, in the pejorative sense:

Love, love, a lily's my care.
She's sweeter than a tree.

('Words for the Wind')

This particular poem ends with a return to Roethke's *Lear* vein:

And I dance round and round,
A fond and foolish man,
And see and suffer myself
In another being at last.

If I felt inclined to psychoanalyse Roethke here, I should say that he was simply deceiving himself about the depth and the reality of the involvement referred to. At any rate, the art produced rings false. It is significant, I think, that the influence of Yeats should predominate in these pages of *Words for the Wind*. Yeats has been a millstone for many poets, with his dangerous doctrine of craft, of making-faking. In the poem that follows 'Words for the Wind'—'I knew a woman'—Roethke states that only gods should speak of her virtues—God, or English poets 'who grew up on Greek'. We could wish for no better confession of the American hunger for 'the real thing'. It is remarkable, I think, that Roethke could surmount the liabilities of this hunger so successfully as to be able to produce 'The Song' in the same collection, the most highly finished yet the most natural-seeming of all his lyrics. Here is that accursed 'Song' preoccupation inherited from Yeats, but exploited with the utmost subtlety, consummating once and for all Roethke's obsessions. The crab—'the quiet breather' of 'The Visitant'—returns, or rather is returned to. The poem begins with an encountered *alter ego*, a terrifying 'ragged man' who

Looked beyond me when
I tried to meet his eyes.

The poet asks him what he has done to him, and

Dust in a corner stirred
And the walls stretched wide.

('The Song')

Once again, as in 'The Visitant' and 'The Lost Son', the tone is more than a little insane: the dust stirs—as the 'bulk of the wind shifted' in the earlier poem—really only in the heightened imagination (apprehending what cannot be apprehended) of schizophrenia. This is a schizoid art, and what is remarkable surely is that while we are unable to discuss it at all without referring to it in quasi-clinical terms, what we are discussing is so indubitably art, not neurosis. This is not, like the poetry of Anne Sexton, for instance, the form of art without the substance; it is purely and simply art—a confrontation-in-transcendence with the human situation on earth.

The confrontation itself is, like all the confrontations in Roethke's better poetry, with a voice that is lodged within the poet himself: it is in this sense schizoid. And once again the poet makes contact with the voice through the medium of introjection into the lowest, most silent, most secret of creatures:

> I stared at a fissure in the ground
> Ringed round with crumbled clay;
> The old house of a crab;
> Stared, and began to sing.
>
> ('The Song')

This is the first time that Roethke's speaking ego has itself done the singing in one of these confrontations: it has previously been the voice of the other that has sung. This, I think, is what lends firmer shape to the whole enterprise:

> I wooed with a low tune;
> You could say I was mad.
>
> ('The Song')

Surely, you could. And this is more than another obligatory shaft of that condign 'self-awareness' that can sicken us in the poetry of the East Coast Confessionals. It is a genuine piece of orientation: yes, this is madness, but the placing of it indicates that the poet is seeing the whole experience from a more detached position, it removes the poet to a higher level of comprehension. He is not only placing an intense and horrible experience, he is also going through it to awareness. The *man* is mad—the poet inside the man is using the madness in order to *know*. For now the poet is answered, and it is perhaps the one moment of true communion in all Roethke's work:

> And a wind woke in my hair
> And the sweat poured from my face,
> When I heard, or thought I heard,
> Another join in my song
> With the small voice of a child,
> Close and yet far away.
>
> ('The Song')

With this communion, this antiphon, comes a strange peace:

> Mouth upon mouth, we sang,
> My lips pressed upon stone.

Roethke remained to the end the lost son.

Part III

The Legacy of Imagism

Chapter 6

Phenomenalist Idioms

Doolittle, Moore, Levertov

In contrast to English poets, American poets of the 1920s and early 1930s proved themselves adept at handling in highly individualized ways the free-verse idioms opened up by the researches of imagism. Imagism was of course initially an English development: Pound took over Flint's and Hulme's brainchild. Moreover, the poetry of the Pre-Raphaelites and of Oscar Wilde needed only the edge afforded by the dropping of the quatrain-form to stand revealed as imagist:

> The yellow leaves begin to fade
> And flutter from the Temple elms,
> And at my feet the pale green Thames
> Lies like a rod of rippled jade.
>
> (Oscar Wilde, 'Symphony in Yellow')

This verse—from a collection significantly called *Impressions*—is imagist in method, and it is hard to say exactly where the 'edge' I have spoken of really begins within Wilde's elegant quatrain. At any rate there is no doubting that when such 'impressions' as Wilde's were allowed to stand forth, without the support of the rhyme-scheme and metre, a decisive shift in emphasis and direction was taken:

> Old houses were scaffolding once
> and workmen whistling
>
> (T. E. Hulme, 'Image')

The 'impression' here is in fact a general observation, yet it *stands forth*: we see the scaffolding when we hear the workmen whistling, and we carry the whole picture in the mind as we savour the thought about time.

There is no doubt that it was at least partly because of the First World War, and its decimation of English poets that the imagist tradition was carried on by Americans. We can point to the best of Flint, Hulme, Aldington and certain of the *Wheels* and *Vortex* poets, and say without hesitation that the achievement there equals what Americans at the time were producing. We could go further and claim that the general technical level of the imagist anthologies is well below that of the English Georgian anthologies. But all this only emphasizes the fact that imagism all but fizzled out in England where in America it transformed itself to become a complex tradition of free verse that left few poets untouched.

Critics are still capable of dismissing imagism as a minor movement.[1] Verbal impressionists with a considerable affinity with contemporary painting, imagists began by being colourists in a fauvist sense—deliberately pastel, and expressly concrete. This was only the doctrine, yet doctrine or no, the ideal of imagism (which is plainly a characteristically refined Anglo-Saxon offshoot of symbolism) has been inherited by the twentieth century as a whole. Why? In its original form, it soon lost ground: it was for the minor to prettify, and historically it is useful to divide the poets concerned into those who did nothing but, and those who became something closer to impressionist. Out of surface art, the concern for bright plain colours, with no 'comment' from the poet, came a poetry of evocation, flexibility, rhythmic subtlety—a different kind of art. The poet developed first a technique of subtle but exact observation; he was interested in impressions, but this always implied something more than arty camera-work. The exactitude in question was not to be confused with the exactitude of Zola or the snap-photographer.

Free verse is, of course, no longer serviceable as a label. It was useful at a time when most poetry rhymed. Now, when very little rhymes, it is hardly possible to attempt classification: it can appear that there are as many varieties of free verse as there are poets practising it. We could, perhaps, usefully follow D. H. Lawrence's general distinction between the 'crystal'-like poetry of the old forms, and 'carbon'-like modern verse corresponding to a conception of the soul as a unique flame-like thing better served by the rapid fluctuating thrusts of verse unrestricted by demands of symmetry and regular rhythm. We could also, perhaps, broadly distinguish between short-lined verse and a longer, slower movement, like that of the later Eliot, approaching and surpassing the invisible norm of blank verse. We could, finally, isolate as an independent idiom or group of idioms the poetry of typographical scatter—that of late Mallarmé, for instance, or Mayakowsky in Russia, or Carlos Williams and cummings in America. Mayakowsky's later verse and Williams's at first sight appear similar. But Mayakowsky's spare, rhythmic ripple—its visual regularity can be appreciated even without Russian in a poem like 'Lenin'—is sharply distinct from, say, Williams's 'Asphodel', where the groupings are designed to slow up the mind and help the eye get the most out of the ruminative ideas. Attempts to classify free-verse effects, however, must inevitably distort and oversimplify. Neither sense-group nor sound-unit works as a basis for categorization. The cutting from line to line must be for many and contradictory reasons, so that we can only postulate, in the most general and unhelpful way, some sort of correlation between the breakdown of social forms with the concomitant growth of

[1] See, for instance, Spender, *Love–Hate Relations,* 117.

anarchic individualism in the twentieth century, and the development of free-verse idioms.

Free verse (as opposed to *vers libre*) may well be described as an invention of Ezra Pound's. In fact no verse was ever less free than Pound's in the decisive years—the years of *Lustra* and *Personae*. Eschewing the traditional sonic devices, Pound took upon himself the task of total sonic tact. His rejection of rhyme and stanza and of an unvarying line-length imposed upon him the most rigorous need for justification within the line. The sonic world of *Lustra* is comparable to the twelve-note system which imposed upon Schoenberg the necessity of avoiding—upon pain of internal collapse—the premature repetition of any note that might suggest a weighting towards a particular key. The artist in each case had to avoid absolutely the clashes and 'accidental' recurrences that had made up the harmonic structures of traditional art. The mastery of *Lustra* is a kind of marvellous avoidance, gathering all the while a delicate assemblage of meaning through tone and idea. The best poems of *Lustra* effect a delicate urgency, restless, without assertion, calm yet never still, never vulgarizing itself into insistence:

> Nor has life in it aught better
> Than this hour of clear coolness,
>   the hour of waking together.

> ('The Garret')

The miracle is that Pound was able to give to this 'clear coolness'—a dangerous aestheticism—a fluid, delicately pulsating life. Pound was often precious, but never dead.

Pound altered irreversibly the relation of sound to structure, and yet the origins of the 'short-line' poetry in America after the Second World War are to be sought less in the rarefied, Pre-Raphaelite researches of Pound than in some of the other poets who found their way into Amy Lowell's anthologies. Pound's larger cultural vision is shorn away in the sensitively raw explorations of some of his contemporaries. Hilda Doolittle, for instance, exploited much of the new glamour of diction initiated by Pound, coating her verse with lavish sweetmeats—pomegranates, peaches, quinces, figs, hyssop, nectarines, beeswax, apteryx, puce—that contrast strangely with the spareness advocated in the imagist manifestos. Yet the crisp freshness still adheres to her imagery, telling us of the excitement she felt in the new aesthetic world opened up by Flint, Hulme and Pound:

> O wind rend open the heat
> Cut apart the heat.

> ('Garden')

In spite of the Hellenic bias encouraged by the liaison with Aldington, Hilda Doolittle's best poetry is instinct with a particularized 'life' which reveals itself in an intense empathy with the natural world:

> The light passes
> from ridge to ridge,
> from flower to flower—
> the hypaticas, wide-spread
> under the light
> grow faint—
> the petals reach inward,
> the blue tips bend
> towards the bluer heart
> and the flowers are lost.
>
> ('Evening')

This stanza lies close to the essence of imagism: we cannot say any longer that the lines mimic or are mimetic of the experience, nor, glibly, that they *are* the experience (they aren't, they're words, and the experience was much more complex). All we can say is that by a combination of line-lengths, pauses, and the direction of the energy of words, something has happened on the page. The re-activation of the still life was one of the most significant preoccupations of imagist and post-imagist verse. We see it, for instance, in Wallace Stevens's 'Woman Looking at a Vase of Flowers':

> Hoot little owl within her, how
> High blue became particular
> In the leaf and bud and how the red
> Flicked into pieces, points of air,
> Became—how the central essential red
> Escaped its large abstraction, became
> First, summer, then a lesser time,
> Then the sides of peaches, of dusky pears.

Characteristically, Stevens philosophizes on the phenomenon in accordance with humanist and almost sentimental needs—

> the inhuman colours fell
> Into place beside her, where she was,
> Like human conciliations, more like
> A profounder reconciling, an act,
> An affirmation free from doubt.

Stevens wants the 'human conciliations', just as he rifles the situation for evidence of an 'affirmation free from doubt'. A different humanism is urged in Hart Crane's still life:

> Put them again beside a pitcher with a knife,
> And poise them full and ready for explosion—
> The apples, Bill, the apples!
>
> ('Sunday Morning Apples')

In other words, the density, the rotund actuality of the apples-just-being-apples, becomes for Crane the revelation of his own (and our own) luke-warm indecision, our lack of any sure existence. Distinct from both these 'humanisms' is the imagist alertness, which lets the still life be itself, drawing from it neither a heart-warming assurance of human significance, like Stevens, nor a desperate warning signal, like Crane. The imagist poet lets the phenomenon invade his sensibility. This is the result of a kind of actively passive intelligence, requiring considerable fineness and mental energy. The true 'concreteness' of imagism is not of the inert, reified variety. The 'concreteness' of Carlos Williams, for instance, is quite distinct from what we find in poets like Marianne Moore and Hilda Doolittle. Their phenomenalism is instinct with awareness: the contours of their poems morphologize the activity of their consciousness. Williams's verse is—from one point of view at least—*more* concrete than theirs: it is inert, graceless as by design, without recognizable organic contour, without the challenge to draw the mind into disappointment by achieving its own obliteration. Williams's verse remains where it was before, during and after reading. It is perhaps this very inertness that has drawn so much admiration from people who manifestly know what they are talking about. But there is often an ambivalence, almost a puzzlement, in the compliments paid to Williams by his contemporaries:

> Nowadays, when the press reels
> With chatterboxes, you keep still,
> Each year a sheaf of stillness,
> Poems that have nothing to say.
> (Kenneth Rexroth, 'A Letter to William Carlos Williams')

Elsewhere in this poem Rexroth refers to Williams as a 'fool'—with due qualifications, of course. It is not difficult to understand the general bewilderment. If we turn from Hilda Doolittle's finely alive still life to a still life by Williams, we cannot fail to be aware of a deadness in the language. This *nature* is very *morte*:

> No rose is sure. Each is one rose
> and this, like another,
> opens flat, almost as a saucer without
> a cup. But it is a rose, rose
> pink. One can feel it turning
> upon its thorny stem.
> (William Carlos Williams, 'Every Day')

Williams hasn't really felt the rose turning at all—hence presumably the tired phrase 'one can feel . . .'—as Hilda Doolittle felt the petals reaching inwards. 'Thorny stem' is naïve, too, merely copying, without changing or excitingly rendering the thing. By contrast with Williams's con-versational casualness, the values of the imagist alertness are clear.

This alertness, passive without being inert, attentive without 'reaching after fact and reason', amounts almost to a mode of awareness in imagism. In no poet is its active inaction witnessed more interestingly than in Marianne Moore. Moore really turned imagism on its head. Instead of the exact urgent plasticity characterizing phenomena, which we have seen to be essential to the imagist still life, her work describes the course that sensibility may describe in phenomena. Her theme is the 'strange experience of beauty', rather than the life of the natural event:

> Below the incandescent stars
> below the incandescent fruit
> the strange experience of beauty
> its existence is too much;
> it tears one to pieces
> and each fresh wave of consciousness
> is poison.

('Marriage')

She experiences elsewhere the touch of Proust's 'air de la chanson sous les paroles', and hovers on the edge of a theory of beauty dynamic and fearful. Regarding her work as a whole, but with special reference to the earlier volumes, we can discern in her poetry a tripartition of sensory experience: what we might call the spear of art, then beauty itself, and lastly, the Gestalt. What is meant by the spear of art? This simply: conscious intervention in three stages, types or aspects, as follows:

1   The incidence of phenomena: this is the direct effect of the imagist revolution—earlier phenomenal experience had been cloaked in introspection, 'the obscure reveries of the inward gaze'.
2   The absoluteness of the compulsive: phenomena draw a bead on the sensibility. Things are witnessed *as* things, as events outside the mind.
3   The fact of motion: this is the possibility of movement, combining elements as it affects the original value-principle. It is the potentiality of movement which renders the fact of conscious intervention acceptable, and makes wrong both the despair of Mallarmé and the notational staticness of the early imagist manifestos.

It is perhaps the final point that makes Moore important. The five-act play and the long poem are not the efforts of the poet to give himself a context for conceiving his insights, but are themselves the investigation of the possibility of movement.

Miss Moore had not the strength to explore the theory she adumbrated: 'it tears one to pieces' she says of beauty, and we have in the phrase the essence of her mind, with its tendency to melodramatic declamation when crisis approaches. But her intuition was right. What was wrong with imagism was its staticness. The way out of the impasse, the way to bring things to life lay in the acknowledgement of the dynamic life of words, not in the superimposition of syntax.

The strange webby tension of the best of Marianne Moore itself reflects the work effected by the techniques and ideals of imagism:

> The barnacles which encrust the side
> of the wave, cannot hide
> there for the submerged shafts of the
> sun,
> split like spun
> glass . . . .

('The Fish')

This could have been neither attempted nor achieved by any of her predecessors: it is neither symbolist nor surrealist, and it stems from the peculiar ethnical slant of imagism. This poetry is American and modern in a much more interesting way than the sentimental urban effusions of an immigrant Whitman like Sandburg. It represents a new precision of sensibility untutored by previous technical decisions, yet supremely aware of its own contours and their relations to the ambient spiritual space, to the last degree intelligent and aware, successively more refined and prepared by its own dross-consuming self-discipline.

This is the true discipline of modern art, and the true sense of the intelligence; it is a far cry from the chronic self-depreciation of academic ironism. This exactitude of awareness—an exactitude unplaceable in any correspondence of verse form to ideal form, but a disposition to reject the inessential part of any experience—the later imagists, via Marianne Moore and Kenneth Rexroth, bequeathed the younger postwar generation.

Marianne Moore actually, for sociocultural reasons, became herself academic, which is not to say merely an academic province (that is the fate of all original poetry). She settled into her own spiritual–mental aims, and she farmed the crops with progressively less sentient interest. The electric contours of her best verse gradually lost their tension (which is to say their spiritual energy), to be replaced by a merely mannered concern with sensibility: no longer 'strict with tension', her verse aspires to the condition not so much of music, as of music played in particularly elegant surroundings—'Like Gieseking playing Scarlatti', as she has it (instead of, say, Kempff playing Beethoven). The spry wit of the early pieces, tutored by Emily Dickinson, disappears, to be replaced by a staid and static hauteur. Compare these witty irreverences of 'To a Steamroller'—

> As for butterflies, I can hardly conceive
> of one's attending upon you, but to question
> the congruence of the complement is vain, if it exists.

with a poem like 'No Swan So Fine' in which she confesses to a preference for the refinement of 'art' over those 'real toads' she had elsewhere spoken of. Versailles has usurped the 'imaginary gardens'—thus, really, pushing the artefactual premises of that poem to their logical conclusion (since the gardens were imaginary, the toads could be 'real' only in a manner of speaking: her ambition to be a 'literalist of the imagination' was perhaps always an ambivalently worded intention to stay in the Pound domain of beauty and form). The tact of sensibility diminishes into aestheticism. Compare, again, this romp—

> the bat
> holding on upside down or in quest of something
> to
> eat, elephants pushing, a wild horse taking a roll, a
> tireless wolf under
> a tree,

—which preserves beautifully that unique tension she could attain between the poetic and the prose voice—with the lifeless formalism of this:

> Arranged by two's as peaches are,
> at intervals that all may live—
> eight and a single one, on twigs that
> grew the year before, they look like
> a derivative—
>
> ('Nine Nectarines and Other Porcelain')

Here only the placing of 'grew' reminds us of her real ability. Now this New England conservatism of mind does not appear in Moore's most alive poetry. This poetry has as its leading-edge a keen sensibility to the rare but intense experiences that lie at the heart of all poetry, but were isolated by the Romantic poets after Wordsworth, and then by the symbolists in Paris, as being what made life specifically worth living. The technical advances made by Moore and others can now be seen for what they are—indispensable elements in the further treatment and integration of those 'gleams like the flashings of a shield'. This is not to deny that her animal poems of the 1920s, which run parallel to Lawrence's great *Birds, Beasts and Flowers* series of the same period, stand revealed by the most cursory comparison with Lawrence as the art of the taxidermist rather than of the natural poet:

> Another armoured animal—scale
> lapping scale with spruce-cone regularity until they
> form the uninterrupted central
> tail-row! This near artichoke with head and legs a
> grit-equipped gizzard
> the night miniature artist engineer is
> Leonardo's—da Vinci's replica—
> impressive animal and toiler of whom we seldom hear.
>
> (Moore, 'The Pangolin')

A guided tour round the local natural history museum rather than the zoo, one would think. The witty pedantry which is Moore's stock-in-trade can certainly tire the most sympathetic reader. Yet there is no denying the skill and the sensibility on display, nor its value for younger practitioners. Perhaps it will be as well to turn for confirmation to the work of an English poet who found it significantly easier to tune in to the American wavelength after the Second World War than to remain inside English tradition. Charles Tomlinson has confessed to coming under the influence of numerous American poets, among them Stevens, and Marianne Moore's most obvious descendant, Elizabeth Bishop. It is difficult to see what Tomlinson can have found important in Miss Bishop, a poet of some charm in whom, none the less, the conversational side of Moore is largely unsupported by the wit and tension of that poet: but when we turn to his best work it is to see in action the natural intelligence of Hilda Doolittle and the best Marianne Moore, allied to Wallace Stevens's concern for 'art' and the human implications of the phenomenon. Here is an instance of Tomlinson nicely riding the divide between the natural event and the art-consciousness:

> It is the sense
>   of things that we must include
>   because we do not understand them
> the impalpabilities
>   in: the marine dark
>   the chords
> that will not resolve themselves
>   but hand
>   in an orchestral undertow
>
> dissolving
>   (celeste above shifting strings)
>   yet where the dissolution
> gathers the echoes
>   from an unheard voice:
>   and so the wood
> advances before the evening takes it—
>   branches
>   tense in a light like water—
> as if (on extended fingers)
>   supporting the cool immensity
>   while we meditate the strength
> in the arm we no longer see.
>   (Charles Tomlinson, 'The Impalpabilities')

I have already spoken of the way in which the imagist observation makes a space for itself in the ambience—the contours of Doolittle's hypaticas and Moore's fish. With this in mind, we could say that Tomlinson's poem is really confined to the lines:

> and so the wood
> advances before the evening takes it—
> branches
> tense in a light like water—

The 'poem' *is* the event that takes place between the words 'and' (in l. 15) and 'water' (in l. 18). The action of the poem is over with 'water', in spite of the obvious care and intelligence with which Tomlinson has related the phenomenon to the commentary. In fact, these five lines could be excerpted and left to stand on their own. The rationale of the poem— that things we do not understand compel our recognition just by being ungraspable yet indubitable—somehow remains unwelded to the event which *is* the poem—though it is, in a strangely moving way, essential to our experience of that event. We may not—as critics—feel wholly satisfied by Mr Tomlinson's 'unheard voice', but as human beings we can hardly fail to feel stirred and moved by the poet's inability to 'explain' the event he has rendered with such exactness. The whole poem throws more light upon the imagist process: the imagist poem is the action of the phenomenon becoming noumenal. And neither Mr Tomlinson's 'Impalpabilities' nor his borrowings from Bartók can compete with anything so momentous.

This poem in fact enacts a conflict: Tomlinson preys upon the experience. But the essence of imagist practice was that the image was allowed to grow through the poet's finger-tips, as if the poet had become for a moment himself pure vegetable. This explains the uncanny effect of imagist or phenomenalist poetry, the precision that attends the best writing of poets like Moore and Tomlinson. We begin to see that the actual precision is really not an end in itself, at least not as the original manifestos had ordained. It is a question of the anterior ideology. D. H. Lawrence wrote as accurately and economically as any poet ever did. Yet Lawrence's realizations of insects, birds, animals and trees are essentially opposed to the spirit of phenomenalist poetry, in spite of the surface similarities that exist between the free verse of Lawrence and that of, say, Marianne Moore. Lawrence fills his subjects with himself: the field of the Lawrence poem is defined by the envelope of Lawrence's own consciousness. That famous 'voice'—which presumably put Lawrence in Pound's bad books—amounts itself to a formal principle: Lawrence communes with his beasts, talks with them, and in the mirror of his conversation we get the life of the thing. In imagism, by contrast, the experience or thing itself dictates the poem's coastline. The shape of the event as it works its way into the poet's consciousness (ideally) creates the shape of the poem. This is the 'true voice of feeling' thesis argued for romanticism in our time by Herbert Read.[2] Like Olson and Pound, Read made the mistake of taking a particular kind of poetry for all poetry, and erecting description into prescription. We would be better off simply assigning to different kinds of poet different psychological labels. Pound in fact argues the case for a specific kind of temperament, the extroverted or impressionistic, or, to use the term I prefer, the phenomenalist. Lawrence, on the other hand, is a true phenomenological artist: he is at work constantly bracketing his experience, much as Husserl and Brentano described the general action of consciousness. Whether or not this psychological labelling helped us to understand the poetry better, it would certainly have the effect of making us pause before consigning certain sorts of poetry to the wastebin simply because they do not conform to our preconceptions of what poetry is.

Since the Second World War, a new phenomenalist poetry—or a series of phenomenalist idioms—has grown up in America, differing as sharply from the New England conservatism of Moore as the raw daylight of Léger and Picasso from the muted bourgeois twilight of Bonnard and Vuillard. In place of the refined poetess sitting isolated among the teacups, socially aligned with her visitors but privately alienated from them, we encounter the poet-father/husband (Kenneth Rexroth) and the poet-housewife/mother (Denise Levertov), whose living-space coincides with their aesthetic space. The old separatism of the *avant garde,* in which the private world of poetic experience excluded the actual grubby world of social living, is replaced by a unified continuum. It is perhaps the most remarkable and significant achievement of American writing in this period (the essence of the American moment) that it finally cancelled the notion of an artistic *avant garde*: the poetry of the American moment is not *avant garde,* though it represents the best and most advanced writing of its time. This will emerge especially clearly in respect of Allen Ginsberg and the Beat poets. But it is hardly less impressively the case with the phenomenalist successors of Pound, Moore and Doolittle.

It was the work of aesthetes like Marianne Moore that made possible the sharp penetrating idiom of a generation of phenomenalist poets, of whom Denise Levertov is an excellent instance. Black Mountain College played an important part in this development, but Black Mountain basically continued the eclectic tradition of the later Pound. In spite of Charles Olson's much-advertised notions of field and territory, Black Mountain represents in many ways a retreat, a withdrawal (as its very name suggests) to higher ground. Its role in sustaining and developing the imagist ideal of *edge,* of a prosody more responsive and pliant than the

[2] Herbert Read, *The True Voice of Feeling* (London 1952). This still seems the best attempt yet made to describe the course of what is arguably the most important technical tenet of Romantic critical theory as it affected the writing of poetry. Read's final resting-point is, logically enough, imagism, and if he is wrong, he has at least brought to the surface what is—in Pound, Olson and others—a pervasive dogma.

E

rhythmical orthodoxy of neo-metaphysical poets like Tate and Lowell, is nevertheless of the first importance. We can appreciate its beneficial influence in the poetry of Denise Levertov. In contrast to Sylvia Plath, who had written little poetry before settling in England, Levertov had already published good poetry in England before going to America. What America gave her was, briefly, the fine raw edge that in her English verse had been swathed in metre:

> Folding a shirt, a woman stands
> still for a moment, to recall
> warmth of flesh, her careful hands
>
> heavy on a sleeve, recall
> a gesture or the touch of love;
> she leans against the kitchen wall
>
> listening for a word of love . . .
>
> ('Folding a Shirt')[3]

It is interesting to see how much of the Levertov we know is already crystallized here: the tone of voice is already unmistakable. But if we turn from this vignette of Levertov folding a shirt to this equally domestic piece, written after she had settled in America, we cannot fail to see how much she has gained:

> The washing hanging from the lemon tree
> in the rain
> and the grass long and coarse.
>   . . . So light a rain
> fine shreds
> pending above the rigid leaves.
>
> ('The 5-Day Rain')

Like Tomlinson's, this verse stems from the subtle precision of imagism. But it is concerned, as his usually is not, with the actual life-style of the poet, with the most banal experiences. In 'The 5-Day Rain', the vibrant tough sensibility revealed in the primary observations exults in a release of insight:

> Wear scarlet! Tear the green lemons
> off the tree! I don't want
> to forget who I am, what has burned in me,
> and hang limp and clean, an empty dress—

This is a superb domestic image, symbolizing with unforgettable simplicity a complex predicament—the predicament of the woman who wants to accept the role of mother and wife, with all the curtailments and

[3] Printed in *Little Reviews Anthology*, edited by Denys Val Baker (London 1949), 152.

sacrifices it involves, without losing contact with that other self that writes poetry and lives intensely. My phrasing suggests a difference between the two personae which contradicts the unity of poet and mother/wife earlier put forward as being remarkable in Levertov. Yet, to the contrary, the really remarkable thing about Levertov is that the poetry comes out of the conflict of the two roles, that the conflict itself could only be apprehended given the acceptance of the unified experience-continuum.

Certainly it is not an easy stance to sustain, when children have to be put to school every day, and the husband's shirts to be laundered. The dilemma is dramatized at greater length, with less intensity but more humour and irony, in 'Matins'. Half-ironically, half-jubilantly, Levertov catches herself—in situations that might be humiliating but aren't— invoking the authentic:

> The authentic! Shadows of it
> sweep past in dreams, one could say imprecisely
> evoking the almost-silent
> ripping apart of giant
> sheets of cellophane.
>
> ('Matins' 1)

What is ripped of course is exactly that veil of the banal behind which the world hides most of the time. If the poem never quite recaptures the sheer excitement of those sheets of cellophane (perhaps the best instance in all Levertov's work of her genius for exploiting the imaginative possibilities in the banal), it does not have to. In fact, the repeated ejaculations of 'The authentic!' are really quite different, and in the difference lies the poem's pathos and drama. The cry that opens the poem, and which suggested the ripping apart of the cellophane, greeted the sudden appearance of the authentic: as one would open the door and exclaim, 'John!' on seeing one's caller. But the cry in the second section of the poem, though grammatically identical, is in fact quite different:

> The authentic! I said
> rising from the toilet seat.
> The radiator in rhythmic knockings
> spoke of the rising steam.
>
> ('Matins' 2)

This is more like 'That's it! Of course . . . why didn't I see that before!'— and of course it is the revelation of the authentic in the first part of the poem that created the situation (provided the frame) for the later exclamations. When the cellophane ripped apart, the banal became intolerable, yet the authentic itself lay precisely in that humdrumness which the poet had perhaps been ignoring, despising, 'taking for granted'. So she once more urges herself to take a tighter hold on the values revealed to her:

> The authentic, I said
> breaking the handle of my hairbrush as I
> brushed my hair in
> rhythmic strokes: That's it,
> that's joy, it's always
> a recognition, the known
> appearing fully itself, and
> more itself than one knew.

('Matins' 2)

'More itself than one knew': as the excitement subsides—she drops the exclamation mark for the second repetition of 'authentic'—so the understanding of the revelation deepens. In the third section she takes up the sound-effect skilfully handled in the beginning of the second section: the knocking of the steam in the pipes had been like a second signal to her —as if the ordinary world were declaring itself to her 'With rhythms it seizes for its own/to speak of its invention'. And the invention is no less than

> the real, the new-laid
> egg whose speckled shell
> the poet fondles and must break
> if he will be nourished.

('Matins' 3)

The next section discourses, by means of remembered images, on this discovery—

> A shadow painted where
> yes, a shadow must fall.
> The cow's breath
> not forgotten in the mist, in the
> words.

('Matins' 4)

These are the things in which 'reality' (the 'authentic') declared itself, and the poet's genius for verisimilitude—saying it like it is—is what 'draws up heat in us'. The 'zest/to follow through,/follow/transformations of day/in its turning, in its becoming' derives from this gift for the verbal transformation of reality: note that although the poet's tone and diction here suggest the disembodied speculativeness of Stevens, Levertov's poem leads back to the banal family-routines that were evoked somewhat wrily and ironically in the early sections of the poem:

> Stir the holy grains, set
> the bowls on the table and
> call the child to eat.

('Matins' 5)

There follows a beautiful, precise yet affectionate description of the getting-the-children-off-to-school routine: Levertov is making her daily routines work for her here. They are the source of the authenticity, which consists precisely in being true to them. Levertov *is* true to them, even down to the structure of this whole sequence: the child having been got off to school, the poet returns, a stage further on in comprehension, to the abstract theme. Section 6, the last but one of the set, reinvokes the authentic, but now admits that it remains elusive:

> it rolls
> just out of reach, beyond
> running feet and
> stretching fingers, down
> the green slope and into
> the black waves of the sea.
>
> ('Matins' 6)

She addresses a 'little horse' (the child's toy perhaps), asking how to follow the 'iron ball' of authenticity

> to the place where I must kill you and you step out
> of your bones and flystrewn meat
> tall, smiling, renewed,
> formed in your own likeness.
>
> ('Matins' 6)

Finally, the poem ends with a direct address to 'Marvellous Truth', begging it to 'confront us at every turn':

> Thrust close your smile
> that we know you, terrible joy.
>
> ('Matins' 7)

Whether or not we are quite clear about the violence thought necessary in the sixth section of the sequence, we cannot doubt but that the structure of the poem is masterly, effortless, natural yet strangely exalted. It is perhaps a minor mode, but we may well think Levertov more successful in practising her minor mode than either Ginsberg or Duncan their major.

It would be interesting to compare the wise cheerfulness of Levertov's poetry with the sour gloom of Sexton and Plath, in whom the banal and the routine are heinous. In general Levertov's verse at its best exploits the fine rough edge of imagist tradition to articulate a sense of life that is closer to the Beat than to the essentially eclectic elitism of Black Mountain. Levertov's verse is sensible, normative, vivid with meaning. Back of it is the Blakean sense of the lambent meaningfulness of ordinary life:

> Let's go
> much as that dog goes
> intently haphazard.
>
> ('Overland to the Islands')

Let us go, in other words, not with aims and ideals, deferring reality
until death or worse, but with intent pleasure in the Now, in the natural
highs dulled out of life by concentration on the wrong things, so that
'every step' is, as she puts it, 'an arrival'. 'Matins' shows how hard it is to
live up to this—or live down to it, perhaps.

As these formulations suggest, with Levertov we shade into the world
of the Beat poets, and it is her distinction, I think, to have put the technical know-how of Black Mountain at the service of the ordinary in a
way that bridges the gulf between Black Mountain exclusiveness and
Beat realism. In a curious way, her voice occasionally suggests that of
Berryman's Mistress Bradstreet:

> Call the child to eat,
> send him off, his mouth
> tasting of toothpaste, to go down
> into the ground, into a roaring train
> and to school.
>
> ('Matins' 5)

As Anne Bradstreet was, Levertov is an exiled Englishwoman, and it's
worth noting both that no-one writes quite like her in the current scene,
and that her particular mix of wit and intensity—of sense and sensibility—
owes much to the native English balance she brought across the Atlantic
with her. She has inevitably perhaps become the victim of her own skill.
The naturalness in the end ceases to penetrate, so that the exciting
incisiveness, the keen noumenal roughness of poems like 'The 5-Day
Rain', tends later to give way to an easy familiarity:

> it is all a jubilance, the light catches up
> the disordered street in its apron
> broken fruit rinds shine in the gutter.
>
> ('Six Variations')

This is that lambent ordinariness, but hasn't it lost some of the excitement of penetration? If we turn from these joyous yet somehow too
neatly ordered perceptions, to this simpler, more primitive description,
the difference is plain:

> They have
> a great space of dark to
> bark across. The rabbits
> will bare their teeth at
> the spring moon.
>
> ('The Springtime')

This sense of barbarous yet ritualistic ceremony has been ironed out by
Levertov's later professionalism. In general the earlier work, less natural,
with more verbal harmonics and overlapping, and a generally greater

hierophantic incantation, owing so much to the example of Robert Duncan, seems more important now:

> It is your loneliness
> your energy baffled in the stillness
>   gives an edge to the shadows—
> the great sweep of mountain shadow,
> shadow of ants and leaves,
>   the stone of the road each with its shadow
> and you with your long shadow
> closing your book and standing up
> to stretch, your long shadow-arms
>   stretching back of you, baffled.
>
>   ('Lonely Man')

Perhaps Levertov's most satisfying pieces are those in which the native English good sense and the ease of her speaking voice are in competition with the more ceremononial manner of Duncan. Naturalness of voice, we are reminded yet again, is not the true end of the poet's aspiration:

> Green snake—I swore to my companions that certainly
>   you were harmless! But truly
> I had no certainty, and no hope, only desiring
>   to hold you, for that joy, which left
> a long wake of pleasure, as the leaves moved
> and you faded into the pattern
> of grass and shadows, and I returned
> smiling and haunted, to a dark morning . . .
>
>   ('To the Snake')

We turn to Emily Dickinson, to Sylvia Plath, to Robert Duncan himself, vainly searching for the delicate, joyous yet exalted tone of this verse.

Chapter 7

Black Mountain Academy:
Charles Olson as Critic and Poet

Denise Levertov is one of a number of distinguished poets in the 1950s who received stimulus and direction from Black Mountain College. Although it's hardly possible to define a very clear Black Mountain style, it is possible to use the label to indicate a rough area of preoccupation in postwar American poetry. America has traditionally lacked—it still lacks—a literary centre on the scale of London or Paris, and it is interesting that at least two important poetic movements have originated in, or centred in, the South. Black Mountain may have owed something of its persistent ruralism to its location in Georgia, but it was never a regionalist movement, like the Fugitives. On the contrary, Black Mountain College was internationalist—*avant garde*, indeed—from the time Josef Albers crossed the Atlantic in 1932, to the time of its dissolution under Charles Olson in 1955. What Black Mountain stood for, as far as poetry was concerned, was the perpetualization—almost, we might argue, the institutionalization—of the poetics of imagism. The phenomenalist modernism described in the previous chapter found a home in Black Mountain College, and there, I should like to suggest, it became academic. In word progressivist and modernist, Black Mountain had become a retarding force in the development of poetry before it was dissolved. It encouraged an elitist exclusiveness, concerned all too often with the display of learning rather than with its spirit, and with erudition rather than with learning. The poetry it fostered tended to be refined rather than energetic, esoteric rather than refined. As an outpost of modernist prosody in the neo-metaphysical 1930s and 1940s, Black Mountain was positive; as a bastion of ideas that were at their most fertilizing in the years just after the First World War, it was negative.

Black Mountain poetics had two important sources, Pound and Carlos Williams. As a poetic influence, Williams was, I believe, negligible. But his prose work *In the American Grain*[1] had an effect second only to that of Pound's seminal critical works—*Guide to Kulchur*, *ABC of Reading* and *How to Read*. From this point in time, *In the American Grain* seems a classic of proud provincialism—a bull-headed asseveration of cultural

[1] W. C. Williams, *In the American Grain* (New York 1956).

independence, like Twain's fiction and Sandburg's verse. As far as Black Mountain was concerned, its most important contention was that the Puritan forefathers served America badly by failing to see the great new continent as a 'place': they saw it ethically, and everything that followed was their fault. Now this is clearly naïve ahistorical day-dreaming, a projection of twentieth-century thought onto seventeenth-century actions, not so much wise as stupid after the event. The fact is that all civilizations, all cultures, were founded by men with 'vision' of some kind—Roman Catholic, Protestant Low Church, Buddhist, Vedic, Aztec, Inca. It is only our time that is stripped of vision. In its disavowal of all myths, Williams's book stands revealed as a piece of outrageously Romantic mythopoeia—a late instance of American new-Adamism. Such a capacity for 'dreaming' has often been presented as an American strength; but in this case, as in many others, it seems more likely to have kept Americans from accepting themselves as they really are. And what they really are is not a nation of pioneering Boones or open-hearted Whitmans but an energetic hard-working European nation descended from seventeenth-century Englishmen with strict notions of conduct and a need for political freedom, who would never have established a society at all if they had tried to wander through the land, as Williams seems to have imagined Daniel Boone did. The Puritans were bad about their witches, but there is no instance of a civilization without some such 'flaw'—as witness the elaborate tortures of the Sioux, for instance, the Aztecs' daily human sacrifices, or the bloodbaths in the Roman Colosseum. To blame 'everything' on the Puritans, as Williams in effect does, is itself outrageously puritanical: the Puritan refuses to accept himself as he is, with his flaws and vices, but must continually excoriate himself, trying feverishly to sponge himself clean. We can see this spirit at work in the American intellectual's migrations to Paris in the 1920s,[2] we see it at work today in his violent denunciation of America as she really is—a strange mixture of idealism and cynicism, ruthlessness and generosity, power and weakness, perspicacity and myopia.

Much of this distraught puritanism reappears in Black Mountain poetry and poetics, most notably in the work of Charles Olson. It is from Williams, in the first place, that Olson takes the notion of 'place'. We saw in the case of imagism that a particular openness of the sensibility, an active awareness, a vigorous patience with phenomena, was an important part of the poetic enterprise. This awareness was largely absent from Williams's somewhat inert 'concreteness', and the reason may well be related to the poet's tendency to erect 'place' itself into a concept, so that the actual vigilance of the sensibility was sacrificed to a faintly chauvinistic cult of 'America'. Williams dramatized this cult in *Paterson,* a long poem which has had many descendants in America. Taken in conjunction with Pound's *Cantos, Paterson* has, I think, helped to slacken the muscles of

[2] See F. G. Hoffman, *The Twenties* (New York 1962), 43–55.

American writing in the postwar period. In the absence of any precise aim, the poet tends to diffuse himself in images: the mystique of 'place' encourages mere notation, observation without meaning, evidently noted down in the belief that the absence of any 'poetic' or metaphysical dimension somehow justifies them.

This general slackness is, to be sure, disguised by Olson in the quasi-dynamic theory of 'projectivism': 'get on with it, keep moving, keep in, speed, the nerves, their speed, the perceptions, theirs the acts, the split second acts, the whole business, keep it moving as fast as you can citizen'.[3]

Stephen Spender is inclined to accept this at its face value,[4] but in fact it runs counter to the rest of Olson's theory, to his own verse practice, and to the tradition from which it stems. Now the same paradox appears between Pound's poetry and theory. Yeats called Pound's verse 'tapestry-like', that is to say, static and flat, a thing of texture and colour with little depth or drive. Yet there is a striking contrast between this (I think correct) conception of Pound's poetry as aesthetic and decorative, and the emphasis of Pound himself on the poetic image as essentially active and dynamic. This was a central idea of Ernest Fenollosa's, taken over first by Pound, then by Olson. Olson paraphrases Fenollosa so closely, in fact, that we can use his words without referring to Fenollosa's text directly at all: the sentence Olson sees as 'first act of nature, as lightning'. Now this account of the sentence, based upon Fenollosa's use of the Chinese ideogram as an 'idea in action', has usually been accepted as an essential part of imagist poetry. Pound, in fact, introduced the idea for the first time in his Gaudier-Brzeska monograph of 1915, that is to say, two years after he had received the manuscript of Fenollosa's essay 'On the Chinese written character' from Fenollosa's wife. The imagist manifesto of 1912 concentrates its attention exclusively on the image, which must be 'hard, clear'. The manifesto makes no reference to the necessity of using transitive verbs or of avoiding similes and the copula. As a matter of fact the original imagist emphasis is true to Pound's own practice, which is closer to the 'exquisite' aesthetic textures of Lionel Johnson and Oscar Wilde than to the 'transitive' drive of Marinetti or Mayakoswky.[5] The entire imagist movement, in fact, from Pound and Amy Lowell down to the Black Mountain group, has never done more than pay lip-service to the idea of the transitive verb in action. An intentness on the image naturally led to a static poetry in the first place; and in the second, action was—as the strident vulgarity of the English vorticists and the Russian and Italian futurists showed—geared to a worship of the machine, and therefore to the idea of social change.

[3] Quoted by Spender in *Love–Hate Relations*, 228.
[4] Idem.
[5] Interestingly, D. H. Lawrence showed himself far more intelligently responsive to futurism. See the letter to Edward Garnett in *Selected Literary Criticism* (London 1956), 17–18.

Pound later came to envisage a social revolution, based upon the redistribution of capital and the establishment of a dictatorship. But it was essentially a retrospective conception, reactionary, conservative, based upon an idyllic vision of feudal contentment, with each man knowing his place. To embrace futurism—or indeed vorticism—the artist had to be prepared to cut his links with the aesthetic values of the immediate past and to throw in his lot with a raucous and raw future, egalitarian and 'progressive' in precisely the sense hateful to Pound. If the criticism talks of action in language, the poetry fondles the past and the unchanging idyll of 'aesthetic' feeling.

In fact, Fenollosa did poetry a disservice by making his famous parallel between the Chinese written character and the language of poetry. Chinese happens to be ideographic, not phonetic; hence, it appears, to the outsider accustomed to a phonetic language, to have preserved primitive pictural events in its signs for objects and processes which in Indo-European languages are referred to by symbols divorced from the pre-phonetic origins of language. To an enthusiastic but naïve Westerner, such an ossified ideographic language may appear a miracle of poetic vividness. In fact, Chinese is obviously just as threadbare to those that use it as our own languages are to us: from every cultural and literary point of view the ideogram is a disaster, which has—if this is not to put cart and horse wrong way about—kept the Chinese insulated from world history, as impervious to intellectual 'progress' as the Boxers thought they were to the effects of small-arms fire. A Chinese proverb has it that 'A picture is worth a thousand words': why, if the language is a running poetic performance, with detonations of active and concrete imagery every time a peasant opens his mouth to ask the time of day? It was Fenollosa's error initially, but it was wholly characteristic of Pound to accept uncritically his diagnosis of a general degeneracy of European language, with no attention to the facts of political or linguistic history.

Charles Olson transfers the Fenollosa fallacy to Mayan hieroglyphs in a later essay, 'Human universe': 'They retain the power of the objects of which they are the images,' he observes.[6] The implication is that our own verbal icons lack this sort of vividness and that we ought to learn from this ancient culture how to refurbish our language. But the parallel is quite factitious. Olson is regarding the hieroglyphs as visual art. To *use* these symbols (pictural as they may be) is at once to sacrifice their mimetic quality, which becomes irrelevant to the needs of the sentence. And we should remember that *qua* hieroglyph the hieroglyph was not intended to have 'power of the object'. To believe that it was, again, is just the outsider's awe. To the Maya, it was a sign, and its visual quality hardly mattered. Certainly it can have no relevance to our own cultural needs. Granted that it may in certain circumstances be desirable to strive after

[6] Charles Olson, 'Human universe', in *The New Writing in the USA*, ed. Robert Creeley (Harmondsworth 1967), 189.

clear imagery in poetry, it's by no means certain that the way to achieve
this end is to concentrate on the 'concreteness' of language. Language
evokes by naming, not by representing, and the events of language are
quite different from those of visual media. Now in fact, every poet using
his language well does charge his imagery with just the sort of trenchancy
Olson found in the Mayan hieroglyph. And here we encounter the
fundamental circularity of Olson's criticism: the apparently descriptive
(and therefore helpful) criterion turns out to be merely an approval-
word, a value judgement. Lawrence was a poet who found little favour
with Pound; but don't Lawrence's animal poems precisely 'retain the
power of the objects of which they are the images'—granted only that the
word 'image', in relation to poetry, must be taken to refer to the combined
capacities of several signs, not to single iconic vocables? What about this,
for instance:

> Till he fell in a corner, palpitating, spent.
> And there, a clot, he squatted and looked at me.
> With sticking-out, bead-berry eyes, black,
> And improper derisive ears,
> And shut wings,
> And brown, furry body.
>
> Brown, nut-brown, fine fur!
> But it might as well have been hair on a spider; thing
> With long, black-paper ears.
>
> (D. H. Lawrence, 'Man and Bat')

There is no twentieth-century volume of verse—there are few enough
from any century—in which there are more verbal signs which 'retain
the power of the objects of which they are the images' than *Birds, Beasts
and Flowers*. Yet the instance only makes us understand that the programme
of transitive verbal power is, in the imagist theorists and poets, pure lip-
service. What we must pay attention to in their poetry is the purpose of
the imagery. Imagism, like projectivism, has a specific *Weltanschauung,*
and the apparently practical methodological side of the movement is
spurious, a smokescreen to conceal a detached, elitist, basically passive
philosophy of life and society.

As far as 'life' is concerned, Olson dutifully embraces a 'dynamic'
theory of the emotions, a theory which partakes equally of D. H. Lawrence
and Ezra Pound. Olson indicates the Poundian bias of his thought by
aligning himself with the Keatsian negative capables against the sublime
egotists. This view of things is not backed up, in fact, by the poetry:
Keats was no less concerned than Wordsworth with metre and regular
stanza form, and the subjective coloration is if anything more pronounced than it is in Wordsworth. But it gives us an idea at least of where
Olson is going. For the remark is followed by the repudiation of the

'subject'—what Pound had rejected as 'the obscure reveries of the inward gaze'. 'Objectism,' Olson says, 'is the getting rid of the lyrical interference of the individual as ego, of "the subject" and his soul, that peculiar presumption by which western man has interposed himself between what he is as a creature of nature (with certain instructions to carry out) and those other creations of nature which we may, with no derogation, call objects.'[7] Now the general evolution of European thought and literature over the past two hundred years has been in the direction of what we might call object-dominance. Europe has moved away from what is in fact a determinate historical phenomenon: that 'under consciousness of a *sinful* nature' of which Coleridge spoke[8]—and which Olson wants to castigate as an aberration, a wilful truancy of the mind away from 'objectism'. Once again we witness the ahistorical bent of Poundian thinking, reducing all ages to the same condition, with no consideration of the peculiar relations which dictate certain ranges of content and attitude in some periods, and outlaw them in others. The basic problem still remains: man is an object, as Olson reminds us, but he is also (and perhaps more importantly) a subject. It is the subjective experience of things which is recorded in poetry. The subject-consciousness of man creates the world he has to live in, in Kantian terms; and the question of what he is to do with himself in it, and how he is best to live there, would not be answered by simply 'recording' the world-as-object, even if this were possible. The rise of object-dominance was a historically governed development, not the sloughing-off of blindness. Man remains a 'soul', and still has a responsibility for himself which cannot be honoured by abdicating from the subjective. The rise of object-dominance records Western man's changing relations with his world, not his gradual emergence out of a subject-self which egotistically blocked his 'vision': this conception of externally existent reality, just waiting to be snapped by the alert eye of the poet, is one of the root-fallacies of imagist theorizing. Neither of its oriental models—neither the T'ang poetry of China, nor the Japanese *haiku*—abjured the subjective, as Olson suggests poetry can. The most engaging quality of Golden Age poetry in China was, as A. R. Davis observes, 'its intimate expression of personal feeling'.[9] The greatness of Bashō, similarly, was based upon his ability to express the profoundly subjective without mentioning or labelling the emotion; the *haiku* was the marriage of the inner and the outer, not the triumph of the outer over the inner. Moreover, the T'ang poets were profoundly influenced by the only alien cultural force before Marxism to make any impact on Chinese intellectual life—Buddhism; and Buddhism was the pervasive presence that made the *haiku* possible. Davis notes that Confucianism, the identifyingly practical social philosophy of China, was

---

[7] 'Projective verse', in *Selected Writings* (New York 1974), 24.
[8] *Lectures and Notes on Shakspere* [sic] (London 1893), 92.
[9] Introduction to *The Penguin Book of Chinese Verse* (Harmondsworth 1962), 23.

superseded during the T'ang dynasty by both Buddhism and the T'ao.[10] Significantly, Pound himself ignored the deeper spirituality of Chinese poetry, and concentrated his attention on the 'unwobbling pivot'— Kung, the social rule-maker. Thus, once again, we see imagism, and its projectivist offspring, as deficient in depth and hinged upon nothingness.

Such philosophy as Olson himself articulates to back up his poetics is crudely naturalistic. If man 'stays inside himself', Olson says,[11] if he is 'contained within his nature as he is participant in the larger force, he will be able to listen, and his hearing through himself will give him secrets objects share. And by an inverse law his shapes will make their own way.' This seems a strangely arcane departure for the disciple of Poundian objectism. But it is of course the old symbolist lore, part Baudelairean *correspondance*, part Nervalesque animism, part Keatsian negative capability. It echoes, too, dimly and confusedly, the ideas of the *haijin*: Bashō's advice to the poet was to recognize in great art the working of the spirit:

> It is a poetic spirit, through which man follows the creative energy of the universe and makes communion with the things of the four seasons. For those who understand the spirit, everything they see becomes a lovely flower, and everything they imagine becomes a beautiful moon.[12]

But this is backed up by Buddhism, it is logical and wholly consistent It is Buddhism that breathes through Bashō, and the doctrines are sense less without the deep faith.

In the case of projectivism, we are left simply with the shallow dogma of objectism, the cult of which has left a great hollowness in American poetry in the postwar period. Projectivism makes a convenient target, merging, as it does, different strands of modern thought in their movement towards a common end of pseudo-primitivism. The *faux-naïf* primitivism, of which Marshall McLuhan was the leading exponent in the 1960s, was the fashionable form of the trend towards object-dominance in the late postwar period. Like McLuhan and William Burroughs, Olson rejects symbol, metaphysics, linear thought, causation, abstraction, logic, etc., all or any of the elements which make up the Western intellectual tradition initiated by the Greeks. We have witnessed this already in Olson's dream of returning to the semantic innocence of the Mayas. The great influence on this kind of thought in the twentieth century is Henri Bergson: nothing Olson writes is free from Bergsonian metaphysics, which lies also behind the thought of T. E. Hulme and Ernest Fenollosa: language with its symbolizing, abstracting, comparing functions, we are to understand, keeps us from 'the active intellectual states . . . analysis only accomplishes a *description*, does not come to grips with what

[10] Davis, Introduction to *The Penguin Book of Chinese Verse*, 3.
[11] 'Projective verse', 25.
[12] Quoted in Makoto Ueda, *Zeami, Bashō, Yeats, Pound* (The Hague 1963), 37.

really matters.'[13] And so on. Bergson had some excuse for his error, of trying to destroy metaphysics with metaphysics. In indicating the 'weakness' of intellectual descriptions of reality which merely 'distort organic synthesis', Bergson failed to appreciate that when we describe a thing in intellectual terms it is our conception of the thing we are getting clear in propositions which mirror the logical fact; we do not pretend to represent the organic thing itself. Now that Wittgenstein has done the job of sorting out the different functions of language, there is no excuse for repeating Bergson's error. Olson distinguishes the 'bad' abstractive processes of traditional 'symbology' from some life-giving variety, in which metaphor or idea enters in at the pores of the skin—how, or under what dispensation, is never made clear. Olson provides the perfect example of the inevitably self-contradictory, self-destructive kind of alienation that has accompanied and proceeded from the evolution towards objectivity. Using a language composed of the general terms he pretends to disavow, Olson patronizes the primitive and assumes the mantle of prophet, and so obscures the nature of the difficulties that confront us today. If the present impasse in thought is to be evaded, it is not through the abrogation of thinking. We must think, and continue to think, acknowledging that the 'universe of discourse', which is nothing but the world of our awareness (or the world we are aware of), comprises a stratification of hierarchical realms, from base matter itself up to the refinement of music and poetry. This means, though, also understanding that in so far as we are conscious of the universe, it is part of our consciousness, and that no matter how hard we try to deny abstraction, merely to refer to matter itself in the simplest terms is to commit ourselves to abstraction; it is useless pretending that in doing so we can somehow return to a Rousseau-esque realm of intellectual innocence. As soon as we use language we are already committed to thinking, with all the linear constructs that that implies.

It was this paradox that Bergson's metaphysics, with its characteristic dichotomies of intensive and extensive manifolds, was intended to solve. It is true, as Lawrence saw so clearly, that an estrangement of mind and instinct accompanies the process of civilization, and that it behoves us to re-feel our consciousness, to regain contact with the life of the body and of the instincts. But he knew that this was not to be accomplished by trying to turn the clock back, by 'going native', by ceasing to think. On the contrary, as he observed of Melville's *Typee*, nothing stinks like rotting civilized man,[14] and civilized man rots if he does not exercise his mind, soul, awareness to its maximum extent. Man will grow by expanding his mind, not by contracting it.

The relative success or failure of poetry is not to be equated with

[13] 'Human universe', 187.
[14] 'Melville', in *Studies in Classic American Literature*, reprinted in *Selected Literary Criticism*, 370.

intensity of belief. In the first place, belief, though it can pick itself up from nowhere—irrespective of the political or general spiritual atmosphere—can also be blinded by a single mote in the eye, or simply by nothing; it can fall away, and a man is dead even in the act of saying, *I believe*. But the imaginative daring that is required to give depth, weight and permanence to the poet's professional 'openness' to experience, is all too often lacking in mid-century poetry. In England, this took the ideological form of a care for self-criticism and sobriety; in America, often, of a mistaken cleaving to the worn-out ethics of imagism. Donald Hall's introduction to his anthology of contemporary American verse, with its characteristically ironist emphasis on colloquial diction, also shared the general post-Poundian bias in favour of the 'good' image against the 'bad' abstraction:

> People talk to each other most deeply in images. To read a poem of this sort, you must not try to translate the image into abstractions.[15]

Whoever would, or did? we might ask. And is it really true (if plausible) that 'people talk to each other most deeply in images'? Don't we need a particular context of expectations and directives to be able to know what they mean, in the simplest terms, and to interpret the images?

In point of fact, this is not really the way either poetry or literature works. And the point seems worth labouring, not in order to condemn Mr Hall of failing to understand its workings properly (we all fail in that task), but because it is a sign of an academicism which has probably gained rather than lost prestige since Hall wrote this preface in 1961. What we might call the imagist academy sponsored a poetry really no less circumscribed, no less in need of spiritual regeneration, than the neo-metaphysical academicism it was supposed to have replaced.

Hand in hand with the cult of the image goes the *breath* fallacy. Olson was a somewhat confused polemicist, but in so far as one can understand his notion of breath, it seems to be equivalent to Pound's notion of *music*, that is to say, the soul of poetry itself. (The same word is used for both *breath* and *spirit* in many languages of course.) Basically, both critics want to distinguish poetry which is merely metrical from poetry which is alive through its rhythm. The underlying relations between metre and rhythm have been part of the English tradition since *Beowulf*, at least, and the reader wishing to understand them more formally will be better off reading Hopkins's introduction to his poems than wandering through Pound or Olson, who really throw no light on the subject at all. *Music* in Pound and *breath* in Olson are simply value terms, conferred on or withheld from poetry as it is considered good or bad, with no other reason given. We know, of course, from reading Pound, which poets Olson will approve of: approved of are the impressionists and the image-notchers of the nineteenth and twentieth centuries, the Elizabethan song-writers,

15 Introduction to *Contemporary American Poetry* (Harmondsworth 1961), 25.

the Romance poets of Provence, and Homer. Disapproved of are the soulful men, the Blakes, Whitmans, Hopkinses and Lawrences. What we have, in fact—clearly in Pound, confusedly in Olson—is a particular psychological type (what we might call the impressionist or the extroverted) erected into an universal norm. Back of the enterprise in Olson's case is Carlos Williams's pan-Americanism:

> Where else can what we are seeking arise from but speech, American speech as distinct from English speech. . . . In any case from what we hear in America.[16]

This is crude but clear, and in its way sensible. Olson obscures the issue by adding to breath and speech his own notion of 'syllable': 'It is by their syllables that words juxtapose in beauty, by these particles of sound as clearly as by the sense of the words which they compose.'[17] But it is equally by their syllables that words juxtapose in their ugliness or their banality (whatever the phrase 'juxtapose in' actually means). Any good poetry will be syllable- and sound-responsive. Once again a value-word has been offered as if it helped us actually describe poetry. Olson quotes the opening lines of *Twelfth Night* and a stanza of 'Westren Wynde' as instances of syllabic poetry, but we are none the wiser: lines from Milton or Whitman could have been substituted without alteration of meaning. It is a waste of time asking what Olson means by saying that the syllable 'dropped from the late Elizabethans': he merely relies on the reader's vague acceptance of the Pound/Eliot dissociation theory to guarantee agreement on a general decline.

The most striking feature of Olson's own verse seems now to be a curious amalgam of imagist notation and wide abstract generality. 'La Torre', for instance, begins with the approved sort of notation:

> The tower is broken, the house
> where the head was used to lift,
> where awe was . . .

Soon enough Olson is paraphrasing Fenollosa:

> Lightning
> is an axe, subject to object to
> order: destroy!

This leads to a sinisterly fascistic tone a little later:

> To destroy
> is stand again, is a factor of
> sun, fire is
> when the sun is out, dowsed . . .

[16] W. C. Williams, 'The poem as field of action', in *Selected Essays* (New York 1961), 289–90.
[17] 'Projective verse', 17–18.

What is 'dowsed' doing here? Somehow the usage epitomizes the Black Mountain style, falsely vernacular, awkwardly 'concrete'. Now 'dowsed' is there, of course, because it is an *action* word: it is as if Olson had caught himself napping with 'out', and added a suitably concrete word to keep up the Fenollosa programme. In fact it only clumsily distinguishes itself from 'out' and so blurs the required contrast between the sun's shining and the fire's neutralized burning. This emphasizes yet again that language is often most effectively 'concrete' when allowed to do its work invisibly. 'Concreteness' in fact is a notion that relates to intension (and intention) rather than to any series of verbal procedures: an intentness on saying something, or rather on the something that needs to be said, is more likely to lead to an impression of concreteness or action in poetry than any imagistic programme of strong verbs and no copulæ.[18] When he is set a 'subject', a bit of 'field' to do, to crystallize, Olson is no more successful than Williams:

> The sheep like soldiers
> black leggings black face
> lie boulders
> in the pines' shade
> at the field's sharp edge:
> ambush and bivouac
>
> A convocation of crows overhead
> mucks
> in their own mud and squawk
> makes of the sky
> a sty

> (Olson, 'Lower Field—Enniscorthy')

It would be no defence of this to say that it was not intended to 'crystallize'. He is 'doing' something here—sheep, crows—and doing it limply and inertly, with neither spring to the language nor point to the observations, which are mainly of the old-fashioned analogical variety (the sheep's legs are *like* soldiers' leggings, etc.). In 'The Moon Is the Number 18', we find this:

> the blue dogs paw,
> lick the droppings, dew
> or blood, whatever
> results are. And night,
> the crab, rays round
> attentive, as the ear to catch
> human sound

[18] Donald Davie, *Articulate Energy* (London 1955), argues this point of view at considerable length.

These lines again lack internal spring, aptitude of image, and sound pattern. One remembers Olson's advice to the poet to listen 'to his own speech', and wonders how anyone aware of the question of sound at all could write so flatly:

> The blue dogs rue
> as he does, and he would howl, confronting
> the wind which rocks what was her, while prayers
> striate the snow, words blow
> as questions cross fast, fast
> as flame, as flames form, melt
> along any darkness
>
> ('The Moon Is the Number 18')

Here is a syntactical movement begging for support from the sound: repeated verbs, complex sentence structure, and it would seem hard *not* to make the sound interlock here. But examination of any given moment or of the whole unit shows Olson to be incapable of making sound work for him. Such sound-play as there is is confined to premature repetition—'blue' and 'rue', 'snow' and 'blow', 'fast, fast', 'flame, as flames'. Like the examples in the previously quoted stanza—'paw' and 'dew', 'round' and 'sound'—these assonances are timed mechanically, and the result is the opposite of what, as critic, Olson seems to have meant by 'breath'. He is reduced to front-office words like 'striate', and tries to lose the reader in a show of complexity: first dogs howl, then the wind rocks what something feminine (the moon, presumably) *was*, prayers do something to the snow, then everything melts into everything else. Hardly a demonstration of projectivist virtues: rather a heavy piece of expressionism. Not surprisingly—to anyone familiar with Pound and the *Active Anthology* poets, that is—the show of projectivist method is then given away in a characteristically knowing use of the copula:

> Birth is an instance as is a host, namely, death. . . .

As critic, Olson had laid great emphasis on the incising of images so that they 'retain the power of the objects of which they are the images.' Yet his verse is either inertly notational in the Carlos Williams manner, or extraordinarily general: few poets of the time sprinkle their verse with quite so many abstract generalizations, ethical injunctions and random *obiter dicta* as Olson.

It will be important for me often enough to distinguish between the poetics of a poet and his poetry, and I wish to make no simple causal relation here between Olson's shaky theorizing and his inert poetry. Yet it does seem that the poetic programme here must take some responsibility for the *kind* of poor performance we get. We could put him down simply as a middling poet. But the pretentious allusiveness, the arrogant tone, the passive pseudo-concrete notation (eschewing a more poetically authentic empathy with the object as somehow datedly Romantic), the sluggish reliance upon ponderous generalities—all these vices of Black Mountain poetry seem predictable from the Poundian foundations of the academy. This is especially true of the superior stance inherited from Pound, the esotericism more interested in displaying its knowledge than in the knowledge itself, which was, I believe, a definite brake on American poetry in the 1950s. Pound's frequent concern with manner and his lack of awareness of deeper matter, along with his pretentiousness, made for a knowing yet oddly superficial poetry. It was not until Allen Ginsberg and Jack Kerouac made the crossing from East to West Coast, I think, that Black Mountain prosody made its biggest contribution. It was new spiritual synthesis that America needed then, not esotericism: the esotericism of Black Mountain encouraged an aloofness the exact opposite of the openness to experience advocated in its theory.

Chapter 8

Robert Duncan
The Myth of Open Form

In no significant poetry of the mid-century do the fallacies of projectivism play a more problematic role than in the work of Robert Duncan. Good poetry, one would have thought, can be written in the shadow of no matter what wrongheaded poetics: think only of the successes achieved in spite of surrealist doctrine in the 1930s. Yet in Duncan's *Passages* and *Structure of Rime* series, there is evidence of a general collapse of mind of the sort encouraged if not actually prescribed by projective theory. That Duncan is highly gifted, I doubt that anyone who has picked up one of his volumes has ever questioned. The capacity not only for powerful emotion, but for entertaining, yielding to and articulating powerful emotion, are promisingly evident in the early collection, *The Years as Catches* (1938), which Duncan saw fit—somewhat indulgently perhaps—to have republished in 1966:

> Years in that everlasting life
> darken, unmoving towards the same time.
> Rooms after death have the same light
> left over, beginning the length of the house.
> This is the end beginning with you
> Long as the light afterwards of noon,
> I have taken me to wife
> and sleep and death the deep of home.
> > ('Mother to Whom I Have Come Home')

A good few of Duncan's trademarks are already in evidence here: the strangely deliberate rhythm at the beck of an easily seduced intuitive faculty, the skill with words of movement and momentum ('Years darken, unmoving towards the same time'), above all perhaps the subtle enjambment ('same light/left over'). More significant in the whole poem is the ambiguous tone towards the subject—tremulous, yet oddly detached, emotional yet narcissistic, self-involved even in its governing concern with the loved object.

To say that Duncan's ability to communicate a pressure of emotion distinguishes him from most of his contemporaries is by no means to consign the work to the *ooh! ouch!* category. On the contrary, it is perhaps the detachment, the air of control, of being inside his own rhythms and his own emotional stream, yet on top of them, that sets Duncan's poetry apart from the professional pain of the East Coast Confessionals: the poetry is the thing, in Duncan, not the pain, not the testament. We are concerned here with a release yet a control of feeling, with feeling released by control, and control obtained through feeling. Feelings have been appropriated by symbols and rhythms, and experience which had remained outside the pale of poetry has been conquered for it. This means in turn that we are concerned with the attitudes and ideologies that subtend the feelings. Those of the Confessionals, like those of their English academic contemporaries, spring from a modified form of an essentially negating principle, the principle of alienation that dominates European poetry after symbolism.

It will not do, as Robert Creeley has pointed out, to define what we find in Duncan as a new Romanticism. 'If one depends on the dichotomy of *romantic* and classical,' Creeley observes,[1] 'one is left with too simply an historical description, itself a remnant from an earlier period.' Yet in fact such labelling is not excessively but inadequately historical: it ignores the essential relation of one period to that preceding it, and the inexorable process of transformation which crushes, digests and renews the matter of the past in grinding through to the future it never reaches. Duncan is not 'Romantic' unless we facilely identify Romanticism with any emotional heat or technical 'freedom' on the one hand, or on the other with the general historical predicament he inherits along with every other man who puts pen to paper in the modern world: post-Romantic, Donald Davie remarks, is what we are.[2] John Heath-Stubbs, like many of the New Apocalypse poets contemporary with him in England, and certain Fugitive elements in America, are Romantic in this facile sense of more or less consciously posturing in what is felt to be a 'Romantic' way, manifesting a certain grandeur of passion, set in a certain exoticism of locale.

Duncan was in fact influenced by at least one major figure of the New Apocalypse, and we can trace certain habits of style to the fact. 'In 1940,' Duncan wrote in the Introduction to the 1966 Edition of *The Years as Catches*,[3] 'it was George Barker's *Calamiterror* that most persuaded me. I used to read aloud rapt in the intoxication of his verse.' Later Duncan remarks that 'Barker's poetry was often polymorphous, perverse in its suggestion and could admit in its tide hints and overtones of a homoerotic lure as well as its heterosexual object, as if intensity in itself were a saving grace for all sexual feeling.'[4]

---

[1] Introduction to *New Writing in the USA*, 19.
[2] 'On sincerity', *Encounter* 26 (4) (October 1968).
[3] (Berkeley 1966), 11.
[4] Idem.

Barker is certainly at his best a powerful poet, offering support for a possibly valid but vague conception of 'form' as a 'tension of contraries, each force holding its opposite in check, in moments of clarity and stasis, when traditional jackets master the surge.'[5] But what is impressive about Duncan is surely that his verse, indubitably as it is founded in a mantric conception of poetry ('essentially a magic of excited, exalted or witch-like (exciting) speech'[6]), conveys the sense not of possession or formlessness or rant but of containment and a curious modesty. Though one of the most professionally rapt poets of his time, Duncan is surely one of the least excited, though certainly not one of the least exciting. We approach here surely the crux of the matter of Duncan's status. There is no doubt in the first place of the general mastery of rhythm, and the presentation of significant motif:

> Reveries are rivers and flow
> where the cold light gleams reflecting the window
> upon the surface of the table,
> the presst-glass creamer, the pewter sugar bowl, the litter
> of coffee cups and saucers,
> carnations painted growing upon whose surfaces.
> The whole composition of surfaces leads into the other
> current disturbing what I would take hold of.
>
> ('Bending the Bow')

I deliberately choose a passage that is different from what a reader flicking through *Bending the Bow* or *Roots and Branches* would be likely to take as most characteristic of the poet. The longer line and the relaxed spillage of domestic images suggest the influence of Philip Whalen or Frank O'Hara (what O'Hara called his 'I do this, I do that' poetry), rather than that of the mantric poets under whose ægis Duncan normally works. The shorter, more mantric line Duncan early learned from the Pound of the Roman *Cantos* does not lend itself to such 'real' fluidities. The general tone of the verse, easy yet contained, derives from the longer line: notice the way he guides the eye along the river reveries, from the 'cold gleam light' on the surface of the table, over the 'presst-glass creamer', the 'litter of coffee cups', finally to the expanding 'surfaces'. Duncan takes the ruminative watching into an internal thought-stream, and in fact the theme of the poem is precisely the interaction (or perhaps the competition) of the important-inner with the trivial-outer ('Day's duties'). The whole poem is launched by the idea of the bending of the bow, 'till the end rimes in the taut string/with the sending'. The bow is in the first place[7] that of Ulysses, and I think Duncan is flirting with the Milton role—

---

[5] Idem.
[6] Idem.
[7] Though not the last: see p. 143 below.

> only in that swift fulfillment of the wish
>> that sleep
> can illustrate my hand
>> sweeps the string.

('Bending the Bow')

Dr Johnson derided his own blank-verse contemporaries for being unable to bend Milton's bow. 'Lycidas' is almost quoted here. Milton's great elegy might justifiably be taken by a homosexual to be at least covertly homosexual. Duncan addresses a woman in the poem, his dead mother, to whom, as we learn from other poems, the poet is in the habit of writing letters. Duncan's letters to her are like Orphic invocations to bring 'The deep tones and shadows I will call a woman' from the shades.

'Bending the Bow' is one of Duncan's most satisfying poems: it has a shapely pedestal structure—two ample, relaxed yet taut stanzas, resting upon a Poundian stem which sprouts to the first direct address to the woman-subject. It ends beautifully with the thudding of the bow-string:

> and I would play Orpheus for you again,
>> recall the arrow or song
>> to the trembling daylight
>> from which it sprang.

The sense in a poem of having its end contained in its beginning is close to being a rule-of-thumb criterion of literary evaluation. Form, structure, shape are all of them unsatisfactory notions (chaos has its own shape, so has the London Telephone Directory, and to attribute 'form' is more or less a circular business, conferring approbation), unless they point to that aesthetic pleasure derived from a statement or artefact which launches a feeling or idea which fulfils itself and concludes itself, each part leading to the next until what had been started is set at rest.

Duncan's best work undoubtedly conforms to this principle. In the poem under consideration, the notion of curvature and tension suggested in the title is enacted in the arc of the poem, and the emotion is called to rest at its most vibrant moment. Something of this is true of a poem closely related to it, 'Such Is the Sickness of Many a Good Thing', which employs a more slender variant of the pedestal structure. The line used is the more characteristic short one, phrase-bound, sturdily end-stopped, and each line rests on the line below, or stands layered over it much in the way Donald Davie described it in Pound,[8] on the whole discouraging enjambment, and forsaking sinuousness and follow-through in the interests of the mantric invocation:

---

[8] *Ezra Pound: Poet as Sculptor* (London 1965), 123.

> All the flame in me stopt
>   against my tongue.
> My heart was a stone, a dumb
>   unmanageable thing in me,
> a darkness that stood athwart
>   his need
> for the enlightening, the
>   'I love you' that has
> only this one quick in time,
>   this one start
> when its moment is true.
>
> > ('Such Is the Sickness')

Like all Duncan's better writing, this verse has a sound-network holding it together: 'tongue/dumb; me/need, *dark*ness/ath*wart*/start; you/true.' The slightly stilted stance Duncan habitually sustains, honouring his deep mantric vows to that 'magic of excited, exalted or witch-like . . . speech', stands him in good stead here. The intensity is kept on ice, the urgency heightened, precisely by his refusal to flop over into the 'honest', normal speech-tone of, say, Ginsberg's 'Aunt Rose'. The poem is of course not *dis*honest in any way, but it is easy for a reader brought up too exclusively on a diet of mid-century confession and self-abasement to mistake Duncan's *heigh sentaunce* for rhetoric. The poem uses well, too, a quasi-sonnet structure; the octet gives us the situation, the poet's inability to say the things he knows will ease his lover. The generalizing begins sharp at the beginning of the sestet:

> Such is the sickness of many a good thing
> that now into my life from long ago this
> refusing to say I love you has bound
> the weeping, the yielding, the
> yearning to be taken again,
> into a knot, a waiting, a string
> so taut it taunts the song
> it resists the touch.
>
> > ('Such Is the Sickness')

(This is that same bow-string—fiddle, lyre-string, gut—of 'Bending the Bow', now, as we shall see later, the property of Hermes Trismegistos.) The carefully gathered sound-skein ('so taut it taunts') is mimetic of the tension of the string, and the poem ends with a beautiful minor chord:

> It grows dark
> to draw down the lover's hand
> from its lightness to what's
>   underground.
>
> > ('Such Is the Sickness')

Now according to a certain view of poetry, this should be typical at least of what poetry ought to aspire to. I do not refer to quality of achievement, but to kind: the achievement of the ordered, intense, personal yet universal voice-statement, formal, internally coherent yet natural-seeming. Stately and direct, the voice of the poetry here could be said to be paradigmatic of the art as a whole. Yet in Duncan, such poems are a fairly pronounced minority, and before rushing to judgement on the rest of his work, we must consider the poetics according to which they are written. I have so far considered two poems—lyric, personal, intense, complete in themselves. The first of the two, 'Bending the Bow', however, makes use of references which would inform us, if we knew nothing else of the poet, of an important electicism in him. I do not mean only the Milton allusion—though structurally this is perhaps the most important one. I mean the allusion to a realm of mythico-anthropological lore and to the poet—translated by Duncan in the same volume—who went further perhaps than any other poet of the modern age towards building an entire and self-consistent hermetic poetry, Gérard de Nerval. The word 'inconsolate' in Duncan's poem gives us the explicit pointer to Nerval's sonnet, 'El Desdichado', cited at the end of *The Waste Land,* and obligingly translated for us by Duncan on page 84 of the volume. The last lines of Nerval's sonnet reveal Duncan's poem as almost a paraphrase:

> And twice victorious I have crossed the Acheron
> Modulating turn by turn on the lyre of Orpheus
> The sighs of the saint and the cries of the fay.
> (Duncan, translation of Gérard de Nerval, 'El Desdichado')

In Nerval's poem, all things are claimed by the poet. But he is 'inconsolé' and 'veuf'. The Orpheus-role is central to the statement: like Orpheus, he has lost the woman who will complete him. Duncan shifts the inconsolateness onto his mother, but he has conjured her with his lyre, as Nerval has twice conquered Acheron.

All of Nerval's *Chimères* are presented by Duncan in the volume, and we find in them the source of much of his own poetry. The Mediterranean mythology and doctrine, given anthropological dimensions by Sir James Frazer, had been available in the *Corpus Hermeticum* since the seventeenth century. Following Eliot and Pound in this respect, Duncan structures much of his poetry on hermetic and mythological sources, rather than on psychoanalysis, for instance, or economics. Now the question is, of course, how do these sources and influences shape Duncan's poetry? We can reject out of hand any purist notion that such arcane sources should have no function in the writing of poetry. Whether the poet's sources are the masters of his own tradition, or the philosophers of an alien one, is irrelevant: poetry, like consciousness itself, is a sedimentation, a layering of past consciousness, and the briefest reading of Frazer, or the Greek myths, or of Ovid—to say nothing of the Hermetic texts—is enough to tell us that at the deepest strata of our beings we respond to forces, drives and symbols present in the ossified form of myth and symbol. So an interest in Hermes Trismegistos, for instance, can clearly go along with a drive towards the understanding of oneself, the world, and one's place in the world. Indeed, if Spencer Lewis is correct in holding Rosicrucianism, for instance, to be itself merely a revival of an order going back to the Egypt of Akhnaton,[9] it would be an overweening tribute to twentieth-century positivism to deny that the loose *congeries* of ideas associated with the Hermetic and Cabbalistic writings can hold any interest for a poet or intellectual of our time. More, the general identifying characteristic of Hermetic and Rosicrucian thinking is a distinct distrust of rationalism and orthodox science. Hermetic writing was geared to *praxis* and was, like alchemy for instance, at once scientific and mystical. It stressed the importance of the laws of attraction and sympathy in the physical world, and held that the cosmos was a single whole, governed by these laws. Thus its very claims to being scientific were responsible for its distrust of the normal science which ignored certain binding laws simply because they did not allow of verification by testing within the technological resources of the time. The reader familiar with the poetry of Gérard de Nerval will by now have recognized this general family of ideas. 'Vers dorés' is one of the key works of modern hermeticism, a rare instance of occult lore turned into something immediately apprehensible both as idea and poetic experience:

> Souvent dans l'être obscur habite un Dieu caché;
> Et comme un œil naissant couvert par ses paupières,
> Un pur esprit s'accroît sous l'écorce des pierres!

Significantly, Nerval's poem has an epigraph translated from the founder of classical geometry, Pythagoras ('Eh quoi! Tout est sensible!'), and yet in its opening phrase throws down the gauntlet to modern scepticism:

> Homme, libre penseur! te crois-tu seul pensant
> Dans ce monde où la vie éclate en toute chose?

One thinks of Edgar Allen Poe ('Edgair Po'), who combined the same elements of mystificatory obscurantism and a genuinely scientific sense of inference and psychological process. The drama of Strindberg is perhaps the greatest nineteenth-century example of hermetic art: alchemist and chemist, mystic and experimenter, poet and scholar, Strindberg was the complete hermetic thinker. Again, Strindberg brings to mind the most important aspect of hermeticism: the need to see everything related and tied together by objectively real laws of sympathy, laws occasionally all but visible as actual threads. And what is important of course is that in Strindberg's case, as in that of Nerval, Blake, Swedenborg and Christopher

[9] H. Spencer Lewis, *Rosicrucian Questions and Answers with Complete History of the Rosicrucian Order* (London 1941).

Smart, the need to feel things related could intensify in the direction either of mystical possession or of neurotic breakdown. The very nature of hermetic thought seems to objectify an actual psychological temperament, one which could push its need for wholeness and unification either into physical science (in which case it produced the pseudo-science inseparable from hermeticism) or into mystical gnosis. For Hermes, as Duncan reminds us, not only 'devised the harp of Apollo and was first in the magic, the deceit, of song. But as Thoth, he is Truth, patron of poets.'[10]

Can we at least in theory, then, isolate a 'hermetic' personality? In Duncan's case there are two problematic considerations. The first concerns the mere 'use' of hermetic or other occult imagery to float or decorate what are little more than ruminations, reaching no firm conclusion and bodying forth no clear philosophy. Nerval's 'Vers dorés' showed how close to the actual nature of poetry itself are the main principles of hermeticism. Like the gnostics, the Rosicrucians and the alchemists, poets in our time have thought to provide another and more important truth than that of science. No reader familiar with the poetry of Wordsworth or Shelley fails to place the insights in Nerval's brilliant sonnet securely within the mainstream of modern poetic development, or needs any special knowledge to understand it. The second consideration concerns something more widely interesting, Duncan's use of hermetic ideas and symbols in conjunction with popularized physics and subatomic physics. Behind Duncan, as behind Charles Olson, is the generally pervasive influence of Alfred North Whitehead. Whitehead influenced Yeats[11] much as Teilhard de Chardin has influenced writers in our own day, by appearing to combine the intellectual rigour of science with a philosophy of process and sympathy lying closer to the tastes of poets, musicians and humanists than the determinism of orthodox science. Whitehead can be called a hermetic philosopher of science, in fact, with his emphasis on prehensions rather than cognitions, on indefinable time-space entities, in his interest in collapsing the perceptual structure that has always seemed indispensable to modern science and replacing it with a quasi-mystical interactive situation somehow more flattering to the human ego. Robert Duncan's 'Towards an open universe' shows his attraction to pseudo-science in general and to Whitehead in particular.

It is difficult now to feel that Whitehead added anything significant to our mental universes. I cannot myself see that Yeats derived any real benefit from Whitehead, apart from a general boost to morale. In the 1930s, humanist intellectuals in general took a similar comfort in Heisenbergian indeterminacy; why, it is hard now to see since, if anything,

---

[10] 'Towards an open universe', in Nemerov (ed.), *Contemporary American Poetry*, 181.

[11] See Robert Snukal's *High Talk* (London 1974). My own opinions on the important issues raised by Mr Snukal are expressed in my review of his book *Yeats Today*, in *Southern Review* (Adelaide) VIII (1) (1975), 74–86.

Heisenberg had seemed to show that the universe which the liberal (and literary) intellectual had traditionally thought it so important should be proved ordered was even more uncertain—in respect of our cognitions of it at least—than Einstein had suggested it might be. But such was the demoralization in the humanitarian camp that it could take comfort from what seemed to be the discomfiture of the scientists. This clutching after straws is surely the heart of the *Trahison des clercs*. Kathleen Nott demonstrated the fallaciousness of the literary exploitation of Heisenberg some years back:

> I should say . . . that there was nothing in the Heisenberg Uncertainty Principle . . . to justify any statements at all about the freedom of the will (individual choice and action). The Uncertainty Principle as Russell says tell us about physical measurements, not about hypostatical entities such as Will and Freedom.[12]

In Duncan's case, the flirtation with science, as popularized by scientists not at their best, and with pseudo-science goes along, I think, with a general inner softness, a certain lack of intellectual and moral rigour, which keeps him from being the major figure some would claim him to be. It is difficult to agree with Macha Rosenthal's view of Duncan as 'in many ways the most intellectual of our poets from the point of view of the effect on him of a wide, critically intelligent reading.'[13] The word 'intellectual' is apt to suggest William Empson or W. H. Auden, and beside both these poets Duncan appears soft-minded if not superficial. And as far as the use of wide reading is concerned, it seems to me that both Philip Whalen and Kenneth Rexroth are better models. Whalen is more acute than Duncan in understanding the peculiarly ambiguous value of a wide reading for the poet today: it is as likely to collapse his frail pretensions by making him extend his capacity for hope and empathy beyond what ordinary life habitually offers. Moreover, it is with this ordinary life that the values endemic to poetry have to concern themselves. And of this fact Whalen is almost excessively aware. Rexroth, I think, makes more skilful and subtle use of a wide mathematical and astronomical learning, learning which gets down to the substance of actual science far more impressively than Duncan's rather airy-fairy dabblings in popularized subatomic physics and hermetic texts.

Hermes Trismegistos may be derived from Thoth, the Knower of Egyptian mythology, 'Truth, patron of Poets',[14] but he is also patron of pseudo-science and obscurantism, and of downright charlatanism. Duncan's hermeticism stands forth proudly when he quotes Carlyle's magnificent peroration on Song from *The Hero as Poet,* and with beautiful simplicity when he cites Keats's 'Grecian Urn' ode. But these statements

[12] *The Emperor's Clothes* (London 1953), 19.
[13] *The New Poets* (New York 1967), 177.
[14] Duncan, 'Towards an open universe', 181.

of the English Romantics had their own problematics: they constitute responses superior to the historical situation which demanded them. Duncan may not be the best American poet of his time, but he represents an essential Americanness more purely than any of his contemporaries. This is what one might justifiably call a central non-problematicness. Is this in fact something 'gloriously' American, something the European needing complexity and qualification to structure his own doubts defines as non-problematic? Is this merely life, hope, the future—before which the negative backward-looking European spits nastily? When Stephen Spender remarked of Whitman that he lacked a sense of evil, was he, too, merely expressing the European's inability to rise to the unflawed and to embrace a universal imperative? Lawrence, we remember, wrote of Whitman's 'essential message. The heroic message of the American future. It is the inspiration of thousands of Americans today, the best souls of today, men and women.'[15] It is as well to entertain the doubt.

When therefore Robert Duncan harks back to the high moment of English Romanticism, it is important surely to think long before deciding that the air of blandness about his words derives from a certain absence of the troublingly problematic which is *limitingly* American, not resoundingly so. For the problematics demanded are not those entailed in automatic scepticism and self-doubt. Whitman, as Lawrence saw, had his own problematics—the soaring of the democratic ideal was a response to a deeply understood historical challenge, and in some such relation the notion of the problematic must be understood to exist. Whitman may have lacked the subtle sense of evil that informed the poetry of William Blake, for instance. But there is nothing non-problematic about the Lincoln Elegy, or 'Out of the Cradle Endlessly Rocking', or 'Reconciliation'. The fact of death in these poems confronts the onward movement of the mind, which is checked but not deterred. The complexity of the poems therefore is problematic, compact of the poet's apperceptive awareness of his relations with the unwonted visitor Death, and a more general awareness of the relations between this problematic and the general movement of society into its democratic, mechanized phase. For these are poems written out of the bitter collision of a great and pure optimism with the obscenity of mass warfare: it was America Whitman saw lying dead in 'Reconciliation'.

The difference between the essentially problematic complexity of Whitman's Civil War poems and the blandness of much twentieth-century poetry in America could not be better illustrated than by passing from 'Reconciliation' to the poetry of Robert Duncan. And if we turn to Duncan's essay 'Towards an open universe' we catch a glimpse of the sort of rationale upon which this blandness rests. For if the citations from Keats and Carlyle are in their fondness authentically nostalgic, the use of scientists like Schrödinger and Heisenberg seems almost in bad faith:

[15] *Selected Literary Criticism*, 403.

'When is a piece of matter said to be alive? When it goes on doing something; moving, exchanging material with its environment.'[16] Duncan tells us that what interests him about this statement of Schrödinger's is that 'this picture of an intricately articulated structure, a form that maintains a disequilibrium or lifetime, whatever it means to the biophysicist to the poet means that life is by nature orderly, and that the poem might follow the primary processes of thought and feeling, the immediate impulse of psychic life.'[17] It is valid enough to take heart from the discoveries of physics, as Lawrence once took heart from relativity theory. But it is surely not valid to allow the thinking of a physicist to tell the poet anything about the way poems are written, or still worse, ought to be written. We have here of course a close approximation to projectivist theory, with its attraction towards the magic words 'environ-ment' (or 'field', to cite Duncan's own favourite), and its emphasis upon 'the immediate impulse of psychic life'. This is much how Herbert Read described the entire Romantic formal principle;[18] it is roughly how Lawrence justified and explained his own free verse in 1920.[19] It is, we could say, the general aesthetic of modernism, what was given its first clear expression in Schelling's *On the Relation of the Plastic Arts to Nature*.[20]

It is not simply the fact that this notion was one hundred and fifty years old by the time Olson and Duncan used it that is troubling (Lawrence made it work anew); nor even the use of scientific discovery to provide analogies for the creative process—this too is a custom, though one perhaps 'more honour'd in the breach than the observance'. What is disturbing is the absence of a moral and imaginative engagement, which might have made of Schrödinger and Heisenberg supporting illustration of a felt reality. It is all very well to move from 'Beauty is Truth' to Dirac on the elegance of mathematical formulae (though this is frankly more what one would expect from George Steiner than from a distinguished poet). For Keats's great statement bears a distinctly problematic relation-ship both to the poem it brings to a climax, and to the historical *moment the poem transcends in being adequate to it*. The 'Grecian Urn' ode is a key docu-ment of Romanticism and it wrestles with the nature of experience as it had been revealed in the new historical and social situation after the industrial revolution. The famous aphoristic line is 'ecstatic' (Duncan's word for it), but it does not rise from a confident sureness of poetic intuition or of recognition, 'our insistent knowing of fitness as we work in the poem'—not at least in the uncomplicated way Duncan suggests.

16 'Towards an open universe', 171.
17 Idem.
18 *The True Voice of Feeling.*
19 Introduction to *New Poems* (New York 1920).
20 F. W. J. von Schelling's treatise, *Über das Verhältniss der Bildenden Kunst zu der Natur,* is translated under this title in *The True Voice of Feeling.*

The provenance of works of art is paradigmatic of the history of consciousness itself: art exists in a relation of exactly ordained freedom, of determination transcended in an adequacy to it. Hence the truly ecstatic cry of great poetry—of Keats's ode here—for the cry of poetry is a gasp, the thud of the blow of knowledge producing the cry of recognition.

Duncan's use of science—if it is popularized by authentic practitioners, popularized it remains—runs parallel to his poetry itself, which achieves so often not the ecstasy of surprise but precisely that 'monotonous rapture' he refers to in the poetry of metrical regularity. It isn't perhaps too unfair to turn Duncan's fine phrase against him here: for it occurs in just one of those passages which gloss on science, suggesting that the poet in writing his poetry can merely let it happen, let it glide, flow out of the cosmic rhythm. Chekhov surely set this sort of thing in the right perspective when he satirized Constantin's silly play in *The Seagull*: 'This sounds like the Decadent school,' Arkadina says after lengthy paragraphs of rambling about the cosmic consciousness. Now if Duncan's explanation of rhythm are contained in the Preface to the *Lyrical Ballads*, his phrasing oddly recalls that of general cultural commentators like Arthur Koestler and George Steiner ('Dance of the chromosomes' might be vintage Steiner). The thinking indeed suggests an earlier Steiner, Rudolf, he of the eurhythmic vibrations, 'getting with' the cosmic energies. At any rate, Duncan's phrase 'the chemistry of death' evokes—in this reader at least— a powerful disgust with these facile jugglings with Big Ideas. This is not science, but, again, pseudo-science: the material may originally have come from *bona fide* science; the use it has been put to is surely pseudo-scientific—the realm of Gurdjieff and Ouspensky, or even of Madame Blavatsky. For we remember that a defining characteristic of pseudo-science is its normativeness, its insistence on describing the universe in a way the acolyte must adapt himself to. Reading Duncan's remarks about regular rhythm, we ask ourselves, so what? The answer could be: so you get with the universe, let it happen. And write good poetry? The first contention—by no means stupid—is specifically American; so, strangely enough, is the second. And this seems important. For here, thinly disguised, is that essential non-problematicness of contemporary America, its one-dimensionality, in Herbert Marcuse's idiom.

Duncan speaks of our consciousness as coming in a 'dancing organization between personal and cosmic identity'.[21] Now what does this mean? It is so plausible a mid-century offering: we have accepted, since I. A. Richards, any statement asserting the nature of a given phenomenon to consist in a 'tension' between two disparates, or opposites. And yet here the assertion means—to me at least—absolutely nothing. Or rather that the man who wrote it is toying with modish counters, swapping around Absolutes to get equations for Life. Now you do not have to be a European sceptic (though it helps) to find this somewhat slick and bland.

21 'Towards an open universe', 171.

Parenthetically, Duncan has assured us that the poem is 'a supreme effort of consciousness': yet there is little evidence in the surrounding matter—and not much more in the poetry itself—that he really attaches much importance to the question of effort. If, after all, the 'amoebic intelligences' and the cosmic iambics come dancing through, why is any effort (supreme or otherwise) necessary at all? The postulation of a supreme effort appears to concede the necessity of a problematic otherwise negated in the eurhythmics.

But in fact if the spell aroused in our minds by the periodic stricture of the 'rising lines and repeating metres' was a reality, if it corresponded to the systole and diastole of the heart (cosmic and personal), where is the room for the aperiodic structure of which Schrödinger was speaking, and which Duncan has brought into use to explain and justify his own irregular metrical practices? We cannot simply change our scientific analogy every time we want to describe a different poetics: Schrödinger was describing something—the second law of thermodynamics—which has always been true, and always will be; not something which has come to be true in our own time, or which, when understood by us, can alter our fundamental life-rhythms. Has man in some mysterious way come to be responsive to entropy as he was not in the old days when the systole and diastole of the heart came pounding through in regular rhyme and rhythms? Or are all these exciting discoveries of science ultimately irrelevant to the writing of poetry, simply playthings or images for poets to work on, with no guidance for the essentially moral and emotional effort required in the activity?

The essential uncertainty of Duncan appears pre-eminently in a certain ontological vagueness. Duncan has spoken of the poet as seeking 'the most *real* form in language', and we can have our doubts about the meaning of this. Language is public and conventional on the one hand, but, on the other hand, 'the divine world' (with which the poet is supposed to commune) doesn't change—it cannot change—and our apprehension of it would seem to close the question of any greater or less reality. In the poems there is a certain rhetorical wistfulness that too often gives up the ghost at the crucial moment:

> The moon climbs the scale of souls
> O to release the first music somewhere again
>   for a moment
> to trust the design of the first melody
>
>   ('Night Scenes')

What is apprehended here? Is there any more meaningful *signifié* in the phrase 'the first melody' than a vague eclectic Pythagorean notion of the music of the spheres? Is this the ecstasy of Keats, or 'monotonous rapture'? For here we have Duncan's religious imagery spread wide. Behind it there is evidence of a strong emotional sense of significance, but only the loosest and most confused intellectual understanding, a patchwork religion, made up of bits of the *Corpus Hermeticum*, *The Golden Bough*, and the more effusive mystics in the Western tradition. Duncan's actual presentation of his poems is intended, one suspects, to suggest a sustained, paean-like emotionalism: the poems in all his collections are printed one after the other without space, so that the volumes are extremely difficult to penetrate. I cannot help suspecting myself that this device is meant also to keep adverse criticism at bay: Duncan seems to be afraid that exposure or isolation of his poems will diminish their significance and reveal them to be less powerful than he had thought. This possibly explains, too, his dislike of being anthologized.[22] He wants us to buy him whole—so that our scepticism will be swamped—or to be kept out.

More importantly, Duncan's individual poems show a distinct tendency to lose their contours, as the poet's mind loses its grasp upon the substance of the emotion. My treatment of the 'pedestal' poems suggests a general attitude towards a fairly substantial body of achieved lyric work in Duncan. But the number of poems which fail to become poems (properly speaking) and slide into one another, so that parts of one seem to be interchangeable without loss with other contexts, is far larger. This is perhaps a result of the 'open field' theory of composition, Olson's dilution of a compositional 'method' Ezra Pound admitted to have failed him in the *Cantos*,[23] one which in the end meant jotting everything down in the hope that a facile formalism had been evaded and a new kind of 'totality' achieved. This fallacy springs from the naturalism of Olson I have referred to above (pp. 132–3): in many important respects, art is not like life; experiencing is one thing, turning experience into poetry another. The fragments gathered together in Pound's *Cantos* do not gather significance, in spite of the more or less fortuitous relations which will inevitably obtain between the random expressions of any given mind. The significance of the whole, like that of the part, can only derive from a series of individual efforts, each one sustained on the swell of an unbroken effort, asking 'not less than everything'. And this groundswell itself cannot be a brute egotistical asseveration: that is mania, of which the *Cantos* divulge much evidence. The 'life-time's effort' of the poet is not merely a matter of blind will; it demands constant vigilance towards the facts, and towards the developments that take place with age inside the human organism. There is little sign that Duncan is capable of any such sustained effort. Too frequently, he takes the first opportunity offered of letting the rhythmic identity of his poem flag, and, with it, the meaning and inscape of the poem. Sometimes this appears simply as a rhythmic indulgence. In the poem 'My Mother Would Be a Falconress',

[22] See D. Allen, *New Writing in the USA* (Harmondsworth 1964), 11.
[23] See Michael Reck, 'A conversation between Ezra Pound and Allen Ginsberg', *Evergreen Review* 12 (55) (June 1968), 29.

for instance, the opening line, Duncan tells us,[24] came in a dream, followed by the line 'And I a falcon at her wrist'. In the written-up version of the poem suggested by this couplet, the tight ballad line is diffused, padded out by the use of one of Duncan's favourite verbs:

> And I a gay falcon treading her wrist.

What does 'treading' do for the verse here? It is a favourite reverberation of Duncan's, a verb he uses well, after the manner of his mentors, Edith Sitwell and Yeats. But the resonance Sitwell and Yeats load onto such words depends materially upon the eschewal of the more literal meaning. Duncan had his picture here ('And I a falcon at her wrist'), and has squandered its pregnancy with a piece of superfluous graphics: 'doing' words aren't always the best to produce concreteness.

The point is well illustrated by the much anthologized piece, 'A Poem Beginning on a Line of Pindar':

> *The light foot hears you and the brightness begins*
> god-step at the margins of thought,
>   quick adulterous tread at the heart.
> Who is it that goes there?
>   Where I see your quick face
> notes of an old music pace the air,
> torso-reverberations of a Grecian lyre.

This is Pound's music, of course (the Pound of 'Homage to Sextus Propertius', according to Rosenthal,[25] the Pound of the later *Cantos*, in my opinion). At any rate, it is a fine stanza in Duncan's best manner, rhythmically well sprung yet stately, balanced yet intense and onward-moving. But what it promises is not later fulfilled. The poem that begins with a line of Pindar (mistranslated by the poet's dream-mind, so he tells us[26]) turns into a rhapsodic homoerotic extravaganza, sparked off by a different artist, Goya:

> In Goya's canvas Cupid and Psyche
> have a hurt voluptuous grace
> bruised by redemption. The copper light
> falling upon the brown boy's slight body
> is carnal fate that sends the soul wailing
> up from blind innocence, ensnared
> by dimness
> into the deprivations of desiring sight.

'This is magic,' Duncan later observes. But what it really is is surely given in the phrase that follows, 'passionate dispersion'. Isn't most of Duncan's

[24] *Bending the Bow* (New York 1968), 51.
[25] *The New Poets*, 23.
[26] 'Towards a human universe', 280–81.

poetry, in fact, passionately dispersed? He sustains the rhapsodic tone, but his voice often divulges banalities:

> In time we see a tragedy, a loss of beauty
> the glittering youth
> of the god remains—but from this threshold
> it is age that is beautiful.
>
> ('A Poem Beginning . . .')

This modulates, or rather deteriorates, into a swipe at the 'U-nighted States' in the approved cummings Protest manner, unhelpful and, at the heart, self-congratulatory. The Pound of the *Pisan Cantos* is consciously acknowledged later in the poem, in the third section dedicated to Charles Olson:

> In the story the ants help. The old man at Pisa
> mixd in whose mind
> (to draw the sorts) are all seeds
> *as a lone ant from a broken ant-hill*
> had part restored by an insect, was
> upheld by a lizard.
>
> ('A Poem Beginning . . .')

What follows is suavely garbled *Cantos*, literary ('Scientia holding the lamp, driven by doubt') and again, ultimately, made up of banalities:

> Cupidinous Death!
> that will not take no for an answer.

The cupidity-Cupid pun (Death-will) is platitudinous, reminding us yet again that irony and verbal 'wit' do not guarantee the full participation of the poet's intelligence. In fact, Duncan's poetic equipment rusts disused in this most 'thought-bound' section of his poem, and something of the sort is generally true of his poetry. He returns to the footfall of the Pindar line, now 'informed by the weight of all things' (how?). Perhaps the finest passage in the sequence comes when Duncan introduces his metaphor of the children dancing in the field, which runs through the title poem of the volume in which this poem appears:

> On the hill before the wind came
> the grass moved toward the one sea,
> blade after blade dancing in waves.

> There the children turn the ring to the left.
> There the children turn the ring to the right.
> Dancing. . . . Dancing. . . .
>
> ('A Poem Beginning . . .')

At the very end of the poem, having once again, in a prose insertion

failed to say why the line from Pindar meant so much to him, Duncan
produces a fine passage:

> the information flows
> that is yearning. A line of Pindar
> moves from the area of my lamp
> toward morning.
>
> In the dawn that is nowhere
> I have seen the wilful children
> clockwise and counter-clockwise turning.

But what the dancing of the children actually means has not, to my
satisfaction, been sufficiently elucidated. We have here echoes of Eliot's
Quartets, as we had in Roethke's 'Lost Son'. And in thinking of Eliot's
characters 'dansynge, a commodious sacrament signifiyinge matrimonye',
and the voice of the children in the foliage, we can hardly fail to find
Duncan's passage emotive, in a limiting sense, and inconclusive. A vague
sense of history's being related to passion, and stemming from some
Platonic cave-dream, and of the passion expressing itself through the
dance and history—this is all powerfully evoked, or rather gestured
towards, by Duncan. But if we return to the spiritual sources—to Yeats,
to Eliot, to Pound—it is difficult not to feel that the masters remain un-
superseded. It is enough, perhaps, to have got that close. But greater
claims than this have been advanced for Duncan, and we have the right to
judge him more severely than his contemporaries. If we think of the
mastery of St John Perse (another source of Duncan's style and stance),
sustaining itself in detail, over the vast stretch of *Vents*, or of Edith
Sitwell's progressive movement towards the condensation of the mantric
style, concentrating itself in the profound and lucid utterance of the
'Dirge for the New Sunrise'—it is, then, easy to to feel that Duncan is
somewhat disorganized, and intense only in patches.

Part IV

Beyond the *Avant Garde*

Chapter 9

Rexroth and Patchen

Alternatives to Breakdown

The regeneration of American poetry in the 1950s was made possible only by a conscious act of self-isolation by a series of poets, by the creation of an infra-culture which ignored the social and academic precepts which had exercised an often damagingly powerful influence over poets like Tate, Ransom, Shapiro, Jarrell and Eberhart. Just as in England much of the finest poetry of the mid-century was written by poets like Dylan Thomas and David Gascoyne who deliberately excluded themselves from the mainstream of English poetic and critical development, so in America certain poets who neither belonged nor wished to belong to the cultural and literary establishment helped to keep alive a more powerful and exalted conception of poetry during the neo-metaphysical winter. There has always been, since the establishment of *Poetry Chicago* in 1912, an official imagist *avant garde* and this has been seen to be important. But apart from this tradition, which itself underwent, at Black Mountain College and elsewhere, a process of refinement that almost killed it, American poetry was helped by the work of certain disaligned radicals. It seems important here to emphasize again that the Nervous Breakdown school drew a large amount of its energy from the affluent and privileged strata of East Coast society. Much of the forcefulness of the American revolution of the middle 1950s came from working-class radicals or members of ethnic minorities.

This is certainly true of two elder poets, Kenneth Rexroth and Kenneth Patchen, whose work seems increasingly important in the context of recent American writing. Rexroth was an established radical campaigner, whose later poetry breathes outdoor independence:

> the cliff
> Falls sheer away five hundred
> Feet to a single burnt pine
> And then another thousand
> Feet to a noisy river
> In spate. Off beyond it stretches
> Shimmering space, then fold on

Dimmer fold of wooded hills,
Then, hardly visible in
The pulsating heat, the flat
Lands of the San Joaquin Valley,
Boiling with life and trouble.

('Time Is the Mercy of Eternity')

Rexroth's poetry celebrates sexual love, the life of the family, the Signature of All Things, set in the context of astronomical reading that seems to have absorbed him much in his latter years. The hallmark of his verse is a phenomenalist accuracy of observation diffused through relaxed, conversational paragraphing structured by a line of three stresses and seven, eight or nine syllables. (The syllable-count here is more relevant than is usually the case with verse in English: often entire poems contain nothing but septosyllabics, regardless of the beat, which is free to wander, contract or intensify within the rigid framework.) The reader readily trades intensity and panache for the quiet fatherly strength and the never questionable honesty of tone; when Rexroth says of his wife,

I have never known any
One more beautiful than you,

he means it and we believe him. But Rexroth's poetry is more than straight talking. It is informed by a belief and trust in the natural world so absolute that it is content merely to describe, and in describing, with no striving after symbolic resonance, to achieve just that more-than-descriptive import that poetry must have:

Now it is night and our fire
Is a red throat open in
The profound blackness, full of
The throb and hiss of the rain.

('Spring Rain')

Or:

Two days ago the sky was
Full of mares' tails. Yesterday
Wind came, bringing low cigar
Shaped clouds.

('Autumn Rain')

Having decided upon a septosyllabic line, Rexroth proceeds with the wise confidence he must surely in part have learned from the Japanese poets he has translated so well.[1] The logic of Rexroth's own poems of course differs radically from the subtle detonation of Bashō's *haiku*. His poetry builds up relaxed yet supple descriptive units. The belief in the physical world as a thing sufficient in itself, without the mediation of

[1] *One Hundred Poems from the Japanese* (New York 1959).

metaphysics or morality, seems to have been influenced by the literature of China and Japan, though equally strongly by D. H. Lawrence and the Christian mystics. Rexroth writes poetry without the need to prove himself: he rejects the cultural impasse of poetry as social vindication. He seems to have written poetry in fact much as he seems to read, steadily avid, or as he might fill buckets with water or chop firewood in camp— something meaningful in itself which nevertheless does not throw into meaningless shadow the rest of the daily round of which life is composed.

It is no accident that so much of his finest poetry is contained in the volume called *The Signature of All Things*, for the peaceable crazy sanity of Jakob Boehme seems close to Rexroth's own mind. His heroes are men who loved the actual world—Boehme and D. H. Lawrence, Dylan Thomas and Homer. His message, in the end, is that 'Our Home Is in the Rocks.' In his finest pages, this deep sanity rides over and through the sometimes quirky erudition, and the *idées fixes*, such as his bigoted anglo-phobia and the hostility to homosexuals, which harden slowly as one makes one's way through the *Collected Shorter Poems*, and make the later longer poems and the *Autobiographical Novel* almost unreadable. The character that emerges from a sustained reading is complicated and not altogether pleasant, in fact. The image of Rexroth presented by Kerouac in certain of the novels (under the name Reinhold Cacoethes) dovetails exactly with the character that emerges from Rexroth's own *Auto-biographical Novel*. Learned, arrogant, cold, even brutal, concerned to excess with the display of knowledge, gnarled by a tough early life into certain bigotries that betray the poet's ethnic-minority background, Rexroth does not endear himself to us in his constant asseveration of his own superiority. We could hardly predict from the caustic autodidact of the *Autobiographical Novel* the sensitive masculinity of the best of his poetry. Yet a sense of soft pulsation—the sympathy with flowing water and small animal life—is really his most enduring quality:

> The mountain beaver, with the face
> Of an overfed angel, eyes me
> With his black jewels of ultimate
> Innocence. Of far feebler folk
> Than the Scripture's coney, he dies
> If touched, so quietly you can't
> Believe he is dead, as he lies
> So still in your hand, breathless, with
> Dulling eyes.

('Our Home Is in the Rocks')

There is enough work of this quality in Rexroth to make him a key-figure in the so-called Poetry Renaissance of San Francisco, over and above his role as convenor and father-figure. The description of the dying beaver, so delicately alive, so responsive to the inward life of the animal, to its hardly apprehensible dying, is managed, as is usual in Rexroth's verse, within the octosyllabic line, only very rarely letting itself add one syllable or contract by one. Another indication of his subtlety with a syllabic prosody is in the second section of 'The Signature of All Things'. The whole section is retailed in lines of seven syllables, except the last line. It is hard to say quite how Rexroth achieves his effect, or in what way the seven-syllable lines impose their music. But there is no doubting the effectiveness of the eight-syllable line that ends the section:

> There, in blotched and cobwebbed light
> And dark, dim in the blue haze,
> Are twenty Holstein heifers,
> Black and white, all lying down,
> Quietly together, under
> The huge trees rooted in their graves.

The rhythmic inscape of each line seems different, but the minute difference of the extra syllable is sufficient, such is Rexroth's mastery, to enable him to modulate from the crisp up-beat of the seven-syllable lines to something of a soft C-Major cadence in the last.

Poems like this depend on a quite different prosody from the neo-imagism of Black Mountain, in accordance with the different philosophy of life they articulate. The aloof disdain of Black Mountain, its mandarin elitism, is replaced in Rexroth by a more rugged, outdoor radicalism. Politically, indeed, he makes a fascinating contrast with the Black Mountain people: his committed radicalism is in sharp contrast to their Poundian elitism. In general, his own more abstract 'experimental' poems—poems in which significantly he jettisons the syllabic line for a free form—are quite unsuccessful, and reveal the somewhat harsh pedantry of the *Autobiographical Novel*. His natural music vanishes, and with it the pulse and life of the verse:

>   a time
>   take one
>   from a pair, a pair
>   from a quartette a quartette
>   from an
>   octette
>   the arrow through the octave
>   and the sun rising athwart
>   the ungloved thighs
>   ('In Memory of Andree Rexroth')

How much more impressive is the easy power of 'Autumn in California'. Rexroth begins in California with one of those relaxed paragraphs that are his real stock-in-trade:

Autumn in California is a mild
And anonymous season, hills and valleys
Are colorless then, only the sooty green
Eucalyptus, the conifers and oaks sink deep
Into the haze; the fields are plowed, bare, waiting;
The steep pastures are tracked deep by the cattle;
There are no flowers, the herbage is brittle.
All night along the coast and the mountain crests
Birds go by, murmurous, high in the warm air.

It is interesting that alone of American poets in his time Rexroth should have imbibed the lessons of the English tradition well enough to write good blank verse. Rexroth exploits the properties of the form, as skilfully as Arnold and Tennyson did, making its apparently informal measure alternately brace and accommodate his meaning:

Once more I wander in the warm evening
Calling the heart to order and the stiff brain
To passion.

('Autumn in California')

The feminine ending of the first line here yields to the first inverted foot of the next, which in its turn spills over rhythmically into the third. The run-over is functional, the rhythm taut and relaxed at once. It is a masterly performance. The idyllic setting causes the poet to castigate himself: he should, he tells himself, be thinking of 'dreaming, loving, dying'. But instead, he is led to think of a strangely contemporaneous political past:

But I hear the clocks in Barcelona strike at dawn
And the whistles blowing for noon in Nanking.
I hear the drone, the snapping high in the air
Of planes fighting, the deep reverberant
Grunts of bombardment, the hasty clamour
Of anti-aircraft.

The present tense relates in fact to the past: Rexroth is regretting the past here as only the genuine radical can. The man for whom political justice is really important will always feel the horror of the Japanese bombs on Nanking:

In Nanking at the first bomb,
A moon-faced, willowy young girl runs into the street,
Leaves her rice bowl spilled and her children crying,
And stands stiff, cursing quietly, her face raised to the sky.

('Autumn in California')

This is a far cry from the solemn self-importance of Stevens's 'Dry Loaf', though Stevens also uses the present tense to evoke the political facts. In this poem, as in 'The Bad Old Days', Rexroth speaks from a deep core of conviction and sympathy. Yet he speaks also with guilt—the guilt of the man who wasn't there, who didn't put his shoulder to the wheel. This is perhaps most beautifully suggested in the scene in Civil War Spain that follows the Chinese scene. Rexroth imagines (or perhaps remembers) the tension and excitement of living in danger and in the best of causes:

> I hear the voices
> Young, fatigued, and excited, of two comrades
> In a closed room in Madrid. They have been up
> All night, talking of trout in the Pyrenees,
> Spinoza, old nights full of riot and sherry,
> Women they might have had, or almost had,
> Picasso, Velasquez, relativity.

('Autumn in California')

It's hard to read this and not think of Hemingway, yet the effect of Rexroth's poem is quite different from anything out of *For Whom the Bell Tolls*, and it is perhaps the wry authenticity of the line about the 'women they might have had, or almost had' that best suggests the nature of the difference. In Hemingway they would be spinning long yarns—or short, self-satisfied ones—about the women they did have. There is nothing in Hemingway evoking the powerful nostalgia of the time, or its marvellous pathos—its danger and its camaraderies—half so well as these lines of Rexroth's. Rexroth remembers the intensity and purity of the commitment with a deep sadness that brings him back to Autumn, and California, safe, and rather dull:

> The moon rises late over Mt Diablo,
> Huge, gibbous, warm; the wind goes out,
> Brown fog spreads over the bay from the marshes,
> And overhead the cry of birds is suddenly
> Loud, wiry and tremulous.

('Autumn in California')

Again, the suddenly shortened line at the end, cutting discordantly through the quiet music of the pentameters, achieves the effect Rexroth wants: this is the voice of the suffering and the afflicted, and it exists now, as it did then.

The whole poem makes an interesting comparison with Auden's 'Spain 1937'. If Rexroth's poem lacks the brilliant verve of Auden's, and also the intellectual skill with which Auden handles the dialectical possibilities, it has by compensation a pervasive strength, a strength available only to the radical who was genuine in a way Auden was not. Auden's Civil War poetry, as I have noted elsewhere, is authentic in its honest presentation of the ambiguities of his own situation. It could not interest us unless Auden were himself on some level in earnest about the politics: this is precisely the source of the tension in the poems. But

Rexroth was not ambivalent, and he wrote of the evils of fascism and capitalism as few of his contemporary Americans did: only Kenneth Patchen perhaps speaks occasionally with the same authenticity.

Kenneth Patchen is in every respect Rexroth's anti-type. Where Rexroth celebrates, quietly and steadily, the body of the world, Patchen works ceaselessly at locating and releasing the world's 'hidden forms', the 'originating forces' he divines beneath the coarseness of physical reality. His intense Platonism stands in direct contrast to Rexroth's responsible Hedonism, and it is not surprising that he chose surrealism in preference to the relaxed realism of Rexroth. Jacques Maritain long ago pointed out the essential Platonism of surrealism.[2] The surrealist acknowledges the reality of a dimension of idea within external appearances, and bypasses these appearances precisely in drawing upon their outward husks. In the same way, Patchen's poetry takes place in an inner world. If it begins in an objective scene, this scene is swiftly forsaken, or submerged within the ideal presences of which it is the outward token:

> Gone silence down lowered sun
> O at this each
> Of everything here
> These poor knotted hands lost
> Under the darkened foam
> Of grass.
> All should
> Be dark.
> And dark on dark forever
> Now.
> Sundown and world, too.
>
> ('Lowellville Cemetery: Twilight')

Alternatively, he maintains a delicate relationship with the scene, the phenomena now gently animated, now lost in the presiding cope of the ideas, only to return discreetly, nudging through the symbolic atmosphere. A complete poem, 'What Splendid Birthdays', will serve as illustration:

> The ears of the forest
> Twitch in the sun
> Flies of cloud
> Are shaken off so carefully
>
> See, they alight again
>
> In confident purity
> And their wings seem to rest
> Against the sky like
> Candle flames painted on a cake

[2] J. Maritain, *Creative Intuition in Art and Poetry* (New York 1955), 66.

Deer in the sunglow

Green ears
Twitching sleepily in the warmth
Of
A peaceful summer's afternoon
Later . . . the herd stirs awake
Antlers purpling
And the first match

Touches the darkling candelabra

If the pulse-beat—skilfully allowed to fluctuate from near stillness (the monosyllablic line 'Of') to the strong stirring of the final lines—is what most distinguishes this poetry from the exquisiteness of cummings, its air of being strongly committed, as well as its warm inward shapeliness, sets it definitely apart from the elegant idealism of Wallace Stevens. The symbols vary from the animistic 'ears of the forest' to the deeply submerged immanence of the final herd–antlers image, and they do not, in spite of their accuracy, give the impression of striving to capture the effect. Instead, they have a kind of archetypal relevance which is a central part of Patchen's poetic achievement. His poetry inhabits a world of archetypes, of natural symbols, which are often deeply archaic, though rarely 'literary'. Thus, his sunsets conceal quasi-classical horses that champ 'bits of gold'; night is made up of 'murmuring rivers', and contains a 'consciousness' of caves. The sky

moves in its whiteness
Like the withered hand of an old king.
('The Snow Is Deep on the Ground')

Loneliness is like riding

back and forth
On
A blind white horse
Along an empty road meeting
All your
Pals face to face.

('Lonesome Boy Blues')

These classical emblems—night's streams and caves, the horses of dawn and sunset, the blind white horse, the old king—move naturally through Patchen's poetry. He beholds them, and converses with them, as naturally as Yeats with his swans or Wordsworth with his rocks and streams. It is important to bear this in mind, I think, because Patchen's symbols are not always derived from observed phenomena as clearly as they are in 'What Splendid Birthdays'. More usually they are, as it were, non-natural, conjured out of the moral consciousness in the surrealist manner, with no immediate objective suggestion. And this is a vital part of Patchen's originality in the American inter-war scene and his relevance, later, to the Beat poets. Something of his sophisticated freedom with non-natural emblems can be observed in the poetry of Gregory Corso. I have described the world of his poetry above as being 'inner'. It would be more accurate to speak of it as transcendental, since he does not retreat into the jungle world of the surrealist imagination, but freely and openly discourses with its symbolic presences in waking reality.

Patchen's relevance to the Beats, though, is not confined to his symbolic precedures. It is the moral intensity of his poetry which pre-eminently makes him a father to the Beat movement. The 'hidden forms' and the 'originating forces' are the mainspring of everything he admires in life—intense purity of passion between man and woman, idealistic scorn of materialism, egalitarian communion of man with man. He rarely describes the joy of sex or of natural communion without relating the experience to the 'hidden forms' or to the archetypal beasts of the universe—the deer, the horses—'even the goat', for he is as dogmatically against the notion of the 'natural man' as William Blake. Where Rexroth believes in the quiet moments of joy afforded to man by his physical being, Patchen postulates the necessity of redemption by the acknowledgement of the ideas, the presiding forms, the 'Unreturning Hosts'. This is the great difference between Patchen and Rexroth. Rexroth's is really a naturalist philosophy: he regards the prime duty of man as being the quest for the maximum sensuous fulfilment in a recalcitrant universe. Patchen's is a metaphysic of Otherwhereness: he seeks after purity in form out of ordure, like all surrealists. Quite naturally and beautifully, he sees and demands obeisance to the great living Hosts of the universe:

> Supreme in the distance, veiled
> As one's own horizon,
> The ancients stand,
> Immutably shadowless in lengthening obliquity.
>
> ('The Unreturning Hosts')

The vision of the forms, the archetypes, tenaciously held to through an often bitter and frustrating life, confers upon Patchen's poetry a distilled cleanliness of line, and at the same time charges it with a fervent moral intensity that lifts it above the restricted symbol-mongering of his academic contemporaries in America and England. Always the archetypes, the forms, govern and purify the moral vision.

This moral vision cannot be divorced from the angry political radicalism he shares with Kenneth Rexroth. Yet social anger does not suit him: there is nothing in Patchen's poetry of protest to match the fine grimness of Rexroth's 'The Bad Old Days' (surely one of the best 'social' poems of its time). Nor is this surprising. Rexroth's sober, down-to-earth sturdiness can take in and express anger much more easily than Patchen's more inwardly oriented, slightly exclusive idealism. There is an almost Shelleyan sibilance to Patchen's protest poems which hardly recommends itself. He is too much involved in his own privileged role really to feel for the social fate of others. Yet, as with Shelley also, this does not prevent him from expressing a much profounder vision of (shall we say) human destiny, or the greater universe of forms which makes that destiny moving in its very insignificance. 'These Unreturning Destinies' (one of the many fine pieces from the *Dark Kingdom* volume of 1942) expresses perhaps better than any other single poem of Patchen's this conception of the walk-on part man plays in the accidental tragi-comedy of history:

> Old dancers sleep
> In feathery cribs, their green rhythm stilled
> By the swaying of stone bells
> In churches of water.
> The figure of a man appears
> For a moment on the steps of the temple,
> Then sorrowfully withdraws to his place
> In the attended shadow.

In the static surrealistic nocturne of eternity, Patchen argues,

> Destiny and youth sleep in the lands
> Of the walking sword.

The essence of surrealist nightmare is of course its strange beauty, the celebration of the calamity it exists to reveal. The surrealist world is non-tragic: it uses the words of the marketplace with the meanings of the marketplace but without its emotional reactions. 'These Unreturning Destinies' concludes with a strangely noncommittal prophecy of violence:

> Here gleeful beasts track each other
> Through lanes of winter and rotting heroes.

This odd equipoise of beauty and horror redeems the potentially moralistic statement that concludes 'Let Us Have Madness':

> Nor ever say
> We wanted more; we looked to find
> An open door, an utter deed of love,
> Transforming day's evil darkness;
>   but
> We found extended hell and fog
> Upon the earth, and within the head
> A rotting bog of lean huge graves.

This stanza incidentally provides ample evidence of Patchen's extraordinarily distinguished rhythmic and sonic sense. Withholding itself from the crashing over-emphasis of Hart Crane, the verse still maintains a strong pulse, assisted by a subtle network of sound-connections, often across several lines: '*more–door, utter–but, extended–head, fog–bog*'. His imagery is equally subtle; a child, for example, has hair like 'watered milk'; sleep is 'full and light and close as outline of leaf in glass of tea'. It is impossible to read Patchen with any kind of attentiveness without refining and heightening one's own verbal awareness.

This refinement of movement and image bespeaks the innocence of vision with which so much of his poetry is ultimately concerned. 'Only the innocent alone approach evil without fear,' he declares in 'The Rites of Darkness', and we may feel that Patchen's own sense of innocence, justified though it is by the rarity of his images, makes his poetry ultimately unsympathetic. I say 'ultimately' because although we must admire unreservedly so much of what he has written, we are likely to miss from his verse the really profound sense of personal confrontation with reality which major poetry must have. There is, that is to say, an element of self-righteousness in his voice which repels sympathy:

> Do you now faintly
> Hear the voice of life?
> I will allow you respect for
> Red apples and countries warm
> With the races of men; peep over
> The transom at China if you like;
> But I will have no hatred or fear
> Entering this poem.
>
> ('The Dimensions of the Morning')

Some of this almost priggish patronage has rubbed off onto the Beats themselves, though on the whole they have imbibed a sufficiently strong draught of irony and humour to ward it off. And indeed Patchen himself is so good at his best (and so accomplished when not quite at his best) that one is more often aware of inspired release than of self-righteousness. This inspired release derives in part from the discipline of surrealism which makes available to the artist a whole dimension of association and awareness closed off to the conventional poet. It is also curiously amoral in technique: surrealism is, as I have observed elsewhere, *à propos* of David Gascoyne,[3] basically a moralist's idiom. Yet its moral probing takes the form of an apparent abrogation of the moral sense, a suspension of the decisional faculties of the moral consciousness, so that for example the properties of evil and despair are laid bare with a surgical curiosity that precludes moral emphasis. Or rather, let us say that it is the moral judgement that is preclusive. For just as surrealism entails a suspension of

[3] *The Ironic Harvest*, 99.

normal seeing, so it entails also a suspension of ethical judgement. Yet the consequence of its probing is the patently moral declamation of Dali's *Premonitions of Civil War*, Eluard's 'Poésie ininterrompue', Gascoyne's 'Rites of Hysteria' or Patchen's 'The Cloth of the Tempest'.

To penetrate the arcane labyrinth of surrealist truth entails the innocence of which I have already spoken in relation to Patchen—innocence, and the dream-freedom of childhood. Much of Patchen's most memorable poetry takes place in the dream-nightmare of childhood.

> Followed by garrulous hunters, the soft children grovel
> Down the valley of sleep . . . so gentle . . . shining . . . but
> Not singing
> Never singing . . . it is the midnight of sense . . . mind's
> Desolate cave
>
> The decayed clock booms out in puffs of sound
> That stagger like drunken apes through the streets,
> Fingering the paint-stripped houses and the wood
> Where death has flung all things beautiful
>
> Watch the fantastic eyelid of that lark
> How enormously lovely . . . hooded like an invisible engine
>   and pulling earth's lustful plow right through the lark.
>   ('All the Bright Foam of Talk')

Patchen's surrealist sureness enables him to penetrate deeper into the subject here than cummings did with his not dissimilar 'proud dream-horse'.[4] The verse burrows down softly and certainly to a Chirico night city, and halts only at the amazing lark image. The soft strength of sleep has of course been a mine of poetic imagery since Keats's 'Sleep and Poetry'. And the association of sleep with snow and the warmth of oblivion does not originate with Patchen either. There is the example of Frost's 'Stopping by Woods', to look no further. But the originality—as distinct from the novelty—of Patchen's treatment of the theme in 'All the Bright Foam of Talk' shows that the innocence of the surrealist eye goes beyond a Dickensian childlikeness. We can allow that the metaphor of the 'puffs of sound' that 'the decayed clock booms out' is, like so much surrealist wit, limited by its very strikingness. (It is in fact extremely good.) The image of the lark, however, is not striking, it is powerfully original, and inhabits a different dimension of significance. Like many images in Patchen it challenges the hermeneutical presuppositions of modern criticism at the most basic level. It is simply not possible to explain this image within the framework of what I have described as ironist criticism—the establishment of Richards, Empson, Eliot, Leavis and the New Critics.[5] It is the kind of image which owes its existence to the closed

---

[4] cummings, 'what a proud dream horse pulling (Smoothloomingly) through' (*Selected Poems* (Harmondsworth 1963), 31).

[5] *The Ironic Harvest*, ch. 1.

intensity of the surrealist imagination. It calls up a realm of imaginative truth that can hardly be referred to in other than its own terms.

The lark image in 'All the Bright Foam of Talk' lies then beyond the reach of conventional hermeneutica—psychoanalytical or ironist. Empsonian unravelling halts helplessly here. An even better example perhaps is to be found in 'Religion Is that I Love You', possibly Patchen's best love poem, and certainly one of the finest of the half-century:

> As time will turn our bodies straight
> In single sleep, the hunger fed, heart broken
> Like a bottle used by thieves

> Beloved, as so late our mouths meet, leaning
> Our faces close, eyes closed
> > Out there
> > > outside this window where branches toss
> > > in soft wind, where birds move sudden wings
> > Within that lame air, love, we are dying . . .

'In what sense', we can imagine the critic demanding, 'can the air be said to be "lame"?' And what, we might well ask, is the critic to make of the heart broken 'like a bottle used by thieves'? To answer these questions we need not the simple algebraic disentangling of Empsonian or New Critical exegesis, but an entirely different emotional and intellectual orientation. It is one without which the new poetry of the present day cannot be appreciated at all.

Chapter 10

Allen Ginsberg
The Whole Man In

In the case of Allen Ginsberg, the danger of substituting sociology for criticism is perhaps greater than in that of any other poet of our time. Ginsberg the poet has become, over the past fifteen years, Ginsberg the public drop-out, the guru, subterranean jet-setter, the King of the May. As a poet he has been, it appears, unable to withstand the extraordinary pressures of modern publicity, pressures ironically far greater than those he had initially dropped out to avoid. The poet has gone under to the entertainer, he has become a skilled performer of works—like '*HOWL*'— originally written out of a passion and intensity which are cancelled by the very professionalism of the 'rendition'. Like Yevgenii Yevtushenko, Allen Ginsberg is a living proof of Herbert Marcuse's account of the one-dimensionality of Soviet-American society, which asserts that the monoliths destroy by absorbing.

This is particularly unfortunate in the case of Ginsberg since there is no doubting his importance in the emergence of a mature American poetry in the 1950s and 1960s. When Ginsberg crossed America and read '*HOWL*' at Rexroth's famous Renaissance reading, he as it were fertilized the Black Mountain school, and the American Moment may be said to have arrived. Ginsberg achieved in '*HOWL*' what none of his predecessors had been able to: to merge the rhetorical voice of American populist tradition with a passionate, personal intelligence and wit. The significance of the achievement is obscured, once again, by some dubious theories of 'voice'.

There have been attempts to return poetry to a so-called conversational tone or speech-tone before. This has been in fact the dominant pre-occupation of most poetic revolutions since the *Lyrical Ballads*. Wordsworth's Preface stated an intention to return to a language spoken by men; and one of the most important elements of the ironist programme of the 1920s was the restoration of the kind of easy conversational manner we see in Marvell, Herbert and Donne. Symbolism and imagism, it is true, concern themselves more with precision of notation, but one of the ways in which later symbolist poets like Laforgue most strikingly differ from the Parnassians, for instance, is in the assumption of a relaxed manner which creates the illusion of cultivated speech. The speech-mystique has been especially important in American poetics. The reason for this is probably that America had no tradition of a cultivated poetic 'speech': there was, as I have observed above, no American Browning, and American poetry before Pound, with the great exception of Whitman, was characterized by an artificial 'poetic' manner, a stiff stilted tone, as of a man on his best behaviour in 'good' society. Dickinson, who might be thought a second major exception to this rule, only substitutes for the pomposities of Lanier and Bryant a nursery-rhyme sing-song. Thus, the imagist rebellion—a remarkably sophisticated one—was, once its centre of gravity had shifted from London to Chicago, an expression of dis-satisfaction with traditional American prosody rather than with anything obtaining in England. It was, in short, anti-provincial. Now, in fact, we might question both the possibility and the advisability of any return to *normal* speech or speech-rhythm. When Charles Olson says that 'from the breathing of the man who writes, at the moment he writes, the line is born', when Robert Duncan speaks of 'the swarm of human speech', when Allen Ginsberg speaks of 'the new speech-rhythm prosody' of '*HOWL*', we must beware of taking them literally. Their poetry is in fact no closer to so-called 'speech-rhythm' than William Cowper's or Walter de la Mare's; '*HOWL*' is not Ginsberg's 'own heightened conversation' except in a sense that guts his words of their meaning: the adjective 'heightened' opens the flood-gates.

The impact of '*HOWL*' needs no demonstration: the poem is a fact of literary as well as of sociological history. It made a permanent difference. But its originality hasn't a great deal to do with speech or 'breath'. 'The thing that balances each line,' Ginsberg writes of 'America', 'with its neighbours is that each (with tactical exceptions) is ONE SPEECH BREATH— an absolute physical measure as absolute as the ridiculous limited little accent or piddling syllable count.'[1] 'In this,' he goes on, 'I've gone forward from Williams because I literally measure each line by the physical breath—each one breath statement, dictated by what has to be said, in relation and balance to the previous rhythmic statement.' This clearly refers back, even in diction, to the preoccupations of Olson, Williams and Duncan. The document from which these statements come is the most penetrating and intelligent analysis and presentation of Beat rhythmics that has yet appeared. On its own it establishes Ginsberg as a serious critic. No-one, moreover, would wish to question the burden of its argument: '*HOWL*', like the companion poems in the volume of that name, sounds much as Ginsberg would lead us to expect it to. Yet his claims about 'one speech breath' cannot be allowed to stand: for one thing it would require the lungs of a bull to encompass a sentence or clause like this:

[1] From a letter to John Hollander, printed in its entirety in *Paterfamilias: Allen Ginsberg in America* by Jane Kramer (London 1972), 163–77.

> who copulated ecstatic and insatiate with a bottle of beer a sweetheart
> a package of cigarettes a candle and fell off the bed, and con-
> tinued along the floor and down the hall and ended fainting
> on the wall with a vision of ultimate cunt and come eluding
> the last gyzym of consciousness,
>
>   ('*HOWL*' 1)

Then, the rhythm of poetry doesn't operate in quite this way. English
poetry has always varied and manipulated the breathing-rate of its readers:
the longer verse-paragraphs of Milton and Wordsworth and the later
Shakespeare compel us to pause and wait and hold on much as 'When
Lilacs Last . . .' does, and indeed '*HOWL*' itself. The long suspensive line
of Whitman forms part of a different approach, to life as well as to the
writing of poetry, from that which informs the sing-song of Emily
Dickinson. It is a question not of 'real' speech and artifice, but of different
kinds of artifice. This understood, we are free to admire the subtleties of
Allen Ginsberg's own manipulations of speech-thought suspension:

> I Allen Ginsberg a separate consciousness
> I who want to be God
> I who want to hear the infinite minutest vibration
>   of eternal harmony
> I who wait trembling my destruction by that
>   aetherial music in the fire
> I who hate God and give him a name
> I who make mistakes on the eternal typewriter
> I who am Doomed.
>
>   ('Lysergic Acid')

The units of this speech vary, flag and revive according to the dictates
of art-consciousness, not of any natural speech mode: the verse recalls
that of 'Ash Wednesday'. The bop model of so-called beat prosody, in
fact, proves it prosody: that Kerouac was inspired by the new rhythms
of modern jazz in itself suggests that the artistic revolution he and
Burroughs had been instrumental in bringing about was very much a
matter of tuning in to new vibrations, new modulations, not of restoring
poetic language to 'natural' language or speech. As a matter of fact, the
opposite is true. It was the academic poets who had mastered the conversational lessons of the Metaphysicals: by the mid-1950s an easy talk-
tone was within the grasp of any poetic talent provided only it was not
too questioning. Academic criticism, from Grierson and Joan Bennett
onwards, had backed it up in this.

The situation in America, certainly, was not in all respects the same as
that which confronted poets like Larkin and Hughes in England. In place
of the deliberately low-keyed talk-tone of their English counterparts,
academic poets in America went in for a muscle-bound rhetoric, for which

the stylistic models were Yeats, Hopkins and Hart Crane. What Berryman took from Hopkins, Roethke from Yeats, and Lowell from Crane and Allen Tate, was a frequently stultifying conception of the poem-as-thing—the well-made artefact. This is in fact another predictable consequence of the excessive absorption of post-Empsonian New Criticism. A poem is all the time—before the act of composition, during it, and in the later work upon it—organizing itself into shape and pattern, but the poet cannot afford to let his awareness of this become an end in itself. If he does, he will lose touch with his own mainsprings—with what it is he needs to say: Hart Crane buries his own insights and feeling under technical lumber far too often, but he never quite loses contact with the man inside the myth, so that even through his densest wranglings the jet of feelings forces its way up into the light. The poetry of American academic poets of the postwar period is informed by a sense of the heroic which is continually being undermined and betrayed by the intellectualist-ironist doubts more honestly confessed to by Auden, Empson and Ransom. Lacking the self-effacing modesty into which English poets of this century have found it easy enough to melt in times of stress, the Americans often resort to a high-pitched scream, and a stilted rhetoric effectively squeezes out the human accent.

In the light of these reflections, Ginsberg's technical discoveries and his talk about speech-breath and even his anti-iambicism make more sense. With Williams, Kerouac and Whitman at his back, Ginsberg created a line which could move easily from relaxation to exaltation without self-consciousness or strain:

> I saw the best minds of my generation destroyed by madness,
>   starving hysterical naked,
> dragging themselves through the negro streets at dawn looking for
>   an angry fix,
> angelheaded hipsters burning for the ancient heavenly connection
>   to the starry dynamo in the machinery of night,
> who poverty and tatters and hollow-eyed and high sat up smoking
>   in the supernatural darkness of cold-water flats floating across
>   the tops of cities contemplating jazz, . . .
>
>   ('HOWL' 1)

The driving colloquial beat of the famous opening to 'HOWL' should not be allowed to blind us to the poem's great flexibility of tone. There is a great difference between the seriousness of this verse, and the humourlessness of, say, Robert Lowell's. Lowell's verse strains after irony, but it is devoid of that real inner balance and confidence of judgement that can make irony functionally appropriate. Ginsberg's greater religious commitment—'HOWL' is about people who have committed themselves irrevocably to a life of perhaps excessive spiritual intensity—releases irony from its academic bondage. Ironically enough, a major consequence

of this anti-ironist revolution has been the reconstitution of irony itself:
Ginsberg and Corso have written distinguished poems—'America' and
'Marriage'—which succeed in being at the same time serious, satiric and
funny. These poems remind us of what had been lost sight of in the
ironist era, the ancient connection between irony, wit and laughter.
'Marriage' satirizes certain aspects of social behaviour and ritual no less
skilfully than Eliot's 'Prufrock', which it draws upon ('And should I then
ask Where's the bathroom?'). But it does so much more amusingly—
and the amusement is of a different kind from what Lawrence Ferlinghetti
seeks to arouse in his piece on 'Underwear', which is cabaret rather than
poetry. The delight one experiences is intellectual. In '*HOWL*', Ginsberg's
ability to move easily from exultation and pain to humour and self-
mockery is radically important: the total impact of the work is composed
of many different sorts of effect. The responses called for range from pity
to terror, through laughter, disgust and contempt:

> who were burned alive in their innocent flannel suits on Madison
> Avenue amid blasts of leaden verse & the tanked-up clatter
> of the iron regiments of fashion & the nitroglycerine shrieks
> of the fairies of advertising & the mustard gas of sinister
> intelligent editors, or were run down by the drunken taxicabs
> of Absolute Reality,
> who jumped off the Brooklyn Bridge this actually happened and
> walked away unknown and forgotten into the ghostly daze of
> Chinatown soup alleyways & firetrucks, not even one free beer,
>
> ('*HOWL*' 1)

Irresistible as it is, it is a complex mechanism: the man who jumped
off Brooklyn Bridge was possibly remembering the Hart Crane poem,
and had seen himself as the bedlamite speeding to the parapets, 'Tilting
there momently, shrill shirt ballooning'. We too are to think of Crane and,
like the would-be suicide, be both outraged and amused by the abysmal
failure of the attempt. The beautiful aside—'this actually happened'—
alerts us to the response we are expected to make; it also tells us that the
whole passage, the whole poem, is at once satirizing the life-style of the
protagonists and celebrating it. Ginsberg has understood and embodied
in language a profound truth about the cultural life, that it is composed
to a large extent of imitation, of conscious affiliation to a culture-myth.

For the culture-hero had been through this process before he emerged
himself. The tradition goes back through Ginsberg to Crane, to Rimbaud,
Baudelaire and Poe. The great virtue of '*HOWL*' is the warmth and
sympathy with which it celebrates what the poet understands is both
sublime and absurd. This is especially true of the third section of the
poem: Carl Solomon went through the whole silly serious routine with
Allen Ginsberg. Yet he did go mad, and what are the alternatives in
modern society?—

I'm with you in Rockland
> where you scream in a straightjacket that you're losing the
> game of the actual pingpong of the abyss

I'm with you in Rockland
> where you bang on the catatonic piano the soul is innocent
> and immortal it should never die ungodly in an armed mad-
> house

I'm with you in Rockland
> where fifty more shocks will never return your soul to its
> body again from its pilgrimage to a cross in the void.

('*HOWL*' 3)

In spite of the silliness, in spite of the farce, the pilgrimage was real,
and the evils of the punitive system we call society no less so. The pity,
the fear and the laughter are inextricably confused together.

At its best moments, '*HOWL*' seems a major utterance in its time. Yet it
presents no less evidence of Ginsberg's weaknesses than of his strengths.
For the humour is sometimes *just* skittish, almost undergraduate, and
Ginsberg seems often more a great parodist than an originator:

> until the noise of wheels and children brought them down shud-
> dering mouth-wracked and battered bleak of brain all drained
> of brilliance in the drear light of Zoo . . .

('*HOWL*' 1)

In this way, Ginsberg plays off the muscular intensity of Hopkins and the
exalted sonorities of Whitman against a genuinely self-mocking pathos.
In the above example, the movement of the verse imitates the sloughing
lurch of the subway train; and Ginsberg's best verse is consistently
humorous and ironical, yet at the same time serious. *HOWL* is, in a way,
satire:

> and who were given instead the concrete void of insulin metrasol
> electricity hydrotherapy occupational therapy pingpong &
> amnesia,
> who in humorless protest overturned only one symbolic pingpong
> table, resting briefly in catatonia,

('*HOWL*' 1)

Many of the poem's best moments come when it breaks down laughing
at itself. The last word in this extract recalls Poe, of course; an important
link, via Crane, with the English Romantics. Poe himself played at being
Shelley; Ginsberg doesn't play at being Poe, but he sees the dangers.

What Ginsberg's poetry lacks is sustained tension and rhythmic drive,
and this doesn't seem unrelated to the vein of fantasy eclectisism that he so
often taps. This may seem perverse: has not '*HOWL*' already been praised
for its chant-tone, enabling it to graduate easily from pathos to absurdity,
from slow thoughtfulness to ecstasy without jar or unease? Yes, and

Ginsberg's effect on the poets who followed him was salutary and permanent. Yet, in fact, he substitutes for the real heroic strength of the masters—Hopkins, Whitman, Blake, Crane—a mad capering rush. Returning to the speech-tone debate for a moment, we could say that the real basis for the rhythm of '*HOWL*' is an illusion of continuous high-pitched talk. As we have seen, this illusion manages—very skilfully—to include within its compass a wide range of ironical and humorous tones: the delivery is really like that of a fast-talking comedian who reckons on his asides gaining maximum impact from there being no alteration of delivery-rate. But there are moments when the high-pitched talk covers up a real flagging of the inner rhythmic momentum:

> with mother finally *******, and the last fantastic book flung out of the tenement window, and the last door closed at 4 AM and the last telephone slammed at the wall in reply and the last furnished room emptied down to the last piece of mental furniture, a yellow paper rose twisted on a wire hanger in the closet, and even that imaginary, nothing but a hopeful little bit of hallucination—
>
> ('*HOWL*' 1)

What is Ginsberg doing here? Behind these words, there seems to be strong feeling; yet the poet has failed to contain it, to nerve it into language. The tone has faltered unsurely, the rhythm flagged, and one is aware that the verse is not governed from within by the strength of a great past. The verse at this point is actually sentimental, closer to the pathos of primitive American naturalists like O. Henry and Dreiser than to the great drive and clarity of Whitman. One is reminded also of the enormous burden the poet places upon himself by committing himself to poetry rather than to prose: to bring one's deepest feelings into poetic language is an almost superhumanly onerous task. The lesser poet resorts to an appeal to the emotions, as Ginsberg does here.

The formal structure of '*HOWL*' encourages or perhaps reflects this tendency in Ginsberg: the pathos of his verse depends heavily upon the recollective mechanism that governs the first part of '*HOWL*' and the whole of 'Kaddish'. Here, the action of poetry is often shelved in favour of mere prose reminiscence. The recollection of poetry ought to take place in the presence of the new phenomenon. The act of prose remembering is closer to ordinary remembering, and necessarily calls upon 'nostalgia'. Here is Ginsberg just remembering:

> But Gene, young—been Mountclair Teachers College 4 years —taught half years and quit to go ahead in life—afraid of Discipline Problems—dark sex Italian students, raw girls getting laid, no English, sonnets disregarded,—and he did not know much—just that he lost—
>
> ('Kaddish')

It is hard to imagine the reason for this kind of inert notation, rhythmically non-existent, artificial yet inept in transition, unnatural and uninterestingly private in content. The brokenness indicates a sort of randomness, never quite listless or casual, but certainly lacking real poetic tension. No new phenomenal appearance or intrusion of life seems to have given the memory significance, it is simply recalled in the manner of Dahlberg's *Bottom Dogs*. It's a kind of randomness one never associates with Kerouac's prose.

Allen Ginsberg's failure to develop beyond the point reached in 'HOWL' can be ascribed, I think, to an amalgam of these reasons. In the volumes after 'HOWL' his poetry divides more and more decisively into two categories: there are 'solid' poems of recollection, and rhetorical poems that tend to disintegrate into spiritual vapour. The poetry of the first sort can become excessively concrete, merely remembered: the remembrances are processed by juxtaposition, each suggesting the memory-trace next door. 'HOWL' itself perhaps tries to carry more luggage than the poet's rhythmic vitality can manage. By 'Kaddish' and 'To Aunt Rose' the recollective systems are clogged and over-burdened. Towards the end of the 1960s (when Ginsberg's entire way of life had altered), even this act of recollection has gone, replaced only by a diaristic notation, the images mere tape-jottings. The poems of the second sort burn out into increasingly gaseous fulmination: the attitudes are peddled and, though sincere in the worldly sense, lack artistic compulsion. Between these two poles, of naturalism and spirituality, his poetry has always oscillated.

It seems reasonable to say that Ginsberg's most successful pieces occur close to the centre of this spectrum, that is, when naturalist perceptions are shot through with spiritual emotion. In these poems—say, 'Paterson', 'Sunflower Sutra', 'In Back of the Real', much of 'HOWL', 'Transcription of Organ Music', 'A Supermarket in California'—the image is considered unhurriedly, until under pressure of the contemplating mind it becomes symbolic. The symbolism accrues from the contemplation, it is not itself sought after. When the phenomenon resists the contemplation, and remains mere phenomenon, we get the opaque memory-collage of 'Kaddish' or the diaristic notation of 'Angkor Wat' or 'Planet News'. At his best, that is, Ginsberg sees the thing in all its grubby essence, yet places it effortlessly in a spiritual dimension:

> . . . the gray Sunflower poised against the sunset, crackly bleak and dusty with the smut and smog and smoke of olden locomotives in its eye—
> corolla of bleary spikes pushed down and broken like a battered crown, seeds fallen out of its face, soon-to-be-toothless mouth of sunny air, sunrays obliterated on its hairy head like a dried wire spiderweb,

> leaves stuck out like arms out of the stem, gestures from the sawdust
> root, broke pieces of plaster fallen out of the black twigs, a
> dead fly in its ear,
> Unholy battered old thing you were, my sunflower O my soul, I,
> loved you then!

('Sunflower Sutra')

If we want to place the superiority of this over the poetic *lingua franca* current when it was written, we shall have to say simply that the last assertion in the extract quoted is fully meant: the flower hasn't been picked on and rifled of its symbolic possibilities, in spite of the literary precedents. On the contrary, Blake's flower is used intelligently, played off against the actual sunflower before the poet with wise and sufficient irony. This *mélange* of religious intensity and wry realism is, I think, Allen Ginsberg's most endearing and enduring gift. There is perhaps a suspicion that the sermon the poet delivers at the end of the poem, though 'sincere', is cooked up in the literary consciousness ('we're all beautiful golden sunflowers inside') and this suspicion, aroused by the title of the poem, is partially confirmed by contrast with the beautiful lyric 'In Back of the Real'. This short piece, included in the '*HOWL*' volume as an early poem, in a way shortcircuits its more famous sister-piece. The progression from 'In Back of the Real' to 'Sunflower Sutra' suggests the direction Ginsberg was later to take towards an ever-increasing religiosity. The situation in the early poem is the same as in 'Sunflower Sutra': the poet discovers the flower at a tired moment on a sunset walk. But the flower is presented with an unaffected simplicity:

> A flower lay on the hay on
>   the asphalt highway
> —the dread hayflower
>   I thought—It had a
> brittle black stem and
>   corolla of yellowish dirty
> spikes like Jesus' inchlong
>   crown, and a soiled
> dry center cotton tuft
>   like a used shaving brush
> that's been lying under
>   the garage for a year.

('In Back of the Real')

In this sense of beat futility and yet of persistent meaningfulness lies the essence of Allen Ginsberg. It is a quality seen also in the early poem 'Paterson', a work which holds much the same relation to '*HOWL*' as 'In Back of the Real' holds to 'Sunflower Sutra'. 'Paterson' handles the same material as '*HOWL*', but with greater simplicity and candour, with none of the self-consciously high-powered religiosity that mars sections of the longer poem, bringing it occasionally closer to pastiche than to original poetry. Ginsberg's poetry testifies to strong religious experience, but his grasp upon it is insecure, his ability to communicate it fragmentary and vague. When he tries to address the absolute directly, a haze of literary verbiage sometimes obscures his spiritual eye—'Immense seas passing over the flow of time' . . . Whitman's 'noiseless patient spider', too—a perfect instance of the natural object persuaded into spiritual significance—becomes a literary property—'[it] hath no name/ Spinneth out of itself endlessly.' This spider never existed on a ledge anywhere. The situation is perhaps rather the reverse of the one described by Professor Fiedler:[2] Ginsberg is basically a Jewish reformer-moralist, trying desperately hard to be an Anglo-Saxon seer—a Blake, a Whitman, a Shelley. His shouting rant deafens truth, and the numinous end of the language spectrum is burned out by over-use. Language itself again needs purging and restoring:

> trailing variations made of the same Word circles round itself in the same pattern as the original Appearance, [etc. etc.]

In the light of this, 'Transcription of Organ Music' assumes special significance in Ginsberg's work. Ginsberg himself describes the poem as an attempt at 'Absolute transcription of spontaneous material, transcription of sensual data (organ) at a moment of near Ecstasy . . .', an attempt to 'transcribe at such moments and try to bring back to the poor suffering world what rare moments exist'.[3] The poem tries to transmit some of the sublime intensity, the exalted pathos of Bach (the natural world in the poem is experienced directly under the influence of the music); yet it never loses contact with the pitiable reality of the poet's own material existence—the flower in the peanut bottle, the lavatory door left open. There is a moving sense of the poet's own awareness of where he stands in relation not only to the religious universe, but to the art of the great masters. 'Can I bring back the words?' he asks. 'Will thought of transcription haze my mental open eye?' No; but what the poet has the power to relay back to the reader is not the experience itself, which is simply referred to—'I had a moment of clarity, saw the feeling in the heart of things, walked out to the garden crying.' We believe that Ginsberg had a powerful religious emotion: the music of Bach lifted him up. But he lacks the power to hold onto the vision and to transmit its quality. And if the phrase in the extract just quoted suggests Wordsworth for comparison, I should say that it is not so much of Wordsworth that I am thinking in placing Ginsberg like this as

---

[2] *Waiting for the End* (New York 1964). Professor Fiedler makes a few quite original errors about the Beats, including the strange assertion that Ginsberg 'created' Burroughs, and not the other way round.

[3] Kramer, *Paterfamilias*, 169.

of lesser poets—say, the Crane of 'Cape Hatteras', the Francis Thompson of 'The Hound of Heaven', and some of Ginsberg's own younger contemporaries.

For reasons of this sort, much of Ginsberg's finest poetry combines the religious and the political. His ability to grasp and embody exalted religious states is limited, it is true. Yet poems like 'Death to Van Gogh's Ear' and 'America' are informed with a zestful humour that derives from a deep source of love and delight which reminds one of some Zen painting:[4] these poems do not attempt the absolute religious affirmation which usually defeats him. They are satirical, critical of organized society, yet qualitatively superior to merely political poetry. They are compact of intense political enthusiasm and deep religious disgust. 'Death to Van Gogh's Ear' is possibly Ginsberg's finest single poem, a politico-religious tract of manic yet deeply sane intensity, achieved with a natural brilliance and economy. Its mode is interesting, an aphoristically witty realization of spiritual perceptions of the sort first displayed by Smart in 'Jubilate Agno' and Blake in 'Auguries of Innocence'.[5] In 'Death to Van Gogh's Ear' the Blakean wit is only intermittent—'Elephants of mercy murdered for the sake of an Elizabethan birdcage'—and there are glimpses still of the pasticheur, the witty undergraduate masquerading as great poet—'Owners! Owners! Owners! with obsession on property and vanishing Selfhood!' But the whole poem is irresistible, a truly revolutionary work. Like 'America', its mode is satirical without being snide: its forcefulness springs from a basically affirmative attitude towards experience and even towards American society, rather than from the negativism which makes most radicalism slightly anaemic and condescending. Nothing is more important in fact than to dispel the notion of Ginsberg and the Beats as fundamentally aligned with protest. Kerouac's novels and Ginsberg's finest poems are based upon acceptance, not rejection, upon affirmation, not negation. This is the primary difference between their work and that of writers like Saul Bellow and Robert Lowell.

In spite of this, however, in spite of the insistence on sexual release and the Blakean programme, Allen Ginsberg's poetry really contains little joy. It is perhaps most alive when fiercely yet humorously attacking the evils of organized society in the Capitalist and Communist worlds, in poems like 'America' and 'Death to Van Gogh's Ear'. Otherwise, his most successful pieces are poems of exhaustion and Beat futility. How sad his world is emerges not only from poems like 'Sunflower Sutra' and 'Transcription of Organ Music', but from a passage in *Paterfamilias* in which he tells of his walks with Carlos Williams: 'I'd show him where *my* epiphanous places were. Places like the river, under the bridge where I

---

[4] I am thinking principally of Sengai.
[5] I am not sure the mode exists outside English. The essence of it really is a kind of paranoid prophecy, the poet striking through to truth by associating disparates with surreal acumen.

masturbated for the first time. Where I kissed that girl who moved away. Where I saw a gang fight. Where I always felt ashamed for some reason. The hedge where I was lonely.'[6] This passive melancholy lies close to the heart of Ginsberg's life and writing. He takes up the hedonistic implication of Blake without apparently understanding how much pleasure Blake took in keeping himself spiritually collected, gathered together in one place, that place the centre of the universe. Dignity and discipline, with their associations of ambassadors and headmasters, do not seem very relevant qualities today: yet spiritual dignity seems very radical to the thought, for instance, of D. H. Lawrence, and a discipline, zestfully renewed each morning, seems incalculably important in the life and work of Blake. Ginsberg takes up the unbridling implications of the later Lawrence—

> It is only immoral
> to be dead-alive—
>
> ('Immorality')

with no appreciation of the fact that this was indissolubly connected in Lawrence's work with ideas of order, sanity, inward peace, and above all a permanant vigilance, without which personal freedom and integrity could not be maintained. Lawrence advised us to

> keep still, and hold
> the tiny grain of something that no wave can wash away.
>
> ('Be Still!')

Ginsberg envisages a vast communal orgy:

> Tonite let's all make love in London as if it were 2001
> the year of thrilling God—
>
> ('Who Be Kind To')

Lawrence, on the other hand, knowing that as things are the results would be something like a German beer festival or a Swedish midsummernight orgy, in which only the pent-up nastiness is released, urges continuous continence—

> Let us contain ourselves
> and rally together
> to keep a sane core to life.

'Why not stay out,' Lawrence suggests to his friends, 'and learn to contain oneself?' The invitation was a genuine one, and his friends—the Carswells, Middleton Murry and so on—were aghast at the prospect of a realization of what they had been glad to applaud in theory.[7]

The catalyst in the formation of Ginsberg's Love doctrine was not

[6] Kramer, *Paterfamilias,* 134–5.
[7] See Catherine Carswell's *The Savage Pilgrimage* (London 1932), 220.

G

Blake but Whitman: the shapelessness, the unarticulated feminine breadth that disperses the self into vapour, derive specifically from Whitman. There is a certain greatness in Allen Ginsberg, the man. Yet in his hands, the Whitman camaraderie degenerates into *loucherie*, in much the same way as the magnificent squealing of Jean Genet suffers a democratized reduction into the vulgar camp of *The Boys in the Band*. And the self-respect that, implicitly in Blake and explicitly in Lawrence, remains indispensable in its drive towards total fulfilment, melts away in the casually begged and ever less satisfying orgasm. It is obvious from commonsense that the human organism requires more than absence of sexual inhibition, that the evils of puritanism are the consequence not the cause of the deeper sicknesses of modern man. There are more people than Allen Ginsberg seems to think already enjoying guiltless and uninhibited sexual freedom: their lives are no more fulfilled and satisfied than those of the parody neurotics who twitch across the pages of Freud, and mutter through the films of Ingmar Bergman. If human fulfilment is a nest of Chinese boxes, each promising to contain the secret, sexual abandon has revealed only a smaller box within. The image of life that emerges from the later poetry of Ginsberg is not one of joy and strength but of exhaustion and despair.

Allen Ginsberg provides final evidence, if any be still thought needed, of the overwhelming importance in poetry of myth—the poet's own conception of himself, and of the dependence of myth upon those poets he chooses to worship and imitate. What Milton and Shakespeare were to Keats, and Marlowe to Hart Crane, Blake, Whitman and Crane were to Allen Ginsberg. There is not only nothing wrong with this process of identification with one's heroes—it is a necessary process. In Ginsberg's case, it helps to account for the surge of released energy which carried him for a few years, perhaps, above the natural level of his own ability. To some extent it is true to say that Ginsberg travelled under Whitman's wingspan, as the wren in the fable borrowed the thrust of the eagle's wings, to stay aloft above his station. The truth is that without the conception of oneself that transcends the limits of the self (without, that is, some form of overreaching) no good poetry would ever be written. Without the projection (and in the projection the forgetting) of the self, the mind is limited to the sum of its sensory particulars. The absence of any transcendent conception of the self is what accounts for the atrophying of the powers of imagination and fantasy in so much twentieth-century verse.

In choosing his gods, Ginsberg made possible one of the most spectacular breakthroughs any poet has achieved since the War: the development from 'On Visions' (1952: printed in *Beatitude Anthology*) to '*HOWL*' is extraordinary. Its releasing impact on the generation of poets who followed more than repays any debt Ginsberg owed culture.

Hardly any of the poetry Ginsberg has written over the past ten years has seemed worthy of the author of '*HOWL*': it has degenerated into tired celebration, orgiastic weariness, almost at times to mental tickertape, breathed into the portable taperecorder *en route* for the next reading. No poet can survive the sort of life Ginsberg has condemned himself to. There is an interesting return to his early Whitman manner in 'Night Gleam'—printed in Gerard Malanga's little anthology compiled for *Transatlantic Review*[8]—in which the 'dull material world' is seen much as it had been in 'A Supermarket in California' and 'Transcription of Organ Music'. It is possible that he may again write poetry as good as he has already written. Otherwise, one's impression is of a keenly intelligent man for some reason talking down to the rest of the world—trying to appear less intelligent than he is. This emerges clearly from Jane Kramer's *Paterfamilias: Allen Ginsberg in America*, a documentation of one period of the poet's life. As important poet, Ginsberg ought to be both master of his own talk and mentor of the young. Instead, we find him so covetous of his 'image'—less guru, perhaps, than groovy elder brother—that he grovels before them, using a language no-one ever spoke, more hippie than the hippie. Talking at Berkeley, Ginsberg sounds like a bad parody of someone acting in a movie of hippie life—one distributed two or three years after it was relevant: 'The things Pound turns you onto are groovy', he says, or 'I get hung up on Bach', and 'I dig Donovan.' People 'connect with Bach.'[9] This is embarrassing and sad from a purifier of the tribe's language. Ironically, later in the scene, a student admits to doing 'Hippie-talk for her anthropology thesis'. The erratic education of the students—wildly esoteric and crassly ignorant by turns, in a kind of Swiftian disavowal of the 'liberal education'—seems of a piece with the abrogation of moral responsibility of a major poet who, at forty-five or thereabouts, simply ought to know better than to kow-tow to people half his age, people who are ironically looking to him for guidance. When a student actually asks him directly for what he proposes in place of the old grey Protestant-work ethic, Ginsberg at last talks straight, though he says little that is of any use to anybody.

What is the significance of this instance of a serious and important poet becoming so pitifully a victim of his own language and self-image? Language is of course inextricably involved with our conception of ourselves—with our 'image'. We speak often not 'from the heart', but in the idiom of the kind of person we want to be, or to be thought to be. Language is itself a mirror of ourselves—or of our self-conception. The psychology of role, of the 'presentation of the self',[10] has been explored more extensively in America than elsewhere, perhaps, and for interesting

[8] *Transatlantic Review* 52 (autumn 1975), 5–29: *An Anthology of New American Poetry*, edited by Gerard Malanga.
[9] Kramer, *Paterfamilias*, 112.
[10] See, for instance, E. Goffmann, *The Presentation of Self in Everyday Life* (London 1969).

reasons. It has been exploited with the utmost brilliance by the advertising industry. I do not know when the word 'image' in its modern sense came into use, or when it was that advertising made the important transition from telling the public that its product was simply better than its rivals', to suggesting to the consumer that he wants to be a particular kind of person, and that the kind of person he wants to be buys this product not another. Role-playing has always been an important part of human behaviour. But the advertising industry has taken an unprecedented part in the formation of self-images, and Americans are fatally vulnerable to its work. The American finds it harder than the European to know who or what he is, and advertising is more prodigiously industrious in America than anywhere else in undermining any durable sense of character, by feeding the consumer with new conceptions of the self, overlaying one role or personality with another.

But the advertising industry is itself simply one of the media, and I am aware of trespassing upon Professor McLuhan's territory. What I am concerned with, as literary critic, is the effect of the media upon language, and upon the living of life that is contingent upon the use of the language. For Ginsberg's case is not isolated. No student of American life can have failed to observe the dramatic increase among American politicians, trade unionists, police officials and businessmen of a self-conscious exploitation of a got-up slang. When Henry Kissinger was threatening to resign in 1974, that most respectable of all American senators, Hubert Humphrey, publicly urged the Secretary of State not to leave his post: 'Cool it. Stay with it. Don't resign.' The message is sufficiently conveyed in the last two words: 'Don't resign.' But Humphrey felt he had to come on trendy, be one of the boys, just as Ginsberg—*mutatis mutandis*—felt he had to with the Berkeley students. The instance could be repeated endlessly. Americans today seem obsessed with idiom of this sort. It is almost as if they feel they have to live up to their reputation they used to enjoy among English lexicographers of coming out with blunt forceful images that somehow went to the core of things. As the Humphrey example shows, bluntness, conciseness, pungency are just what have been lost in the new media-saturated language of America. Where it used to be functional and direct, American slang is now concerned not with *ex*pression, but with *im*pression—the speaker wants the listener to understand what kind of person he wants to be considered. At no time has the poet's role, as Mallarmé saw it, 'donner un sens plus pur aux mots de la tribu', been more important.

Chapter 11

The Development of the New Language

Wieners, Jones, McClure, Whalen, Corso

Even if we see Ginsberg as a wren who used the cover of Whitman's wingspan to fly higher than he could have flown unaided, the fact is that he *did* fly higher—higher than he could have flown had he not had the intelligence and the energy to exploit the various influences that lay in the background; higher than his older contemporaries, the liberal academics who were still cramped and twisted up with the self-consciousness endemic to the ironist tradition. He evaded the grip of the attitudes which were stifling the creative forces of American and English poets—the obligatory alienation, the by now stultifying isolationism, the cowardice of irony, the negativity which eventually congealed into the poetry of nervous breakdown. Ginsberg's breakthrough, such as it was, was a matter not so much of technique as of ideology. The cult of the nervous breakdown is, I have suggested, a phenomenon of affluence, like the extreme self-consciousness of modern America.[1] In this sense it seems relevant to describe the cult of the nervous breakdown in poets like Lowell, Berryman, Roethke, Sexton[2] as ideological symptoms; their varying academicism is only secondarily a technical matter. It is primarily a question of outlook, purpose and belief. If we turn to Allen Ginsberg's poetry or Kerouac's fiction we shall not need to look far for evidence of the spiritual suffering and nervous exhaustion which are part of life in an over-organized but chaotic society like America. The first line of 'HOWL' prepares us for the saga of sickness and pointless debauch we duly get; Kerouac's novels are the reverse of orgiastic: *Big Sur*, for instance, offers one of the most harrowing experiences available to the modern reader. Yet still, 'HOWL' is as different in purpose and impact from Berryman's

---

[1] See page 86 above.

[2] This list of names may suggest to some readers A. Alvarez's *The Savage God* (London 1971). It was not meant to, and I should regard that book too as itself symptomatic. Sylvia Plath's apparent self-sacrifice to this cult is only a particularly fierce example of the feedback: nervous breakdown, the post-Freudian version of Romantic agony, becomes itself not a symptom but a cause of behaviour. Mr Alvarez fails to see the difference between the poetry of nervous breakdown and that of Ted Hughes.

Dream Songs, or a more recent work, like Galway Kinnell's *Book of Nightmares,* as *Big Sur* is from *Herzog.* Ideologically, Ginsberg and Kerouac are in a different age from Berryman and Bellow. And this difference is to be understood less through technical analysis than through an appreciation of a subtle, decisive shift in emphasis and direction. The nightmare is no longer hugged, as providing identity; the isolation no longer clutched, the alienation no longer cherished, the agony no longer needed.

Clearly, a significant element in this change of direction has been the 'feminine' attitude that lies within the counter-culture: to reject order, political or moral, is to deny control. Control demands sustained effort, strain and discipline. There is, perhaps, a causal connection between the Beat rejection of Western, Christian technological civilization and the espousal of an ethic of maximal gratification. No poet better illustrates the new direction taken by poetry in the 1950s and 1960s than John Wieners. Wieners learned his craft, so he says, from Charles Olson.[3] But there is little of the Black Mountain cool about Wieners's own poetry: it is a fascinating instance, in fact, of the interplay between Beat and post-imagist poetics. Much of the technical skill of Wieners's poetry derives from Charles Olson; the actual substance of the poetry owes muce more to Allen Ginsberg, though Wieners bears a closer resemblance to Robin Blaser, perhaps, than to any other poet. In the interestingly neo-Platonist Preface to his *Selected Poems*[4] Wieners observes that 'Verse-making is more than a continuum of principle resting on feminine phenomenological apprehension.' It's the actual occurrence of the notion of the feminine apprehension rather than anything Wieners goes on to say about it that is interesting. The poetry that follows certainly confirms one's expectations of an art from which masculine strain and striving have been eliminated (Ted Hughes's strenuous lines, for instance, seem to belong to a different century). I am not referring to Wieners's passive homosexuality—though this cannot be irrelevant—but rather to the way the poet's sensibility is offered to whatever comes—in his own words, 'The real one of many, the illusory far and near intersect to push behaviour's stream dependent on questing, producing revelatory postures for men, animals and stars.' (The prose is meaningless but not incomprehensible, by the way: its reliance upon a fluent metaphysics—Plato and Bergson filtered through Whitehead and Olson—makes its ellipses and leaps of meaning easy enough to accept.) What follows this *Preface* is painful—lonely, wretched, hung-up, abandoned—but it is not the old Romantic agony, still less old nervous breakdown. The suffering is accepted, as it were, at the point of the mind's growth, the poem takes place at the

---

[3] 'I first met Charles Olson on the night of Hurricane Hazel, September 11, 1954, when I accidentally heard him read his verse . . . and I ain't been able to forget' (*Selected Poems* (London 1972)).

[4] (London 1972).

meeting of the sensibility with phenomena, so that there is something of the imagist freshness and excitement redeeming and renewing the old pain:

> Dirt under my nails,
> my hands hardcaked with
> abuses of lust, despair
> and drugs.
>
> Night a foreign place
> without sound or shadow . . .

(John Wieners, 'Deepsea')

There are as he says, later in the same poem, 'No poems or romance/left, only churning/without image.' He feels that there is nothing to do 'but go on led by flickering of a/flame I cannot name'. It is extraordinary how close the metrics are to Black Mountain without ever evoking the Black Mountain ethos: lacking the perceptual programme behind Black Mountain, Wieners's verse lacks also its tautness, but has by compensation an intimate tender quality. Like Ginsberg, Wieners conveys a sense of being—or feeling that he is—at the centre of what is happening in the world, and it is just this sense which distinguishes Beat poetry and prose not only from academic poetry and prose, but also from the consciously isolationist work of the Black Mountain school. The poetry can safely assume an entire philosophical orientation—not, be it observed, a coherent philosophy, but an orientation, a sense of knowing where one is and of having confidence in a certain loose set of ideas and values. Paradoxically, this art of loneliness and despair is more truly humanist than the well-padded neuroticism of the nervous breakdown school.

Wieners generally succeeds when the metaphysics of romance and reality underlying his verse is held in tension with his own subtle awareness of the grubby world in which he lives. The later work (from *Nerves,* which is, I think, over-represented in the *Selected Poems*) has become trapped in language which shows signs of dangerous over-inflation, and often in sound-play which has little to do with his real subject-matter:

> Better than a closed martinet.
> Better than a locket
> in a lozenge.
> At the market, try and top it
> in the Ritz.

('What Happened?')

Wieners always had a weakness for a rather slack Romantic rhetoric. By now the reader will be aware that the author of this book is committed to disapprove of neither Romanticism nor rhetoric. What other pejorative terms do we have left though, to indict this sort of thing:

> If thou in me the full flush of love see
> Know it comes from the rose that magnifies
> To breath in some corner of that sure sky,
> A coarser blossom than eternity. . . .
>
> ('Mermaid's Song')

Yet the weakness is itself significant, being an invocation not of the Metaphysicals, but of the Romantics. The reorientation was needed. A measure of how precise Wieners's craftsmanship usually is, in fact, can be derived from a comparison of the stanzaic formalism of his Romantic vein with his more natural manner, the manner learned from Olson. 'An Anniversary of Death', printed along with two other poems in *The New Writing in the USA* (1967), has been reissued, with significant alterations, in the *Selected Poems* of 1972. The poem was initially in the form of four quatrains, complete with rhyme-scheme and constant syllable-count. In the second version (which could well be a return to an earlier version), the quatrain-form has been broken up at the end of the last stanza: the third line of this stanza now reads 'because changed, now not the same' instead of 'because now they are not exactly the same'. The alteration is masterly. The need to fill out the pre-ordained quatrain had led Wieners to a slack academicism of expression: the adverb 'exactly' is not only rhythmically feeble, but actually superfluous, since the degree of exactness of change, the agent being time, was not in question. In the same way, the last line of the original version—

sun shines and larks break forth from winter branches

is now broken up into two shorter lines, marshalled according to Black Mountain prosody with the pedantic connective 'and' replaced by a rhythmically powerful caesura and a poignant adjective, 'sad':

> sun shines sad larks break forth
> from winter branches.

We could hardly wish for a better illustration of the difference between the controlled, sensitive prosody of Black Mountain and Beat poetry, and the chained syllable-count of academicism.

At the same time, it is to me distressing that Wieners or his editors should have chosen to exclude from the *Selected Poems* the two beautiful poems ('Not Complete Enough' and My Mother') which accompany the 'Anniversary' in the Penguin volume: a general trend towards a tidier, more presentable poetry seems to be indicated. The excluded poems are both about his mother: they are extraordinarily moving and delicate pieces, utterly without falsity or gesture. In 'My Mother' he watches her 'talking to strange men on the subway': she

> doesn't see me when she gets on,
> at Washington Street

> but I hide in a booth at the side
> and watch her worried, strained face—
> the few years she has got left.

When the poet leans across and says hello, she turns coy:

> She says in an artificial
> voice: Oh, for Heaven's sake!
> as if heaven cared.

How much of us love what we love enough to be able to expose it to the ridicule of truth? The poem ends with a wonderfully natural symbol, not sought for, but inevitable:

> But I love her in the underground
> and her grey coat and hair
> sitting there, one man over from me
> talking together between the wire grates of a cage.

We have to go back to the early Lawrence, it seems to me, to match the quality of this verse. Certainly there is nothing else like it in American writing.

Some indication of the range, subtlety and variety of Beat poetry can be gleaned by turning from Wieners to this poem of Leroi Jones:

> I move slowly. My cape spread stiff & pressing
> in the first night wind off the Hudson. I glide down
>   cautiously
> onto my own roof, peering in at the pitiful shadow
>   of myself.
>
>   ('The Turncoat')

And later in the same poem,

> I dream long bays & towers ... & soft steps on
>   moist sand.
> I become them, sometimes. Pure flight.
>   Pure fantasy. Lean.

The poem to some extent resembles Dylan Thomas's earlier surrealist flights. But where Thomas conveys a sense of having been on a night mission alone, Jones knows that his poem will be read by a community sharing the spiritual values intimated in it. ('Pure flight. Pure fantasy. Lean.') If Jones works often with a short-line technique reminiscent of *The Waste Land*, he has a musicality, a blues sound that is purely his own:

> I am thinking
> of a dance. One I could
> invent, if there
> were music. If you
> would play for me, some

> light music. Couperin
> with yellow hillsides. Ravel
> as I kiss your hair. Lotions
> of Debussy.
> I am moved by what? Angered at its whine;
> the quiet delicacy of my sadness.
>
> ('The Death of Nick Charles')

The techniques again are often those developed from surrealism and symbolism with their emphasis on the primacy of free association:

> Or under the jungle bars, the shadows would
> get in your eyes. More faces. More leaves. A farm sits
> there for years.
>   What do you want now? The street
> disappears. Night breaks down. Dogs bark in blue mist.
>
> (*The System of Dante's Hell*, 2)

The novel, of which this is an extract, in fact gathers strength as Jones drops the associationism, and deals more matter-of-factly with the key incidents. The dual derivation from Rimbaud's *Illuminations* and William Burroughs is interesting and significant.

If we turn from the heavy-handed condescension of most domestic verse, to the exquisitely detached love of Jones's 'For Hettie, in her Fifth Month' we shall be reminded forcefully and in an unexpected way of the superiority of Beat poetry to the verse it displaced. The poem demands quotation in its entirety:

> Aha! what's this?
> because the sky
> is red/& something
> resembling a moon/is
> leaning on the belltower.
> You assume yr. hang-dog look?
>
> Into the room
> not one thing on yr. mind
> (maybe the moon, who knows?)
> but sulking about my head
> curling the pages of the book
> sometimes even whistling/so
> un-ladylike/yr. mother'd frown.
>
> Then pace the room
> chair to chair, in soft spurts
> (leaving a trail of magazines)—
> it's not desperation. But you got to
> go somewhere? (accent last syllable
> for ethnic identification) & smile.

& somedays, not an inch—
(after dragging through the door, tongue out
folding into a chair, staring helplessly
into the kitchen.) Or
in a chair by the window
one finger holding the blind back
so that what sun's left
washes into your womb.

Yr. liabilities? (O, witch of Endor)

A slit in the flesh,
and one of Kafka's hipsters
parked there
with a wheelbarrow.

With its rich complex of attitudes—humour, affection, curiosity, mild irritation—and its sophisticated mix of accuracy and wit, the whole achievement is effortlessly spontaneous and controlled: which is to say, the poet was actually interested enough in a pregnant woman's restlessness to see her behaviour with the detached love of poetry. Jones pays his wife the compliment of actually looking at her with fascination, without shutting off his poetic apparatus as Stephen Spender for instance does when he addresses himself (dutifully) to the domestic front. Love makes 'concern' otiose. Significantly, the next poem in the volume in which the poem appears[5] also refers to Hettie's pregnancy, but in terms honestly off-handed, such as could not appear within the confines of the Confessionals' confessions:

Suddenly one is aware
that nobody really gives a damn.
My wife is pregnant with *her* child.
'It means nothing to me,' sez Strindberg.

('Look for You Yesterday')

The Confessional poets, for all their habitual 'self-awareness', could hardly permit so straight and natural a reflection: we become aware that Beat poetry made not only for a superior life and energy in the writing, but actually for a more direct and meaningful self-knowledge. Precisely because we feel that Leroi Jones, for example, does not cultivate self-awareness as a principle, we accept his words in good faith when he observes:

I am a mean hungry sorehead.
Do I have the capacity for grace?

('Look for You Yesterday')

---

[5] *Preface to a Twenty Volume Suicide Note* (New York 1963).

The question is of a kind that could easily be raised in Confessional verse, but there it would be egotistical, ironical or self-conscious. Precisely because we feel that the Confessionals do not really respect themselves, their confessions are worth less than they ought to be. The dimension of grace established in Jones's question conversely throws the radiance of truth and good faith onto his self-accusation. The distinction involved here, again, is that between self-awareness as an end (which is corrupting) and self-knowledge as a means, achieved through the right exercise of the Self in action.[6]

Jones's combination of qualities—rhythmic subtlety and impressionistic deftness, warm rich physicalness and metaphysical finesse—once again reminds us of the complexity of response of which American poetry became capable in its best moments. It also emphasizes the importance of the feminine element in Beat. Jones's particular 'relaxedness' is partly just black: it is something white poets have learned themselves from modern jazz and its exponents. But it also relates to the Buddhism pervasively present in Beat writing, and to its exploitation of drugs. In Jones's case, it is especially important to understand the complexity of the influences at work, for he is also a peculiarly tense poet. The *racial* awareness was there in his work long before it became rac*ist*. Being black, in fact, constitutes itself an extra dimension in Jones's work—it is itself a vocation. We slight his poetry if we don't see how its subtle packed musicality is put at the service of a preternatural awareness of the unconscious ideology of race. All these matters are raised by what is probably Jones's most often anthologized piece, 'Way Out West'. In a way, this poem epitomizes Beat. It is dedicated, significantly, to Gary Snyder, the hero of Kerouac's *The Dharma Bums* and the most committed Buddhist of the whole movement. I have sufficiently emphasized the significance of the Buddhist orientation of Beat, with its implicit renunciation of order, society, responsibility, guilt and duty. Jones's poem presents the Beat-Zen-Jazz consciousness with incomparable subtlety, in rhythm as well as in syntax:

> As simple an act
> as opening the eyes. Merely
> coming into things by degrees.
>
> ('Way Out West')

That is, waking up from mad Europe's nightmare of will, determination and ambition into truth, the truth of just being. The poem makes the upper-case abstraction a lower-case reality. Awakening to truth means coming to awareness, awareness for instance of

> The leaves. Their
> constant prehensions.
>
> ('Way Out West')

[6] See *The Ironic Harvest*, 19.

Black Mountain imagism is behind this edge. But Jones's poem is warmly, humanly committed as little imagist verse is. And the commitment begins with race: 'Way Out West' is about race-consciousness. It is, by genre, the kind of poem Corso liked to write (viz. 'Poets Hitchhiking on the Highway'), but being black must greatly have complicated and intensified the obscure hostilities the vagrant poets aroused in the small-town mind. 'Way Out West' makes no mention of this: its sensitive courage is a condemnation of narrow intolerance, and a justification, surely, of Jones's later choice of violence. He had so obviously tried, tried so much harder than white people were prepared to try. This awareness perhaps helps to explain the unique quality of the poem, its mix of roughness and sweetness, ancient awe and sad modern futility:

> There are unattractive wild ferns
> outside the window
> where the cats hide. They yowl
> from there at nights. In heat
> & bleeding on my tulips.
>
> Steel bells, like the evil
> unwashed Sphinx, towing in the twilight.
> Childless old murderers, for centuries
> with musty eyes.

('Way Out West')

The poem is also a valediction to tolerance and liberalism. For the time being Jones was prepared to forget, to seek an oblivion of awareness, and the poem ends with a miraculous inversion of its opening:

> Closing the eyes. As
> simple an act. You float

The use so many Beat poets made of drugs also clearly formed part of its basic orientation towards non-striving, passivity and femininity. The experimentation with different drugs carries on the long tradition of *avant garde* spiritual exploration. But the ideal of the narcotic mandarin is a passive world, in which people do nothing because there's nothing they want to do but turn on.[7] It's at this point that one usually starts talking about a new consciousness. It would be better to talk about a new orientation than a new consciousness. Consciousness does not alter: the psychedelic facts still have to be sorted somewhere in the human control-tower. An interesting confirmation of this is Michael McClure's first 'Peyote Poem', written down the day after the experience:

> I KNOW EVERYTHING! I PASS INTO THE ROOM
> there is a golden bed radiating all light
> the air is full of silver hangings and sheathes

[7] See Aldous Huxley, *The Doors of Perception* (London 1954).

I smile to myself. I know
all that there is to know. I see all there
is to feel. I am friendly with the ache
in my belly. The answer
to love is my voice. There is no Time!
No answers. The answer to feeling is my feeling.

It is exhilarating and the moral authority assumed by the poet guarantees
a consistent air of seriousness. It also brought McClure a following: he
seemed in the mid-1960s the poet closest in intention to Timothy Leary.
But this poem is really not typical of the sort of effusion it helped to
encourage from so many other poets.

There is of course a sameness about all mystical and narcotic experience
—or at least about the reports mystics and drug-users have given of it.
Whether the experience is gained through a natural oddity of bodily
chemistry, whether it is deliberately induced or involuntary, whether it is
celebrated in awe or suffered in terror, whether it is mystical or
schizophrenic—the experience of the world we are here concerned with
has certain unvarying properties: we may be familiar with McClure's
intense lighting effects, his sense of great significance and his feeling of
being at the centre of the universe from the works of Blake, De Quincey,
Boehme, Swedenborg, Strindberg—or from a psychiatrist's casebook.
Mysticism and extreme schizophrenia depend as much on the body's
chemistry as the hallucinations of the drug-user. The important variable
is the intellectual context in which they take place—the use, in other
words, which the victim of these bodily states makes of them. This is not
the place to discuss the implications of these ideas. Whether a poet uses
hallucinogens or not, the only question that concerns the reader of what
purports to be poetry is, is the poetry produced good, bad or indifferent?
Nor need this inquiry stay academic. It may be more significant than at
first appears likely, for instance, that Michael McClure's poetry is by no
means always as good as its tone suggests it must be. Poetry—for Michael
McClure as well as for F. R. Leavis—is important beyond the performance of certain linguistic skills. If, to put it bluntly, poetry fails certain
acid-tests, the conclusion critic and reader are justified in drawing is that
there is something more radically wrong with the utterance than some
technical incompetence. This is commonplace. But it needs re-stating
here, I think: for Michael McClure, in the volumes that followed the poem
quoted above, makes certain assumptions, certain claims, which, if
justified, undercut a great deal of conventional intellectual and spiritual
life: the poet, it is claimed, is able with the use of hallucinogens to
penetrate to a layer of experience, of reality, which lies within or beneath
'normal' vision, and is, in some sense 'more true', more real. So the
normal version of the dogma runs. I have already indicated my opinion of
the metaphysical bases of this dogma: hallucinogens cannot be said to

make contact with reality, or truth. They simply change the body's chemistry and thereby its perception, which reverts, unless the equipment is damaged in the process, back to its former state (which we may therefore call 'normal') upon the cessation of the narcotic effect. The most that could be claimed is that it is somehow morally better or healthier to perceive and experience hallucinogenically than in the ordinary way. Rimbaud's *Une Saison en Enfer*, the decline of Coleridge and the testimony of William Burroughs suggest otherwise, but this is not, as I have said, the place to discuss that question. What is relevant here is the question, how do the aesthetic facts bear out the metaphysics? Why, and how, does McClure's verse fail? What are the moral implications of the aesthetic facts?

If McClure had been right, he ought to have hit a poetic gusher: there ought to be no difference between one poem and the next, whereas in fact there are enormous differences—of quality, tone, effect—even within one passage of one poem. Excellent as McClure's best drug poems are, there is little evidence of his having achieved the goal of every poetic mineralogist: the level of his verse fluctuates wildly, it moves from near-sublimity to near-bathos from one line to the next. This is so in the peyote poem already quoted. This, for instance, is the note hit so monotonously by psychosis—'I KNOW EVERYTHING!' McClure's poetry, like Christopher Smart's, moves into and out of relevance, while itself apparently remaining convinced of its own oracular profundity. The nuttiness of 'I KNOW EVERYTHING!' is familiar to many users of hallucinogens, to say nothing of alcohol. Everyone who has ever been drunk or high knows this feeling of *significance*: the things said in this state—afterwards recollected to have been quite trivial—seem at the time to be tremendously, ultimately, profound. Later, in the same poem, McClure tones it down and drops the block capitals—'I know all that I need to know'—arrogant still perhaps, but not absurd. The second statement occurs after a passage of considerable beauty—

> The dark brown space behind the door is precious,
> intimate, silent, still. The birth-place
> of Brahms.

('Peyote Poem')

That is an adjective sequence, we feel, which might have come into being without the peyote, though it's unlikely that the actual instigation—the space behind the door—would have caused it. Not so the Nerval-ish pretensions of 'I read the meanings of scratched walls and cracked ceilings'. This is surely private—an attestation only. Poetry comes into existence in the space between the poet and the world, between his experience and ours. McClure's over-use of upper-case type is a telltale sign of exasperation, an inability to communicate. But poetry, to say it another way, is not—much pseudo-symbolist claptrap to the contrary—concerned with the incommunicable, but with the *otherwise incommunicable*. Chairs are inexpressible, if you like, but our experience of them, or what this experience means to us, is not. In the same way, McClure's poetry succeeds when it is not trying to gesticulate towards the INEXPRES-SIBLE, but precisely when it concerns itself with the frontier-land between the experience of drugs and his own waking consciousness, between his extraordinary experience and our own more ordinary. It is, in other words, half-critical, half-comparative. It is blasphemous to seek to 'say' God, to say what should be left unsaid. The true mystic's concern is what his experience teaches him and his readers about the whole meaning and conduct of life itself. Much of McClure's poetry invalidates itself in trying to declare the undeclarable. So, in the peyote poem under discussion, the interesting and comprehensible statement,

> Here in my Apartment I think tribal thoughts

(we think of Wise Indians smoking pipes of peace, of the wholeness the white man has lost), is followed by a straight line ruled across the page, and then the single word 'STOMACHE!!!' It is hard to know which is funnier, the upper-case type or the triple exclamation marks. Here, truly, is the absurd of drunkenness, the ludicrous conviction of *significance*. It is a phenomenon which could be illustrated at random from any of McClure's longer poems, those sprawling numinous extravanganzas. This is the sort of thing 'poor Kit Smart' stumbled on in his madness: 'STOM-ACHE'! In this instance, McClure immediately goes on to fish out a genuinely fascinating emblem from the unconscious—

> I am visited by a man
> who is the god of foxes
> there is dirt under the nails of his paw
>   fresh from his den.
> We smile at one another in recognition.

The episode is strangely meaningful, though its significance is hard to define without talking in Jungian terms about archetypes and collective memories. Anyway, McClure's memory becomes ours here: the weirdly alarming beauty of childhood is skilfully conjured up. Almost at once—so drastic are McClure's transitions—the scene vanishes: the poet closes his eyes—'Closing my eyes there are flashes of light—My eyes won't focus but leap.' The reporting here is interesting and to the point: the physio-logical facts are relevant at this juncture. We want to know what it feels like, what actually happens, and he tells us, with a frank courage which is an important part of McClure's make-up. It doesn't seem important in the same way to know that he then felt he had three feet. But the odd detail—'I see seven places at once'—has a factual authenticity which tells us something we ought to know about the trip. Throughout this passage, indeed, the reporting is absorbing and pointful, probably because it keeps the inner narrative closely related to the outside world. 'Seeing the loose chaos of words on the page'—we all know that aspect of language. In the middle of the passage there is another hilarious interjection—'STOM? ACHE!'—which must, but can't, be ironical; then, after another line ruled across the page, McClure again tells us solemnly of his feelings about his belly:[8]

> My belly and I are two individuals
> joined together
> in life.

The conclusion of the poem, however, returns to the archetypal world to which it is McClure's peculiar gift and privilege to be able to penetrate:

> I stare into clouds seeing
> their misty convolutions.
>
> The whirls of vapor
> I will small clouds out of existence.
>
> They become fish devouring each other.
> And change like Dante's holy spirits
> becoming an osprey frozen skyhigh
> to challenge me.

('Peyote Poem')

Those ospreys, like the fox-man, earlier and the lion men in the beautiful short poem 'The Child', come from an impersonal realm, a timeless symbol-bank, which sets all the rest of the hallucination in a meaningful context. All McClure's best verse connects his drug-experience with some deeper, broader metaphoric layer, and in just this connection lies the poetry:

> COLD COLD COLD COLD COLD COLD COLD COLD
> COLD AND FAR AWAY
> and we are not cold in our space and not cool
> and not indifferent. And I do
> not mean this as a metaphor or fact.
> Even the strained act it is.
>
> Bending by the brook and filling cups.

('Peyote Depression')

The last line suddenly makes contact with Chinese religious thought; at the same time, it provides a metaphor for life itself which is at once ancient and original. The 'fact-act' echo here reminds us again of McClure's verbal subtlety, subtlety evident more in a non-narcotic piece, like 'Canoe: Explication' which reveals most strikingly McClure's provenance from Robert Duncan:

---

[8] Peyote characteristically produces intense stomach pains, which McClure has duly—but unpoetically—honoured.

G*

> It's the imagined song, the concept
>   of anarchy set to music
> Wavering, symmetrical, unsymmetrical
> Pointed and strange as a matchflame
>   Held in sunlight.

The almost invisible image (so much more apt than Olson's shot at the same thing) beautifully captures the elusiveness of the thought. The same delicacy is applied later to the motion of the canoe:

> A volta appears—the serene charged pause.
>   Thought alone wonders
>   At the connection
> And the duet begins again.

The simple yet subtle physical event—canoeing—has been 'explicated' by the metaphor of music, just as the experience of hearing music has been enlarged by the physical analogy. The slightness of the theme produces a poetry of equal delicacy. McClure is a poet with or without drugs.

Whether he has realized his enormous potential is another matter. Since he came down from his narcotic plateau—a decade ago now— McClure has written a great deal of good poetry. Its sheer quantity indeed makes it impossible for this kind of survey to do it anything like justice. It is enough to say that at its best it achieves a poise and a sinewy delicacy rarely to be found in recent American writing. Its essence is a clarification and refinement of the archetypal symbolism which emerged so excitingly from the highs and lows of his peyote poems.

His best poems balance on a needle-point, yet are as sure as rock. What we might perhaps question is their power to engage our deepest human interest. Here is a more recent instance of this quasi-Blakean mode:

> EACH
> MAMMAL
> does
> a
> small perfect
> thing
> like
> to be himself
> or herself
> and to hold a new creation
> on a shining platter
> as he
> (or she)
> steps towards
> the waiting car.

('For Robert Creeley')

A derivate of Duncan's pedestal pieces, this poem has the shape of a baroque fountain. But one wonders whether it doesn't also share that non-problematicness essential to Duncan's often rather bland celebrations. The central assertion of the poem—that each created mammal (especially, by implication, man) is in itself perfect and in need of celebration—is finely illustrated by the final clause—the step towards the waiting car. No matter how trivial or transient the act, the poem asserts, we are in ourselves at any point perfect. But little of that complexity of all good poetry is generated out of the combination of the two major elements of the poem: we look in vain for that tension of contraries that gives Blake's smallest poems such force. Beat poetry offered Blakean celebration as opposed to existentialist nihilism. But it also offered at its best—in McClure's best peyote poems, in 'HOWL', in Corso's 'Mutation of the Spirit'—an awareness of the foulness and complexity of the conditions against which the capacity for joy has to strive. I have noted above that Whitman himself shortcircuited exploration by the expedient of mass-acceptance—acceptance which really accepted nothing, since it did not *know* what it was claiming to accept. Much of Michael McClure's later poetry, like much of Duncan's, seems to me to limit itself by a desire to say 'Yea', or, still worse, to tell the rest of us that *we* ought to say 'Yea'—yet without admitting all the facts. There is a feeling that the affirmativeness has been too easily acquired.

That vital intelligence characteristic of the best Beat poetry of the 1960s has gradually gone under to an elegant and stylish blandness. The impression is reinforced rather than gainsaid by the obligatory abuse of easy targets—the Pentagon, the Man in the Grey Flannel Suit, and so on. But McClure is still—comparatively—young, and we have not seen his best.

No poet illustrates the sophistication of Beat poetry more strikingly than Philip Whalen. Whalen's stock-in-trade is an attractive self-awareness, a wry, biting humour, a negligent familiarity with the numinous that contrasts interestingly with Michael McClure's solemnity:

> The trouble with you is
> That sitting on a bench in the back yard
> You see an old plank in the fence become
> A jewelled honeycomb of golden wires
> Discoursing music, etc.
> (Whalen, 'Denunciation, Or, Unfrock'd Again')

The subject-matter of the poem is much the same as in McClure's verse; but the psychedelic experience, the mind-changing effect of the drug, is not dashed down in rapt awe. It becomes a source of self-mockery:

> The trouble is aggravated by the grass
> Flashing alternately green and invisible

> Green and non-existent
> While the piano in the house plays
> *The Stars and Stripes Forever*

The self-mockery is more fertile, more purposeful than we had been accustomed to expect in modern verse. There is no covert self-satisfaction in the self-unmasking:

> The trouble with you is you keep acting
> Like a genius: Now you're not a genius
> You're nothing but a prick ... in fact you're
> Not even that, you're nothing but a son-of-a-bitch
> GET OUT OF MY HOUSE!

Whalen obviously does find himself absurd, yet remains quite confident of the significance of what he has experienced:

> What plant put out those
> Tall thin stiff green leaves? Lines
> Drawn from the tip of each one
> Would describe the surface of what
> Regular solid polyhedron?
> You don't dare invent a name.

So closely are Whalen's satiric wit and his intellectual insight related. Once again, we are reminded of the significance of the new release of humour and wit: here surely is something like the wholeness of sensibility it was the design of intellectualist criticism to guarantee with irony? Behind Whalen, as behind Leroi Jones, is the complex efficiency of Black Mountain imagism, with its subtle sense of vegetable life:

> Bud-clusters hang straight down from the sharply crooked
> Geranium stem like strawberries, the wild mountain kind
> These flowers almost as wild right here
> Barbarous thick-jointed tangle, waist-high
> Escaped once for all from the green-houses of the north
> A weed, its heavy stalks jointing upwards and winding out
> In all directions, too heavy to stand straight
> The neighbors clipped some out of their yard
> The stalks lay in the gutter and grew for days
> In the rain water, flowering
> Ignorant of their disconnection.

> ('Soufflé—Take IX')

The endless 'takes' and jottings do, to some extent, betray a disorganized mind. Whalen has never produced the *magnum opus* he seems intellectually qualified to have written. Instead, there are the shorter ironic pieces ('For C', 'Fond Farewell to the *Chicago Quarterly*') which are often perfect, and the longer, fragmented works which only occasionally achieve the moments of penetrating insight:

The wind increases as the sun goes down
The weight of that star pulling air after it
Naturally the prune trees blossom now
And some kind of bush with pink trumpets flowers
All the other trees except acacias have quit.

('Soufflé—Take III')

It seems to have been Whalen's destiny, his function perhaps, to accept a kind of failure. We may speculate once again on the influence of the feminization of the mind encouraged by Buddhism. It is unlikely that a forthright Christian ethic of duty, obligation and striving would have been able to give us the things Whalen has given. If we compare him with Roethke, for instance, whom he resembles in many ways (they write the tragicomedy of obesity), Roethke's labour and strain seem inadequate recompense for the loss of the humour and the play of mind Whalen's detachment affords him:

All day Christmas the sea whirled this tangle—
Spruce logs, redwood stumps, fishboxes and lightglobes—
A big eddy at the creek mouth
Carting back several tons of debris back and forth
          across a hundred feet of beach
In water maybe a foot and a half in depth.

('Letter to Mme E T S, 2.1.58')

Curiously, many of Whalen's most strange and powerful perceptions are, like this, entirely unmetaphoric. It is enough, he intimates, merely to observe. There is, in my opinion, nothing in Carlos Williams or Olson to match the eerie reality of these things in Whalen. 'All that comparison ever does,' Olson had observed,[9] 'is set up a series of reference points: to compare is to take one thing and try to understand it by marking its similarities to or differences from another thing.' Yet Olson's own verse swills around pointlessly, unless some metaphor creeps in.[10] It is to Whalen that we must turn for evidence of the power of annotated reality.

This is especially true of the earlier work. *Like I Say* (1950–58) still seems his best collection. The wryness is already there. But the intelligence about himself (what we have come to regard as intelligent behaviour in a poet this century being largely a matter of laughing at himself) is displayed as much in the mental energy that vaults beyond itself in order to see itself as it is in the self-deprecation. Whalen notes his failure—his obesity, his never getting anything done—with an athletic intellectuality strangely inconsistent with it and with the image of himself that he otherwise projects in his verse. This intellectual energy was what made possible the notation of unadorned reality just noted as being so important in

[9] 'Towards a human universe', 187.
[10] Viz. 'what blows about and blocks a hole where the wind was used to go?'

Whalen's verse: the logs swilling about in the tide, the cut-off flowers still growing—these things are comprehended by an act of the imagination, in Coleridge's understanding of the term, not copied by a prose-camera. In his best pieces Whalen sets these natural images in a sound-pattern of considerable subtlety and a very complex intellectual frame. 'Homage to Lucretius' (written in 1952, printed in the *Evergreen Review* of 1956, included in *Monday in the Evening*, 1961) suggests a systematic scheme in the title which is belied in the characteristic throw-away manner:

> It all depends on how fast you're going
> Tending towards light, sound
> Or the quiet of mere polarity

But the casual manner is supported here (or it supports) a very wide-ranging and economically presented argument. 'We want crystals,' he observes, but 'can't easily imagine another world'—and the reason is that this one (we remember at this point the atoms of Lucretius) is itself 'barely/Visible'. Enough to say that this genuinely philosophical inquiry lacks altogether the portentousness of Robert Duncan's pronouncements, but also that it succeeds in giving the abstract speculation a natural expression: the root-experience, which, I imagine, gave rise to the poem in the first place, is now disclosed, to fill out and illustrate the Lucretian speculations which were in fact suggested by it:

> We lined up and pissed in a snowbank
> A slight thaw would expose
> Three tubes of yellow ice. . . .
> And so on. . . .

The last phrase is disarming, and—of course—charming: we are meant to be delighted by the performance, and we are. This seems to me to be close in many ways to William Empson's more successfully philosophical explorations. What is characteristic of Whalen is not just the colloquial casualness which he shares with Empson, but the ease with which he succeeds in giving the insights—the piss frozen into tubes yields an insight into 'A world not entirely new, But realized . . .'—a greater context of meaning. And the point is this meaning, not the attractive casualness, which is merely instrumental.

At his best, Whalen succeeds in relating this order of intelligence to the random events of a life—wasted, according to the world's view, in meditations, reading, and staring out of the window—and in holding it all in one perspective. The best of these complex efforts to marshal everything is, in my opinion, 'Sourdough Mountain Lookout' (1955–1956), which displays, in its moments of inertia and fatigue, as much as in its explosions of mental energy, a wholeness rare in contemporary writing:

Then I'm alone in a glass house on a ridge
Encircled by chiming mountains
With one sun roaring through the house all day
& the others crashing through the glass all night
Conscious even while sleeping. . . .

The poem exercises a fine virtuosity of feeling, moving from sharp imagist observation, instinct with life, to the inward world, the relations between which are Whalen's real theme. The intellectual vitality which holds together the details and the percepts is revealed also in the apparently random reading which structures the poem: Heraclitus, Byron, Empedocles, Buddha—the sources and influences file into and out of the poem according to a rhythm of walking, resting, climbing and reflection. When he is tired ('pooping out, exhausted'), the ironic awareness of himself comes to the surface ('Remember smart guy there's something/Bigger, something smarter than you'). And this wry self-ridicule—what a reader fresh to Whalen is most likely to take away from the experience—is a product of his intellectual vigour as much as the ability to 'get round'—come round the back of—his wider intellectual interests. He concludes with a generalization that holds the whole of what has gone before easily within itself:

What we see of the world is the mind's
     Invention and the mind
Though stained by it, becoming
Rivers, sun, mule-dung, flies—
Can shift instantly
A dirty bird in a square time. . . .
                    ('Sourdough Mountain Lookout')

Such reflections upon the relations between the mind and the outer world constitute Whalen's major theme. It is a slippery ramp to get on: it is easy to feel, in moving through *On Bear's Head*, that Whalen is too clever for his own good. He does not work up the excitement in the face of the world which we see in the best of McClure; he cannot, it could be, put all the bits together right. He finds it easier to negate what he has just said than to find reasons for moving from it onto something greater. Scepticism is his essence.

It was Gregory Corso, perhaps, who suggested most powerfully what Beat was to be capable of. He stands in relation to Allen Ginsberg as Burroughs does to Kerouac. Where Ginsberg is all expression and voice, Corso is calm and quick, whimsical often, witty rather than humorous, semantically swift rather than prophetically incantatory. His early verse carries on the wit of Dickinson, with a fine surrealist fantasy:

The light that makes us a friend of eagles
has made our poor wounds an interval of clouds,
slow and creeping, calm and sad,
in the skyful dungeon of things.

('One Day')

The surrealism is taken as lightly and deftly as it should be: collocations like 'pie glue',[11] 'telephone snow', 'cat shovel', 'Firestones! Gas! Couch!', 'old Dutch shoes', 'nineteen twenties Norwegian stamps', 'twig smear', 'Roman coin soup', 'Christmas teeth', 'apple deaf', are meant to throw light on things, to illuminate the experiences of which they are severally composed. This has been commonplace poetic practice since the symbolists: Rimbaud's violent yoking together of opposites was applied systematically by the surrealists, and in essentially the same spirit. But Corso's orientation is quite different: the surrealist, following the symbolist, built up a hermetic wall around his sensibility: his creative identity depended upon the mysteriousness of his own words. He was afraid he would cease to exist—in his own mind—if his utterances became less cryptic. The Romantic poet's claim to be an unacknowledged legislator of the world had become strangely transmuted over the intervening hundred years. From the time of the symbolists, the poet had taken to cherishing his alienation as his last surviving claim to existence. The *avant garde*—for all its affectation of disgust for bourgeois obtuseness —had in fact always striven rigorously to repulse any attempted bourgeois fraternization: the public's acceptance of an *avant garde* idiom was always the sign for a rapid withdrawal to higher ground. The artist since Flaubert and Baudelaire has not tried to make himself understood by the bourgeois: on the contrary, he has worked hard to preserve his obscurity, while all the time capitalizing on the bourgeois's sociopolitical guilt to make the bourgeois itself feel responsible for the 'gap'. The gap has now been obliterated: there was no going beyond Pollock's painting and Cage's 'music'. It was the Beats who first made possible the *rapprochement* which has transformed art and literature over the past decade. The Beats were never an alienation movement in the *avant garde* tradition. On the contrary, theirs was primarily a spirit of acceptance, of celebration, of optimism. It was openly enthusiastic for a way of life which yielded more spiritual sustenance, more sheer well-being than the life of the organization man. But it avoided the limiting non-alignment of the liberal intellectual; because he really subscribes to (that is, coheres with, lives in, fails radically enough to dissent from) the values of the society he is intellectually committed to deploring, the liberal intellectual is thrown back upon irony. The question is, again, basically ideological. The tortuous (ironical) writings of writers like Bellow, Lowell, Roethke, Auden and Empson can be explained satisfactorily only in terms of

---

[11] 'Pie glue' is exceptional, in fact—a satirical version of 'I do'.

ideology. And only ideological considerations can make complete sense of poetry like Gregory Corso's.

This could be illustrated in some of the poems from which the already cited neo-surrealist collocations are taken—'Marriage', for instance or 'One Day'. In the first, we find that the relations between poet and society are quite different from what we find to be the case in T. S. Eliot: the poet's satiric humour allows compassion for 'Mrs Kindhead', whose community chest *is* well-meaning and, as far as it goes, admirable. The poet's rejection of marriage does not have the muted bitterness of Eliot's 'Prufrock'. Its laughter is, indeed, infectious.

But the point will emerge more impressively from a consideration of a later, more mature poem.

Mutation of the Spirit (1967) synthesizes his best qualities with a new seriousness. It opens with a breathtaking paragraph that seems almost the only verse since written to rival the ease, poise, sophistication and rapidity of *The Waste Land*'s opening run-in:

> Last night a white apple fell from the loneliest
>   tree in the world.
> Today the field is green the sun bright and warm knit
> Children attend their spirits the old knit knit
> Chicken cries Sacramental sobs from the chapel a
>   window closes
> Loneliness grandeur and blue lambs whorled eyes
>   rinsed light
> Swimming deer and now the long hike back to the city
> Smells of rats and pasty poisons horizons of fuming
>   domes dynamos
> Vast sick sense smudgepots gasping black smoke
> Cheese-cloth faces dead carts bells a white arm
> A long pale arm falls across the port.

The section that follows provides a list of Blake–Smart definitions that imply a maturation of Beat ideals: instead of the usual opting for craziness and the mad, Corso's definitions insist on a severe normality:

> Imperfection may discredit the rare the odd
> Yet shall perfection honour the typical
> Blemishes humiliate the outlandish the unique the strange
> Yet excellence extols the orthodox the natural

Corso's direction at the head of the poem claims that these pages of verse may be read in whatever order one chooses. Yet I fancy he would rather have it read in the order in which it is printed. The first line *is* a first line if ever there was one, and the alternation of lucid density in the first paragraph with the abstract norms of the second recalls the procedures of *The Waste Land*. The action of the poem is also a setting of lands in order, like Eliot's poem:

It's no longer When will I break through this dream
        suddened upon my by questioning life
No longer is it A life unquestioned
        did well enough unquestioned
No the signals are clear I can hear
        and I can ask
        Who is that man whose snip-snap
        makes him more than that mark madcap
        Please who is he tell wild salvo

The mutations involve pop mythology ('Dusty Bright'—a sexually
ambiguous figure who 'is to the sun what the sun is to the earth the sun's
sun') and sinister figures from the declining days of Rome. In fact the
whole poem is poised between a sense of civic disaster ('S is axed from P,
and Q from R is tore') and an extraordinary elation of spirit, exulting in
symbols and images of ecstatic cool transcendence:

O there is burning snow flickering the air
and white velvet sloths in the falling sun
and flamewhite bears tip-toeing across the trees
and oh there are streams of luminous fish in mountain winds
and seldom beasts winking in snowclouds
O zero zoo invisibility

There is throughout a sense of having to make the final decisions—
'come standby spirit my spirit fails'—in other words, a mature but not
disabused reckoning, the kind of spiritual setting forth John Bunyan
made once. As in Kerouac's *Big Sur*, the Beat life itself, which is what is
in a way being placed (if not rejected), enabled Corso to get to this starting-
out point.

The basic elements of his earlier work appear transformed in this poem.
There are the mythic personages—the Ares, for instance, of 'Ares Comes
and Goes' becomes 'real opportunity', the new friend the poet says he's
'gonna follow to the end'. By means of such devices Corso has much
freer access to regions of behaviour and decision than is afforded by
conventional introspective methods. In fact Corso had always shown great
sophistication in his use of archaism, allegorical figures, fantasy and wit.
All these elements of his art lend their weight to *Mutation of the Spirit*.
The peculiar balance of the poem—its intensity and coolness, its force
and delicacy, its urgent expectancy and moral seriousness—expresses
Corso's own sensibility. But it expresses as well the intelligent flexibility
of the poetic tradition to which it seems at the moment something like an
apogee.

Ten years before it would have been unrealistic to expect from poetry
in English a statement as mature and yet as joyously alive, as generally
relevant and yet as unpompous as this:

> Everywhere here and way beyond there
>   suns glow with accordant liberties
> Paradise even pervades Hell cleansing like a bell
> The final gong deafens the sacrosanct room from its door
>   from its halls its rooms Paradise evermore
>   glowed with laughing liberties
> A hell-less universe is on its knees

(Mutation of the Spirit)

This seems to me to possess the classic strength, the clear joyous clash of great poetry. Every poem today is written under the eye of the Bomb. Between the fake demonic celebrations of Doom, and the sturdy pretence that it isn't there, between shaggy Beat gloom-consciousness and square commonsense, Corso's poem finds what seems to be the only true path. It is saturated with an awareness of imminent destruction, that emerges in a halo of ultimate purity (the 'burning snow', 'blue lambs', 'rinsed light', 'swimming deer'). Yet it enjoins neither *carpe diem*, nor despair, nor carelessness, nor irresponsibility. 'Come adorned in sun foliage in the final mutation in this God-closed age,' Corso exhorts. 'Ahead is black' and 'The decencies of life have lost their way', but still, total engagement is all that can be urged. As the poem begins, surely and beautifully, so it closes on a sure final cadence:

> Arise new spirit unroll a nadir wool
> From tip to top the source is measured full
> The eternal exists as well in the ephemeral
> Air is everywhere and life is changeable
> In the yard of the old sun retired spirits sleep
> Into the pool of night the swimmer of light leaps.

(Mutation of the Spirit)

Chapter 12

Devices Among Words

Kinnell, Bly, Simic

The poetry of the Beat period is urban, swift, cutting across the face and body of America, and opening up its potential. It neither begins nor ends anywhere—but its first important statement is '*HOWL*' and it comes to a climax in *Mutation of the Spirit*. Proliferation was abundant, production reckless: ease and sophistication were acquired, if force and drive were lost, as a plurality of traditions merged. Perhaps its most important *rencontre* was the one documented in Kerouac's novels *The Subterraneans*, *The Dharma Bums* and *Desolation Angels*: the confluence of the New York energy and the always more pastoral, reflective Black Mountain tradition, sophisticatedly sure of its spiritual orientation, as it surfaced at San Francisco. Although the East Coast writers, principally Ginsberg, Corso and Kerouac, were in a minority and in the position of novices at the feet of Duncan, Snyder, Rexroth, Whalen and others, it was largely their energy and moral seriousness which touched off the revolution, such as it was, that arguably took America finally and for the first time out of cultural provincialism. For, if the younger poets had taken what they needed—by way of a refinement of the coastline of feeling—from Olson and the Black Mountain group, there is reason to believe that the poetry of the West Coast, learned and relaxed and faintly superior, would soon have foundered under its own inbred wisdoms.

Yet although the sheer volume of the poetry since published deters confident generalization, it seems to me now that a deceleration has taken place, and that the swift, intelligent and essentially human poetry of the Beat period has been replaced by a more self-assured, ruminant and safe verse. There can be no turning the clock back, of course. As in France after impressionism, everyone has been affected. The old academicism has gone for good, just as the *Pompier* painting that had previously filled the salons of middle nineteenth-century Paris simply disappeared over the last decades of the century. A certain freedom of manner, genuinely 'colloquial' and honest, and a certain loose *congerie* of attitudes based on the Beat–Black Mountain ideals (religious, affirmative, critical, exalted, rather than dour, downward and ironically self-probing) have been absorbed into what would have been the academic establishment, so that a once easily recognizable enemy is no longer there to be smoked out. Nevertheless, the American moment has, it seems to me, passed, much as it seems to have in painting. The dense, often turgid complexities of Pollock and de Kooning on the one hand, and the urgent release of Barnet Newman's abstraction on the other, have evaporated, leaving us with the beautiful emptiness of Morris Louis and Helen Frankenthaler, the cool vacuity of Dan Flavin's strip-lighting. The dangers of a too-easy acquaintance with the Absolute were early foreseen by Harold Rosenberg: 'Never so many unearned masterpieces! Works of this sort lack the dialectical tension of a genuine act, associated with risk and will. When a tube of paint is squeezed by the Absolute the result can only be a Success.'[1] In poetry, as well, a void opened up towards the end of the 1960s.

The clearest sign of this is the element of reaction, less in the production of a different kind of poetry than in the more general endorsement of certain poets who had practised during the Beat period. Without the masterworks of the period (*Mutation of the Spirit, Big Sur, The System of Dante's Hell, The Naked Lunch, 'HOWL'*) really having been acknowledged, the American literary establishment has confirmed its election of new representatives. Of Galway Kinnell's poem 'The Avenue Bearing the Initial of Christ into the New World', Selden Rodman wrote: 'I do not hesitate to call this the freshest, most exciting, and by far the most readable poem of a bleak decade.'[2] John Logan called it 'a remarkable 450 line poem hard to match in American literature, drawn from contemporary life around Avenue C in New York.'[3] James Dickey, finally, remarked that 'It is not entirely impossible that the Wave of the Future may turn out to have begun at Avenue C, or some place within walking distance.'[4]

These judgements show more than the persistence of the American craving for the Great American Poem; they amount, I think, to a repudiation of Allen Ginsberg and the Beats as a whole. (The 'bleak decade' Rodman speaks of was among the richest in American writing this century.[5]) Once again, the American literary establishment has failed its poets, as it had failed Crane, Lindsay, Rexroth and Patchen before. For all the conservatism Americans are inclined to impute to it, the English establishment has not characteristically been guilty of this order of blindness. Eliot and Pound were more rapidly established in London than it is likely that they would have been in New York or Chicago; and the best poets born in Britain—Dylan Thomas, Spender, Auden, Gascoyne, Sitwell— were, with few exceptions, more or less immediately recognized.

[1] 'The American action painters', in H. Geldzahler, *New York Painting and Sculpture: 1940–1970* (London 1969), 346.
[2] *New York Times Book Review*, 18 September 1960, 50.
[3] *Commonweal* 73, 4 November 1960, 154.
[4] *Poetry Chicago* 97, February 1961, 319.
[5] The decade included Ginsberg's *'HOWL'*, Duncan's *Roots and Branches*, Levertov's *The Jacob's Ladder*, Rexroth's *The Defense of the Earth* and Patchen's *The Cloth of the Tempest*.

When we turn to Kinnell's poem, what do we in fact find? Something 'drawn from' the life around Avenue C in New York indeed—drawn from it as Paul Hogarth might 'draw from' Peking or Shanghai a notebook of sketches for *Tribune* or the *Guardian*. Kinnell sees New York and its exotic Jews much as a tourist might savour Amsterdam's fleamarket or London's Petticoat Lane:

> In sunlight on the Avenue
> The Jew rocks along in a black fur shtraimel,
> Black robe, black knickers, black knee-stockings,
> Black shoes. His beard like a sod-bottom
> Hides the place where he wears no tie.
> A dozen children troop after him, barbels flying,
> In skullcaps. They are Reuben, Simeon, Levi, Judah,
>   Issachar, Zebulun, Benjamin, Dan, Napthali, Gad, Asher.

('The Avenue Bearing the Initial of Christ into the New World')

There seems more than a suspicion that Kinnell is using people here, these dramatically poor Jews whose exotic headgear and outlandish names have to be pointed out.

> The Downtown Talmud Torah
> Blosztein's Cutrate Bakery
> Areceba Panataria Hispano
> Peanuts Dried Fruit Nuts & Canned Goods
> Productos Tropicales
> Appetizing Herring Candies Nuts
> Nathan Kugler Chicken Store Fresh Killed Daily
> Little Rose Restaurant. . . .

This whole passage (there is as much again in the same vein as I have quoted) fails in its purpose to evoke the 'rich' life of the neighbourhood; it is a jumble of assorted names; rhythm has vanished, and the phenomena and names named merely clutter what they are meant to illumine. Poetry is a viciously exacting art: we apprehend as irrelevance not any technical offence against a norm of economy, but the poet's fundamental lack of engagement in the subject. Kinnell has tried to conjure up a ghetto here, in the way that Tadeusz Rozewicz conjures Warsaw, William Saroyan Chicago, or Izaac Babel Odessa. The poet here simply has not 'seen' or appropriated these things, because he has not loved them enough. He is exploiting them, even if he is doing it 'sincerely', and the result is offensive, especially when he comes to refer to the Nazi concentration camps.

The point is reinforced when we come to consider what Kinnell can do well, what he does see, as he has not seen these Jews in their historical agony. For Kinnell specializes, inevitably, in bits of observation 'well done' in the mid-century manner, though somewhat after the manner of Crane's 'The Tunnel':

> The motherbirds thieve the air
> To appease them. A tug on the East River
> Blasts the bass-note of its passage, lifted
> From the infra-bass of the sea.

('The Avenue Bearing the Initial of Christ into the New World')

Later, 'A propane- / gassed bus makes its way with big, airy sighs.' (ll. 15–16) and 'a crate of lemons discharges lights like a battery'. Such effects are competent in themselves, but they are certainly not welded by a presiding consciousness, or made to play their part in a scenario of values. They sacrifice what vitality they might have had to the demands of an unrewarding context.

What this means is that Kinnell—at this stage, at least—has no real voice or creative personality. The verse is free of rhetoric, it eschews the 'poetic' as studiously as the Pre-Raphaelites sought it, and seems to think that in doing so it has done its job. But in fact no matter how rhetorical (Milton) or hieratic (Eliot) it may be, verse can only live through 'voice', and Kinnell has none to offer. It has a certain egotism in place of the reserve of the older academic—this much has been gained. So what? The successes in Kinnell's later poetry are in the Eberhart neo-Platonist vein. An example is the last poem of the sequence 'Flower Herding on the Mountain':

> In the forest I discover a flower.
> The invisible life of the thing
> Goes up in flames that are invisible,
> Like cellophane burning in the sunlight.

The piece as a whole is one of Kinnell's most successful, though it is characteristic of his manner that one is constantly reminded of other poets—of Levertov here and her 'almost–silent/ripping apart of giant sheets/of cellophane'. No-one of course has a monopoly on the word 'cellophane', but there is a disturbing similarity in the two poets' exploitation of its transcendental possibilities. Levertov's angle on the transcendental is altogether more natural, human and involved than Kinnell's. Kinnell's metaphysicality reminds one rather of René Char:

> Terre en quoi l'orchidée brûle,
> Ne le fatiguez pas de vous.

('Poème pulvérisé')

As in Eberhart's 'The Groundhog', the phenomenal flower (hog) is conceived in its Platonic essence as it burns its way to purity. Behind this way of thinking is the late symbolist tradition: the Valéry of 'Cimetière Marin' and Valéry's French successors, Supervielle and Char himself. Levertov, we recall, included a version of a Supervielle poem ('A Horse Grazing') in her collection, *The Jacob's Ladder*. Thus, Kinnell's poem takes its place in a complex enough tradition, but one which always founded its validity upon the poet's being able to draw the Platonist themes into direct relationship with himself and his own destiny. Valéry's great poem comes to a climax in the pained reflection, 'Il faut tenter de vivre'; Levertov—humorously, half-mockingly—catches herself out: 'The authentic! I said rising from the toilet-seat'. And the whole sequence ('Matins') turns upon the poet's need to redeem from banality a life which at all times threatens to subordinate the identity of the poet within that of the housewife.

It is this kind of relevance that Kinnell's verse characteristically lacks, and the reason is not so much that he hasn't thought about it or doesn't care enough, as that he has not really got an identity or a 'destiny' to relate it to. In this he is typical of a great majority of contemporary American writers.

In 'The Supper After the Last', the egotism referred to above lends a certain weight to the poem: the Valéry-ian platonism is there, but the sexual encounter the poem celebrates gives it body. Once again, there is a curious hiatus between the platonism—'the illusory water' which, among islands, 'bears up the sky'—and the man witnessing it. For the transcendent, as Valéry's poem proves, has also to be witnessed before it can be apprehended as transcendent. Kinnell's first section 'sets the scene'; his second introduces the eschatological properties that are to figure in the allegory he will adumbrate:

> a chair,
> Vacant, waits in the sunshine.
> A jug of water stands
> Inside the door.

But nothing attaches—as far as this reader is concerned, at least—to the chair's becoming 'less and less vacant'. A harmless gag, perhaps, but the general tone is portentous: the word 'host' seems to take both its meanings seriously. Follows the supper itself, a good solid piece of mid-century realism, reminiscent of the verse of Seamus Heaney, in the thoughtful effects, as in its general indebtedness to the early Ted Hughes (e.g. 'the red-backed accomplice busy grinding gristle'.) The fourth section announces the message:

> Opening
> His palms he announces:
> I came not to astonish
> But to destroy you.

The host-seducer disabuses the victim of her 'lech for transcendence'; he teaches her that she is created

> In the image of nothing,
> Taught of the creator
> By your images in dirt.

In the final section, the poet attempts to accomplish what has been promised. The 'Saviour' has promised that he would not 'Astonish but destroy': now in the dusk, everything dissolves:

> The witnesses back off; the scene begins to float in water;
> Far out in that mirage, the Saviour whispers to the world;
> Becoming a mirage. The dog turns into a smear on the sand.
> The cat grows taller and taller as it flees into space.

It is worth noting that such effects are very much Kinnell's own: eclectic as he is, he has his own way with certain physical transformations and he can show the physical turning into the immaterial as few modern poets have.

But the metaphysics nevertheless seem confused. The Saviour says he will 'cut to your measure / the creeping piece of darkness / that haunts you in the dirt'. Having had this done, the victim will be able to 'Step into light'. The saviour/lover will 'make (her) over', and 'breed the shape of your grave in the dirt'. The Saviour, that is, will 'destroy' her/humankind and in doing so, release her/it into death. It comes from an old and tried religious philosophy; but Mr Kinnell hardly endears himself to us by the tone with which he casts himself as Saviour, 'wild man' etc. The whole poem is too evasive to make it easy to attribute identities and roles, but the impression is of a heavy egotism—the speaker/saviour/Kinnell figure is clearly meant to be admired if not revered, and it is a tone we don't easily accept from anybody. Certainly nothing of the guru's authority comes through here, and to succeed the poem badly needed something like it.

Nevertheless, 'The Supper After the Last' is one of the best poems in *Poems of Night*,[6] and the eclecticism so characteristic of the poet is comparatively well absorbed. Crane and Frost are relevant forbears. But one thinks of many others as one works through the volume—Shelley, James Joyce (*viz.* the ubiquitous Bloom figure in section 11 of 'The Avenue C'), the English transcendentalists—*à bien d'autres encore!* Every poet needs his precursors and heroes, and an intelligent recognition and selection of them are a significant part of any young poet's maturation. But all too often Kinnell fails to absorb his influences: he will 'do over', say, Levertov, or Shelley (witness the moon 'crazed with too much child-bearing' in Kinnell's 'Freedom, New Hampshire—3') or Hart Crane (witness the liberal borrowings from 'Harbour Dawn' in Kinnell's 'The River That is East'), much as he consciously 'does over' Robert Frost in 'For Robert Frost'.

What emerges is the care to get the description right which is so typical of mid-twentieth-century verse on both sides of the Atlantic, what we see in Richard Wilbur in America or in Geoffrey Hill in England. This is one of the more distressing symptoms of mid-century *malaise*—a copying of externals, after the methods of the older masters, without any of the

[6] (London 1968).

significance-conferring transcendentalism of those masters. In Kinnell's case, it is again 'The Avenue Bearing the Initial of Christ into the New World' which best demonstrates the point. At the end of the poem Kinnell strives after movement, movement springing from conviction and imparting authority:

> Listen! the swish of the blood,
> The sirens down the bloodpaths of the night,
> Bone tapping the bone, nerve-nets
> Singing under the breath of sleep—

So far so good: it is a distinguished passage, but one needing to lead somewhere for its implications to be redeemed. Kinnell needs to open up America here. And he tries to do so:

> We scattered over the lonely seaways,
> Over the lonely deserts did we run,
> In dark lanes we did hide ourselves. . . .

Presumably what is striven after here is something of that camaraderie of the night so warmly evoked in '*HOWL*'. The mention of Ginsberg's poem—which gets steadily more remarkable as we withdraw from it in time—is enough to demolish the card-house Kinnell has been with some skill putting together. The burning conviction of having lived a confused but spiritually rewarding life that generates the tension and drive of '*HOWL*' has given way to a slightly self-congratulatory in-group feeling: 'We scattered over the lonely seaways. . . .' Reading '*HOWL*', an intelligent square ought to feel stopped in his tracks; reading Kinnell's poem, he could be excused for shrugging, 'So what?'

There may seem to be something of a paradox in having chosen this poem of New York life to represent a poet himself chosen as a representative of a new regionalism. But of course the paradox is, like most others, only skin-deep. It's precisely because Kinnell remains the 'small boy' from Illinois of his 'First Song' that the New York *magnum opus* fails in its purpose. What is best about Kinnell—his often subtle Platonist sense of mutation and transmutation—has its roots in long-mulled-over rural experience, and has no chance to show itself when the poet is on tour in the city. It would be dangerously simplistic to suggest that a significant poetry today has to be spiritually anchored in the city, but the deceleration in American poetry I have spoken of seems to go hand in hand with a tendency to turn aside, and to follow less turbulent paths. (The tendency antedates the Vietnam involvement, incidentally, as Kinnell's work shows.) The Beats were more remarkable than we thought, and America has failed to provide the constant stream of intelligent, dynamic, spiritually adventurous poets which the earlier Beat anthologies seemed to suggest it might possess. In fact, the American establishment has hardly slackened its grip on the creative imagination of its poets.

Kinnell's poetry shows that it is possible to satisfy a good many of the accepted critical criteria without really touching the nerve of human feeling, and that there is a huge difference between ease of movement and voice, between absence of rhetoric and the communication of a human personality. It is superficially impressive and occasionally it is impressive without being superficial, but its absence of any real creative personality, of any deeper spiritual orientation, is typical of much American poetry of its time.

When we turn for instance to the poetry of Donald Hall's anthology,[7] it is to find that the fluency of the poets of the 1920s—Stevens, Moore, cummings—has been to a large extent regained. The pretentiousness, the rhyme- and metre-bound stiffness that characterized the poetry of their immediate academic forbears—Berryman, Roethke, Lowell, Carruth, Shapiro, Eberhart—has been jettisoned. But correspondingly often, the poets have lost the sense of engagement which lifts poems like 'Homage to Mistress Bradstreet' and 'The Quaker Graveyard in Nantucket' into momentary greatness. The traditionally clogging techniques have disappeared, along with the rhetoric and the self-conscious playing upon words, the ironies and the 'daring' conceits. Starting with Richard Wilbur, American poetry re-acquires the facility of the Stevens generation. It becomes obsessed with the duty to avoid the rhetorical gesture and the betraying literary note. Yet the truth is—as we saw in Kinnell—that the ease and freedom that often result seem achingly void of human personality:

> Taking the hands of someone you love,
> You see they are delicate cages. . . .
> Tiny birds are singing
> In the secluded prairies
> And in the deep valleys of the hand.
>
> (Robert Bly, 'Taking the Hands')

Poise, assurance, naturalness, ease of movement—they are all here. It amounts to a new mandarin language—what we see in British poets like Norman McCaig, George MacBeth and John Fuller. Yet why, in the case of the Bly poem, as in so many others, does the verse fail to move us, fail to amount to a significant extension of our emotional compass? Is it that this 'naturalness' is in fact largely negative, a successful evasion of known academic measures—absence of rhetoric and of artifice being proffered as a fulfilled 'naturalness'? And what is 'naturalness'? The questions demand that we go beyond the confines of this discussion, and I must be content to summarize. Milton is 'natural' when he says

> Methought I saw my late espoused saint
> Brought to me like Alcestis from the grave. . . .

[7] *Contemporary American Poetry* (Harmondsworth 1962).

The Chorus in Marlowe's *Faustus* speaks naturally,

> Cut is the branch that should have grown full straight
> And burned is Apollo's laurel bough.

Milton's archaic 'methought' (try 'I thought' for contrast), and the latinate inversions in the Marlowe, not only do nothing to destroy the impression of a direct and powerful utterance, they are precisely what create it. In each case a man is speaking to us, soul to soul, and such an impression is the goal of all art, no matter how rhetorical or ornate its manner.

It is considerations of this kind presumably which led Hazlitt, in a passage which incurred the wrath and ridicule of T. S. Eliot,[8] to discriminate between the 'natural style' of Milton and the 'artificial style' of Pope and Dryden: Eliot's reply was tart and contemptuous, and I am sure he was right; but Hazlitt was more right in his wrongness.

When Robert Bly accordingly informs us that

> There are longings to kill that cannot be seen
> Or are seen only by a minister who no longer believes in God,
> Living in his parish like a crow in its nest.
>
> ('As the Asian War Begins')

I see nothing that could not have been seen in the columns of an aesthetically enlightened *Christian Science Monitor*, the *New Yorker* or a celebrated nineteenth-century diary. In style, idiom, syntax, the sentence is, from one point of view, 'natural': it has nothing literary culled from metrical manuals or books of rhetoric. But the point of view from which it is natural is not the poetic. Whitman is far more 'natural' when he says

> Out of the rolling ocean the crowd came a drop gently to me,
> Whispering and *I love you, before long I die,* . . .

Robert Duncan shows his distinction of mind when he asserts that he took the art of poetry to be 'essentially a magic of excited, exalted or witch-like (exciting) speech, in which the poet had access to a world of sight and feeling, a reality, deeper, stronger, and larger, than the world of man's conventional concerns, and I took the craft to be a manipulation of effects in language towards that excitation.'[9] The early influences Duncan cites, too—George Barker, Dylan Thomas, Hopkins, Edith Sitwell, the Pound of the Chinese *Cantos*—confirm a conception of poetry much broader and more intense than the new academicism, prosy, informative, cool, of which Bly and Kinnell are examples. The real model for Robert Bly's poetry is not normal speech, but certain kinds of prose. There is a style for the pulpit and a style for parliament, and one will not do where the other belongs; there is a journalist's style which will not go in the private

---

[8] *Selected Essays* (London 1932).
[9] *The Years as Catches*, iii.

letter. Bly's 'style' is not easy to place in its stylelessness. A 'terrible detachment' may be the aim: and it is occasionally achieved:

> The city broods over ash cans and darkening mortar.
> On the far shore, at Coney Island, dark children
> Play on the chilling beach: a sprig of black seaweed,
> Shells, a skyful of birds,
> While the major sits with his head in his hands.
>
> ('The Great Society')

Like half the poems in *The Light Around the Body*, 'The Great Society' is overtly political, its technique a montage of synchronous though politically weighted happenings in the manner of Auden's best poems in the 1930s. But Auden's shots are breathtakingly effective, each one chosen with wit and intelligence to epitomize the ethos and the time. Auden never shirks from telling us where he stands. Yet he is far better able than Bly to create the impression of objective veracity:

> Hearing of harvests rotting in the valleys,
> Seeing at end of street the barren mountains,
> Round corners coming suddenly on water . . .
>
> ('Paysage moralisé')

This is a manner we have seen exercised more recently, with hardly less skill, by a number of English poets—in Philip Larkin's 'Here', for instance, and Roy Fuller's 'Pleasure Drive'. It is something English poets excel in, perhaps because the impression of witty finesse in fact derives from a peculiarly subtle sense of social nuance: Auden can moralize his landscape, just as, for instance, Horst Bienek can politicize the landscape of Germany, because of the feeling and inherited instinct that ties him to it. That is to say, the German and the English poet know their place in the world they inhabit and observe, as an American poet hardly knows his, except in the semi-mystical way Robert Frost wed himself to (an in fact alien) Vermont. We touch on an important issue here, one that concerns the content and direction of contemporary American writing in general. Returning to Robert Bly, we are aware of a certain one-dimensionality, even a certain callowness in the political tone:

> Underneath all the cement of the Pentagon
> There is a drop of Indian blood preserved in snow:
> Preserved from a trail of blood that once led away
> From the stockade, over the snow, the trail now lost.
>
> ('Hatred of Men with Black Hair')

Perhaps it is simply that pity in itself is a faintly insulting emotion to declare, perhaps that Bly does not pity enough; perhaps it is that the air of clever objectivity somehow contradicts the emotion avowed; perhaps it is rather that the poem is claiming not to pity, but to indict with objectivity while exploiting the properties of pity (the drop of blood, the

I

pathos-laden incident recalled from a romantic past)—for any, all or some of those reasons, Mr Bly's poem not only fails to move, it positively irritates with its assumption of enlightenment. Now clearly this is an important question, in the light of the political events of the past ten years. The Vietnam involvement has given American poets a dangerous weapon —dangerous, that is, to the survival of their own integrity. The Vietnam war was something on the face of it quite easy to be simply 'right' about. Yet poetry is not the same as political action, nor should it be calculated to lead to political action. To march against the war, to agitate against it was one thing; to write 'a poem' either about it or touched off by it, quite another. If we look back over the political poetry of the past we shall find usually that a certain ambivalence of attitude, or an ambiguity in the situation, or simply a conceptual pluralism, relating the poet to the events or the events to a still greater context, provides a framework which completes the political emotion and at the same time makes it politically heretical. To put it bluntly, there will always be something in the most apparently overt political poem which in a certain sense suborns the immediate political issue, even in being brought to birth by it. An excellent example is Auden's 'Spain 1937', which it has usually been smart to dismiss as agit-prop poetry. In fact, the poem is marvellously delicate in its handling of various ambivalences: it conveys, as perhaps no other poem of its time does, the sheer excitement of the *engagement*, impossible without genuine radical idealism; yet its very time-schema—*yesterday, tomorrow, today*—suggests a greater context, ultimately annihilating the immediate concern. Moreover, the neural rapidity of the verse (Auden never surpassed the controlled momentum of rhythm he achieves here) communicates itself as a lucky dedication of self to an event noble enough to swamp that vacillating individual self which yet remains the vital centre of interest:

> 'I am your choice, your decision; yes, I am Spain'.
> (Auden, 'Spain 1937')

The poem manages, miraculously enough, to be about that decision, yet to be totally authentic in its humanitarian and political dedication. It is nervously 'personal', yet intelligent in its understanding of the historical issues involved; it never loses sight of its intellectual goal, yet it is fully alive to the *ennui* and banality which will—to the poet-intellectual—always be inseparable from utopia and the welfare state:

> Tomorrow perhaps the future: the research on fatigue
> And the movements of packers; the gradual exploring of all the Octaves
>   of radiation;
> Tomorrow the enlarging of consciousness by diet and breathing. . . .

No doubt to the Commissar—even a Lunarcharsky—the poem is hopelessly heterodox, bourgeois in its preoccupation with itself and its own participation. But this is surely the point. The poem should infuriate the Commissar: to be a poem at all, it must explore and express all the spiritual possibilities implicit in the subject, and it can never hold back from any meanings that might detract from the immediate end, the poet's ends being always ultimate, the politician's always more or less immediate.

It isn't fair to expose Mr Bly to Auden near his best: it is a test few modern poets could survive. But it does seem fair to point out the one-dimensionality of Bly's vision of things, his refusal to see, or pretence not to see, the complexity of American life: 'The Great Society' would delight a Commissar. The air of self-congratulation implicit in the cataloguing of America's evils, too, surely goes along with the blinkered vision: Auden, after all, with all his awareness of the evils of capitalist society, never shirks from registering his own complicity in its advantages; indeed the resultant ambivalence informs all his political poetry. Even when he committed himself to some sort of action, as he did in Spain, he never lost sight of his real position, its self-defeating complexities and its obscure ambiguities. Indeed, the nervous excitement of 'Spain 1937', controlled and lucidly expressed as it is, derives much of its pressure precisely from Auden's consciousness of the political heterodoxy of his own participation in the events. Perhaps it would be enough, by way of contrast, to indicate the apathy of Mr Bly's ruminations under farm-house roofs in Minnesota, and the relative complacency of his indictments. And although I have dealt at some length with Auden as contrast with Bly, I could have referred almost as well to Kenneth Rexroth's 'The Bad Old Days' or to Allen Ginsberg's 'America'. The fierce disgust of the Rexroth poem, and the amused amazement of the Ginsberg, become part of a much more complex judgement: they thrust beyond and through their perceptions, and generate energy transcending them in giving them articulation.

But to say these things of Bly—one could say them of a dozen poets of his time—is to go beyond the confines of politicality: as I have observed above of 'Taking the Hands', Bly remains emotionally aloof even in his most personal moments. His 'personal' poems are dominated by a group of sad ideas about evolution, the coming end, degeneration, relapse into barbarism. In fact, for an American poet, they are remarkably hopeless ideas—Spengler without the tension, Toynbee without the grace, T. S. Eliot without the passionate despair:

Some men cannot help but feel it,
they will abandon their homes
to live on rafts tied together on the ocean;
those on shore will go inside tree-trunks,
surrounded by bankers whose fingers have grown long and slender,
piercing through rotting bark for their food.

(Bly, 'Written in Dejection near Rome')

The articulation of the details, as so often in Bly, is skilful. But there seems something confining and oppressive about this very skill: it is a virtuosity of the unclean, practised with a morbid disillusionment that is really a superior stupidity. Well, Mr Bly was dejected: Shelley was dejected, near Naples. But what radiance comes through Shelley's dejection, the dejection that often ensures truthfulness and objectivity, and an exclusion of the ego's more misleading schemes:

> The sun is warm, the sky is clear,
> The waves are dancing fast and bright,
> Blue isles and snowy mountains wear
> The purple noon's transparent might. . . .
>
> (Shelley, 'Stanzas Written in Dejection')

If Shelley's dejection is like this, we might ask . . . But of course, the pristine clarity of the vision, like the final wisdom of its findings—'the sun shall on its stainless glory set,/Will linger, though enjoyed, like joy in memory yet'—is directly related both to the absence of illusion implicit in the dejection, and to the new candour that has stripped off all the veils the phenomenal world is often forced by consciousness to wear.

In Bly we have something entirely different: his dejection is bowed down, as Shelley's was buoyed up, by an implicit ideology. It is an ideology that seems on the face of it very un-American, and so it is, according to a certain image of America that has always been proffered. Yet in another way, it seems very American: through an excess of self-consciousness, modern America is in the process of destroying itself because it has been forced, by the weakness of Europe and by its own technological and economic power, to fill a role it was really quite unready for. That freedom from tradition, that absence of clogging British inhibition, which has always seemed to be such a positive advantage, may in the end prove to be its downfall. I have written elsewhere of the debilitating effects on a generation of English poets of a too strict sense of self-awareness.[10] But incapacitating though it was in Auden and Empson, it was in no danger of eradicating the sense of Englishness which in fact gave rise to it. William Empson, for instance, has remained almost eccentrically English, more himself in his self-ridicule than many a saint through self-affirmation. In the case of America, there has simply not been time enough to build up an intangible but unbreakable core of inward certainty: American poets, thrown back on themselves in this century, have either lacerated themselves, with increasing sterility (Berryman, Lowell, Sexton, Roethke), or, like the regionalist academics, simply lost that sense of themselves which paradoxically they had sought to attain. Self-consciousness is more or less a will-o'-the-wisp. In the case of European writers like Empson and Sartre there was always enough sheerly inherited Englishness or Frenchness—accreted layers of unspoken, subconscious

10 *The Ironic Harvest*, ch. 2.

myth—to make the search for the self at least an amusing hunt for an echo in a labyrinth. And if the echo prove likely to be the sound of the hunter's own footsteps, then the seeker—Beckett, Joyce, Auden, Sartre—could always simply laugh at himself.

When we turn to poetry like Kinnell's and Bly's, we are confronted by one of the possible results of the American quest for a self: nothing. Consider, for instance, a straightforward observation poem like 'Looking at New-Fallen Snow from a Train'. It is constructed antiphonally, a 'descriptive' stanza being followed in each case by an inset quatrain, universalizing the descriptions. It may be that Bly's description simply lacks the quintessential wit to lift it from the ordinary:

> Snow has filled out the peaks on the tops of rotted fence posts
> It has walked down to meet the slough water. . . .
> It rests on the doorsills of collapsing children's houses,
> And on transformer boxes held from the ground forever in the center
>   of cornfields.

At any rate, the antiphonal strophes, good as they are, fail to make us see new-fallen snow again, or to deepen our awareness of our every-day experience:

> A man lies down to sleep.
> Hawks and crows gather around his bed.
> Grass shoots up between the hawks' toes.
> The sword by his side breaks into flame.

Surely this is that technical playing-safe of Theodore Roethke or Geoffrey Hill. The poem, the poem's inner pulse, breaks down into smaller and smaller discrete units, each of which passes muster, and though Bly does not play the sorts of tricks Berryman plays with his broken units, he still takes no risks in assembling them. In this case, the criticism is sharpened by the 'Absolute' content of the units—'Each blade of grass is a voice', 'The sword by his side breaks into flame'. The timeless present tense, moreover, in which so much of Bly's poetry is purveyed, reinforces the impression of a man all the time refraining from making a statement, from committing himself: what does it mean that 'the sword by his side breaks into flame'? Of course, one can understand easily enough the onto-logical schema Bly is adumbrating; but such a schema is in fact empty, its variables unequipped with values, unless the poet step forward and declare himself. And lest I be misunderstood, I should emphasize that by declaration I do not mean anything necessarily vocal, oratorical or ex-pressionistic. Some extra content or accent in the images must give them direction and supernal identity. In Bly's poetry, such accent is more or less wholly absent. So that when Bly exclaims, for instance, 'What a joy to smell the flesh of a new child!' (in a poem sadly entitled 'Evolution from the Fish') I personally experience a distinct chill: the utterance seems inhuman, at least it would, if it were really an exclamation at all, in a real human voice. But this is not a voice, not a human being speaking, but a factitious literary convention, an assemblage of vocables, a device among words. And in this, Bly's poem, like his poetry in general, is characteristic of the transatlantic academic mainstream.

Introducing his *Contemporary American Poetry* in 1962, Donald Hall chose Robert Bly and Louis Simpson to illustrate his notion of 'a kind of imagination new to American poetry'. But the two instances he gives us remind us irresistibly of the not dissimilar claims Cleanth Brooks made thirty years before on behalf of the Fugitive poets. In Bly's lines

> In small towns the houses are built right on the ground
> The lamplight falls on all fours in the grass . . .
> ('Driving Towards the Lac Qui Parle River')

we have surely precisely the kind of metaphysical conceit Allen Tate occasionally brought to a high pitch of intensity:

> The singular screech-owl's tight
> Invisible lyric seeds the mind. . . .
> (Tate, 'Ode to the Confederate Dead')

The more literal-minded animism of Bly's image perhaps suggests rather the fog-cat figure in Eliot's 'Prufrock', but the general indebtedness to the academic conception of the metaphysicals and the symbolists is surely too apparent to justify Mr Hall's talk of a new kind of imagination. And Louis Simpson's 'angel in the gate, the flowering plum, / Dances like Italy, imagining red' surely comes out of Stevens ('Here and there, an old sailor, / Drunk and asleep in his boots, / Catches tigers in red weather'), if not indeed out of Andrew Marvell's 'Green thoughts in a green shade'.

From Emily Dickinson, through Frost and Stevens to Ransom and Warren, American poetry has always been fertile in such conceits, and one would have thought that Simpson's image crossed too narrow a terrain, linking too little together, to stimulate the palate jaded on the curries of mid-century metaphysics. Hall's mention of Trakl in the context has its point, as we see occasionally in Bly:

> The split-tailed swallows leave the sill at dawn;
> At dusk, blue swallows shall return.
> (Bly, 'Where We Must Look for Help')

But the German poet's 'blaue Luft' crosses more frontiers, uniting more diverse possibilities than Bly's swallows. They are surely too carefully 'split-tailed', and once again we have notice of that mild, over-careful accuracy we can trace everywhere in the mid-century. We are talking, as always, of presiding spirits of feeling and belief, and these take their scale and identity from the conceptual framework. They are not—by any means —to be simplemindedly equated with a raw crudeness of belief. The example of Charles Simic provides interesting contrast.

Simic seems to me a better poet than either Bly or Kinnell, yet his poetry's most distinctive quality (I hesitate to say straight out its strength) seems actually to be its most signal limitation. This is a brilliant fluency of invention that enables him to sustain a uniform texture through a whole poem and a whole collection of poems—*Dismantling the Silence* [11]— without its ever offering much substance for the mind to feed on. One would call it a natural metaphysics, except that the word suggests the essentially knotty poetry of the English seventeenth-century poets, and of their modern imitators, poetry which rewards the reader's intelligence with flight, and his diligence with release. The metaphysical conceit detonates in the mind at some depth from the surface, and the labour taken to unravel its complexities generates a light which is logically but mystically related to the substance of the figure chosen. In Charles Simic we have something totally different. He was born in Yugoslavia and in a very material sense has remained a Slav rather than become an American. If we opened his book *Dismantling the Silence* at random, knowing nothing of the author but the verse offered, we could be forgiven for supposing it the work of some unimaginably brilliant translator, whose Balkan originals were blessedly free of the machine-age and of Americanization. For even the substance of his verse—its material referents—are European and rural rather than American and urban. Simic has 'taverns', 'fabled highwaymen', 'hermits', 'gallows', and so on. He speaks significantly at one stage of 'my migrant's bundle'. Otherwise, the world his poetry creates—or rather with its brilliant semantic evacuation *de*-creates—is that of central Europe—woods, ponds, peasant furniture (even the word 'table' has an archaic ring in Simic). We could say that he de-creates his world in an effort to forestall its non-existence: he makes mysterious the actual (America, now) and then de-materializes the mystery. So, his basic modus is the fairy-tale or *skazka*. There are faintly Audenesque allegories (in 'Explorers', especially), but in the main Simic practises his fabulous transmogrifications of the real after the fashion of the European poets he so often recalls—Juhasz, Kocbek and Popa. The peasant simplicity (which can comprehend so much subtlety) from time to time brings Sergei Esenin to mind:

> Outside they are opening
> Their primers
> In the little school
> Of the cornfield.
>
> (Simic, 'Summer Morning)

[11] (London 1971).

Compare the symbolism of this with Esenin's beautiful 'Easter':

> Of pine and willow smells the air;
> Heaven slumbers now, now sighs.
> In the pulpit of the forest there
> A sparrow reads his Psaltery.
>
> (Esenin, 'Easter' [my translation])

The difference is that Esenin's metaphors are guaranteed by a basic, simple Christianity, where Simic's serene hedonism owes no allegiance to any creed or Church. It is the mid-century natural religion that breathes through these lines:

> Further ahead, someone
> Even more silent
> Passes over the grass
> Without bending it.
>
> —And all of a sudden
> In the midst of that silence
> It seems possible
> To live simply
> On the earth.
>
> ('Summer Morning')

Yet at the same time as the verse breathes like Rexroth's the beneficence of the grass, it is strangely hellish, almost as if it is expecting at any moment to break into the black-and-white horror film to which it is the technicolor contrast. In poems like 'Marching', Simic writes as a European in a more than technical sense:

> Blood rose into my head shaking its little bells.
> In the valley the glow died in the udder of the cow.
> The trees ceased playing with their apples
> And the wind brought the sound of men marching.

An American poet cannot, of course, know such things, as the occasional efforts to imagine them (Stevens's 'Dry Loaf', for instance, or service poems like Eberhart's 'Fury of Aerial Bombardment') inform us. 'The worst is still to come,' Simic begins, in 'For the Victims':

> Then, at last, we'll get a true taste of ourselves.
> The ear will crawl back into the eye
> Like Jonah into his whale.

The modus is that of Bosch or Dali. Simic creates a world in which only emptiness finally exists: it is a world of silence, waiting for the unspeakable to happen, or subsisting in the limbo left afterwards:

And always someone's missing
and the light left for him in the window
is now the oldest one on earth
and still each day his shirt, bowl and spoon
are washed by his mother and sister
and the front door is unlocked just before nightfall
because that's the time
when the ones who have been gone so long
like to return.

('Invention of the Invisible')

Except that no-one *is* going to return, ever. The 'place' that is invented (or that invents—the genitives are both subjective and objective) is hellish and beautiful at once, like the summer of 1939, emptied of adults, witnessed by children who register the menace without really being able to experience it:

Two uniformed men
stroll along the empty streets,
solemn and slow
they advance, stopping
to look in shop-windows,
into parked cars.

One of them wears a brass whistle,
the other hides a gun with a silencer.
There's no-one left on the earth.

(Simic, 'Invention of the Place')

The scene might be present-day midwest America; but it isn't. Or perhaps it is a limitation in Simic, here at least, that he doesn't make enough of the possible correlations: the past is re-imagined, it is not really seen in its relations with the present. He invents finally 'Nothing':

I didn't notice
while I wrote here
that nothing remains of the world
except my table and chair.

('Invention of Nothing')

The dimension of menace in Simic becomes metaphysics in itself, and if we compare his handling of certain motifs with that of Kinnell, for instance, we surely cannot doubt his superiority:

And this chair will reveal itself
As the exact shadow of someone
Who stood here all this time

(Simic, 'For the Victims')

The chair in the Kinnell poem ('The Supper After the Last') was merely waiting for a seducer: as Simic uses the image, it takes its place in an evocation of a world of political happening. Yet again, Simic finds in 'nothing' a strange beauty:

> Why am I so quiet then
> and so happy?
>
> (Simic, 'For the Victims')

Few things are so chilling as this happy peace resting on a surface tension of fear, and Simic's nothing is outlasted by 'the throat of an empty beer-bottle'. It seems strangely appropriate that this brilliant yet oddly vacuous volume should end with a *jeu d'esprit* on *'errata'*.

Conclusion

Towards Decadence

This book began, somewhat apologetically, with sociology, and with sociology it is obliged to end. Or rather, perhaps, with a warning about sociology. In the final analysis, there is no real explanation of the rises and falls that take place in the history of art. We cannot really say, for instance, why it was that French poetry was (on the whole) better than English towards the end of the nineteenth century; any more than we can explain to any satisfactory degree why English poetry was (on the whole) more interesting than French at the beginning of the same century. The question of the 'maturation' of a literature is a different matter, as I have tried to explain already. Nobody—arguably—was 'better' than Melville in 1850. Yet the literary critic would be failing in his job if he did not establish that Melville was 'provincial' as Flaubert, say, and Dickens were not.

The reasons for the arrival of 'the American moment' might perhaps be accepted. But such an acquiescence would by no means commit us to the view that American writing is always going to be as impressive as it was ten years ago. We must admit finally just that 'it comes and it goes': America produced good poets in the 1950s and early 1960s; now it seems to me that the exciting edge has gone, to be replaced by a cool cleverness. Inevitably, the Vietnam war will be offered as in some sense explanatory. But the war could explain only the origination of poetry, not its quality—the direction, not the scale, of achievement. The war might be taken to explain the attitudes in the poetry, not the poetry fostered by those attitudes. Thus, the sociologist could point to the fact that America indulged in an orgy of what the Russians call *samokritika* ('self-criticism' seems bland for the purpose) that lasted from the late 1960s to the middle 1970s. With the humiliation of withdrawal from Vietnam, the nation to all appearance relapsed into an equally consuming orgy of self-congratulation. Black rebels quietened down and even recanted, students stopped rioting, people started to say 'The system works', and so on. The sociologists and social historians of the future might plausibly describe the mood of America in such terms. Yet, although some kind of sociological analysis is essential to any thoroughgoing understanding of literature, it would really be valueless to draw up a list of sociological factors of this kind, relate them to the literature corresponding to them, and think that one set of facts has 'explained' the other. There seems, on the face of it, no reason why American poetry and fiction should be less good now than it was twenty years ago. What we can profitably do, nevertheless, is to warn against the effect upon American writing of certain developments in American society which may, as an evil byproduct, inhibit the emergence of new literature of the highest quality. There is a real danger, it seems to me, that the academic proliferation since World War Two is generating a quite spurious set of values, erecting factitious masterpieces, and preventing the recognition of the real ones.

Nothing can make good works come. The masterpieces of the next twenty years may be in formation now in a backroom in Manchester or a semi-detached house in Belfast or a seminar-room in Ithaca. Nothing, equally, can stop their coming. But there is a genuine threat—a threat the more dangerous because from an unexpected quarter—in the appropriation of much of the traditional territory of creative writing by the universities. To some extent, this means that the 'values' in the literary work are at the mercy of the Foundation that sponsors the university. This is a familiar equation of culture–sociology, and it is a situation artists have on the whole been able to cope with: it places the work produced in the 'free' world in the same category as that produced in the totalitarian states in which all writers are 'protected'. But it also means that the writing is dependent on the taste and judgement of academics. Without pretending that we can describe all academics in the same way, we can say that literary academics are simply better at judging the work of the past than that of the present. That is to say, they are safe when the 'life' of literature has hardened into tradition. They recognize value more easily when it is dead. They can see what *was* the life of a work of art. But when it is alive and new, they tend to be blind to it. The academic *qua* human being is just as capable of responding to the life of live art as anyone else. Not *more* capable, necessarily: there may well be describable empirical reasons why certain sorts of intelligence avoid the island of university life, and certain sorts (strong perhaps in some regions, weak in others) choose it, rather than let themselves go in the sea of ordinary life. The academic, that is to say, may have more in common with the botanist or the philosopher than with the poet or even the journalist-critic. He tends to excel at the study and classification of certain recurrent features of his particular phenomena (which happen to be works of art) rather than with the response to them as living organisms. To recognize something as new and alive requires of itself a sort of creative spontaneity —spontaneity of a kind which is often an embarrassment to the academic critic. Moreover, his profession demands more than can properly be given as 'response'. As literary academic, he is required to *process* what he experiences in literature—to make out a good case. Now the essence of the living work of literature is that only with time does it harden into fully apprehensible shape. With time, its values can be apprehended as form. But at the time it is created, the truth is that it cannot be described formally. Hence, the academic feels happier with work that is already canonized.

We may note than even with the work of the past, its essential value, what makes it alive among so many dead imitations, is precisely what is most difficult for the critic to describe. Sooner or later, he must get down to a value judgement, and a value judgement is primarily a cry, a grunt of recognition, an ostensive gesture rather than an articulated utterance. This is perhaps why so many literary critics in America have loftily disdained the value judgement as being irrelevant to the practice of the literary critic. Perhaps it is so; it depends how we conceive of the critic's task. There would appear to be a certain dishonesty in concentrating upon the 'analysis' or 'description' of works of art which are only identifiable as such by the exercise of a value judgement. But this does not matter so long as the critic concerns himself with the work of the past, when he can pretend that he is the critic that walks by himself and all works are alike to him.

When we come to the work of the present, these unanswered questions about the nature of criticism do matter. Now, over the past decade, the whole structure of university life in the 'free world' has altered, and with it the relations between the university and the society in which it lives (and on which it ultimately depends). No longer is the literary scholar exclusively concerned with the past, with cataloguing, transcribing, editing, describing the works already canonized as the tradition. Increasingly, the literary academic in America—as indeed elsewhere—is concerned with what is being produced *now*. They are also, increasingly, themselves responsible for the production of what is studied. Because of the nature of the processes involved, the work that is applauded is work which is designed to please the class that applauds. It used to be said that American poetry was written by professors for professors. When the professors involved were men like John Crowe Ransom and Allen Tate, the main result of this syndrome was a quietly inbred conservatism, feeding on itself and on the works of the past that occupied so much of the poets' waking attention—largely in disdain of the contemporary world, which was an unpleasant, grubby place from which the professors were avowed fugitives.

The situation confronting us now is quite different. If we compare the poetry of the American neo-metaphysicals with that of their English contemporaries, I have suggested, we can hardly help being struck by the difference between an academic verse which had lost contact with the 'real' world, and a 'political' poetry which applied its academic and intellectual researches to the real world which formed them, or rather perhaps to their relations with that world. Today, the contrast we are called upon to make is between the literature of the academic circuit and that of the poets and novelists who exist outside it. The neo-metaphysicals had a reasoned and deeply felt social basis: their very conservatism was moral— like that of F. R. Leavis—so that the concern with the poetry of the past cohered with their outlook on the present. Today, no such coherent good faith informs the academic poet. He is caught up in a self-perpetuat-ing machinery of 'values' which have increasingly little to do with the actual needs of man. The contemporary academic writer is remorselessly trendy—to use that handy English term which mocks what it denotes— but he shares the limitation of vision endemic to the academic mind in general: he recognizes values only when they are dead, and, therefore, reproduces updated parodies of the past and offers them as life. The past it updates may be very recent: Robert Coover's *Prick Songs and Descants* takes the brilliantly witty routines that erupt throughout Burroughs' *Naked Lunch* and turns them into heavy parables—pabula, in other words, that the academic mind can digest. The product is empty, heartless, brutal: but it is also mercilessly satirical—an 'indictment of the violence of our society' and so on—so that its very heartlessness and brutality are qualities the academic feels pleasure in savouring. For the really sick thing about Coover's pieces is not the subject-matter, but the fact they are meant to be enjoyed in the academies: the enjoyment has a 'moral' and intellectual justification. The work has none of the ruthless brilliance of the earlier Burroughs, none of that savage humour that makes *The Naked Lunch* one of the funniest as well as one of the most penetrating books of the postwar period. The living moment, the impulse of dis-covery that is 'immortalized' in the work of art, in other words, has been processed into attitude. *The Naked Lunch* is violently obscene; *Prick Songs and Descants* is mere dirty-jokery—the more so for its laboured messages about the brutality of the police and the idiocies of conven-tional morality.

The gap between the living art of the present and its intelligent recep-tion by a large public has been closing fast ever since the end of the 1950s. The old *avant garde* schism—that gulf so carefully preserved by the artist and so necessary to the production of the work—has been narrowing since the first successes of the absurdist dramatists in Paris: the long runs of Beckett and Ionesco proved that the relations between the absurdists and their progenitors—Joyce and Artaud—were becoming tenuous. The public is still a limited one. But the situation is nevertheless radically changed from what it was: the elite group that likes hard-edge painting and electronic music is, still, a public. The old *avant garde* isola-tion has gone for good, and with it the particular tensions that held the art of Europe together over a whole century.

The central argument of this book has been that American writers and painters were responsible for breaking down the *avant garde* separatism. Sociologically and culturally, it was an achievement of enormous significance—not only for America but for the whole world. It was also an achievement beyond the reach of any European culture, and in itself deeply related to the American sociocultural experience. It was almost as if American writers—I think at this point particularly of Ginsberg, Burroughs and Kerouac—had to have the courage of American vulgarity before they could most effectively exploit their own creative gifts. Kerouac's first novel, *The Town and the City*, is written in a formal, correct third-person narrative; Ginsberg's early poems—'High Scholars of the Sublime', for instance—are polite and rather studious; Burroughs's *Junkie* was a brilliant but formally constricted piece of first-person reportage. In all three cases a technical breakthrough (Kerouac's totally honest' first-person style, Ginsberg's Whitman chant-tone, Burroughs's anarchically free hallucinations) accompanied an inner release, a new sense of values. The resultant development of the pop culture of the 1960s is part of modern social history, and I am already conscious of having trespassed into the territory so well mapped by Theodore Roszak. The point I wish to make here is simply that the world in which the intellectual listens habitually to music not so far removed from (and in many cases the same as) the music listened to by people who used to be called low-brow, is a world from which the old *avant garde* structure of alienated artist and ignorant moneyed populace has largely disappeared, and this is a significantly American achievement.

It is also a matter of historical and technological evolution, and it has set the artist new problems. The problem facing the American writer today is twofold—the increasing monopolization of new writing by academics, and the new roads to big financial success undreamed of by the old *avant garde*. Because his profession requires a certain kind of performance from the academic critic, he himself prefers the poem or novel in which the 'point' has already been made by the writer, i.e. which is already academic. But the real life and newness of the alive, new poem are precisely what can't be processed, formalized according to academic satisfaction. Later, when the work has been absorbed into the tradition, the academic can go through the motions of 'formalizing' the poem, translating its life into symbols so that it all sounds inferential and 'scientific'. This is an old ruse: the response is assumed, the work's external properties are enumerated and described as if the value judgement tacitly assumed were *necessarily* entailed. In fact, the real life of the poem—the source of its value—cannot be tabulated, and the value judgement can never be entailed. Literary criticism, except where it confines itself to 'scholarship', invariably uses rhetoric to disguise its slide from 'is' to 'ought'.

The art of poetry in the academies, therefore, becomes trapped in a cycle of production–appreciation–analysis–reproduction. The new factor, of course, is that those who sit in judgement and confer the approval that—somewhere along the line—leads to livelihood are, increasingly, those who also produce. Those who produce are chosen on the strength of qualities which appeal to those who judge. And so on. Added to this is the new trendiness: academics today eschew the 'academic', the studious, the archaic—the emotional even—like the plague. So a meretriciousness has got built into the cycle: increasingly, the work set up for approval is empty, facile, smart.

This is of course a vision of possibilities rather than a description of the state of affairs. But there are all too many signs that much of its content already exists: a great deal of what is sometimes referred to as the New Fiction seems to me to be of this kind—vacuous contrivance without real life. It is, moreover, almost avowedly disposable. A culture which allows itself to flaunt an ephemeral literature seems to have run into serious trouble. What is disposable is, after all, simply trash. Clearly a statement of opinion without the supporting argument required in this sort of territory can carry little weight of itself. Yet one is surely to be allowed one's prognostications: mine here is that the New Fiction is largely without real importance, that it is badly overrated, and that the foreign critic has to be more than usually careful in this instance to keep his head before he swallows the euphoric sales-talk of an establishment that seems to have entered a phase of cultural imperialism.

Finally, another judgement that must excuse itself as prognostication: American culture seems at this moment to be in grave danger of orienting itself excessively towards criticism. American criticism is impressive in its range and energy, but it *is* criticism, and, *pace* Northrop Frye, criticism is, so far as the life and endurance of a culture are concerned, parasitic. Literature can do without criticism (though it would be bad for it to have to do so) but criticism cannot—logically—exist without literature. Beneath the restless dissections of American criticism there is something, perhaps, characteristic to the nation, a puritan refusal to accept experience and the world as they are, a dissatisfied sense that the work of art is not enough in itself, and that there must be some theory to make the experience it offers seem more important. The disease is of course by no means unique to America: it affects all cultures now. But, like most disorders of the technological era, it has tended to get out of hand more spectacularly in the United States than elsewhere, and the United States, after all, has still a more precarious hold on its own cultural identity than the European societies which will never, with the worst will in the world, quite be capable of competing with American extravagance.

Bibliography

John Berryman

Poems (Norfolk, Conn.: New Directions 1942)
The Dispossessed (New York: W. Sloan 1948)
Homage to Mistress Bradstreet (New York: Farrar, Straus & Cudahy 1956; London: Faber & Faber 1967)
His Thoughts Made Pockets & The Plane Buckt (Pawlet: Claude Fredericks 1958)
Seventy Seven Dream Songs (London: Faber & Faber 1964)
Berryman's Sonnets (New York: Farrar, Straus & Giroux 1967; London: Faber & Faber 1968)
His Toy, His Dream, His Rest (New York: Farrar, Straus & Giroux 1968; London: Faber & Faber 1969)
Love and Fame (New York: Farrar, Straus & Giroux 1970; London: Faber & Faber 1971)
Delusions, etc. of John Berryman (New York: Farrar, Straus & Giroux 1972; London: Faber & Faber 1972)
Selected Poems 1938–1968 (London: Faber & Faber 1972)
Recovery (London: Faber & Faber 1973)

Robert Bly

Ducks (Menomonie, Wis.: Ox Head Press 1967)
'Silence in the Snowy Fields', and other poems (London: Cape 1967)
The Light Around the Body (London: Rapp & Whiting 1968)
The Morning Glory: Prose Poems (San Francisco: Kayak Books 1969)
Forty Poems Touching on Recent American History (Boston: Beacon Press 1970)
The Teeth-Mother Naked at Last (San Francisco: City Lights 1970)
The Sea and the Honeycomb (Boston: Beacon Press 1971)
Jumping Out of Bed (Barre, Mass.: Barre Publishers 1973)
Sleepers Joining Hands (New York: Harper & Row 1973)
Old Man Rubbing His Eyes (Greensboro, NC: Unicorn Press 1975)
Selected Poems (Middleton, Conn.: Wesleyan UP 1975)
Translations:
Neruda and Vallejo: Selected Poems, ed. Robert Bly; trans. Robert Bly, John Kneopfle and James Wright (Boston: Beacon Press 1971)

The Fish in the Sea is not Thirsty, by Kabir (Calcutta: Writers Workshop 1972)

Gregory Corso

'*The Vestal Lady on Brattle*', *and other poems* (San Francisco: City Lights 1955)
Gasoline (San Francisco: City Lights 1958)
The Happy Birthday to Death (New York: J. Laughlin 1960)
Long Live Man (New York: J. Laughlin 1960)
The Geometric Poems (Milano 1966)
Elegiac Feelings American (New York: New Directions 1970)

Hilda Doolittle

Sea Garden (Boston: Houghton Mifflin 1916; London: Constable 1916)
'*Heliodora*', *and other poems* (New York and Boston: Houghton Mifflin 1924)
Collected Poems of HD (New York: Boniand Liveright 1925, 1940)
Red Rose for Bronze (New York: Random House 1929)
The Walls Do Not Fall (New York and London: Oxford UP 1944)
The Flowering of the Rod, by HD (New York and London: Oxford UP 1946)
Selected Poems by HD (New York: Grove Press 1957)
'*Bid Me to Live*', *a madrigal by HD* (New York: Grove Press 1960)
Helen in Egypt (New York: Grove Press 1961)
Hermetic Definition (Oxford: Carcanet 1972)

Robert Duncan

Selected Poems (San Francisco: City Lights 1959)
Roots and Branches (New York: Grove Press 1960; London: Cape 1969)
A Book of Resemblances: Poems 1950–1953 (New Haven: Henry Wenning 1966)
The Years as Catches: First Poems (1939–1946) (Berkeley: Oyez 1966)
Bending the Bow (New York: New Directions 1968; London: Cape 1971)
Derivations: Selected Poems 1950–1956 (London: Fulcrum Press 1968)
The First Decade: Selected Poems 1940–1950 (London: Fulcrum Press 1968)
The Opening of the Field (New York: Grove Press 1960; London: Cape 1969)
Caesar's Gate: Poems 1949–1950 (Berkeley: Sand Dollar Press 1972)

Allen Ginsberg

> '*HOWL*' *and other poems* (San Francisco: City Lights 1959)
> *Empty Mirror: Early Poems* (New York: Corinth 1961)
> *Reality Sandwiches, 1953-60* (San Francisco: City Lights 1963)
> '*Kaddish*' *and other poems, 1958-60* (San Francisco: City Lights 1967)
> *TV Baby Poems* (London: Cape Goliard 1967)
> *Planet News, 1961-1967* (San Francisco: City Lights 1968)
> *The Fall of America, Poems of These States, 1965-1971* (San Francisco: City Lights 1972)
> *First Blues: Rags, Ballads and Harmonium Songs, 1971-1974* (New York: Full Court Press 1975)

LeRoi Jones

> *Preface to a Twenty Volume Suicide Note* (New York: Totem Press 1961)
> *The Dead Lecturer: Poems* (New York: Grove Press 1964)
> *Dutchman* and *The Slave: Two Plays* (New York: Morrow 1964)
> *The Baptism: A Comedy in One Act* (New York: Sterling Lord 1966)
> *Blackart: Poems* (Newark, NJ: Jihad Productions 1969)
> *Black Magic: Sabotage, Target Study, Black Art; Collected Poetry, 1961-1967* (Indianapolis: Bobbs-Merrill 1969)
> *It's Nation Time*, by Imamu Amiri Barak (LeRoi Jones) (Chicago: Third World Press 1970)

Galway Kinnell

> *What a Kingdom It Was* (Boston: Houghton Mifflin 1960)
> *Flower Herding on Mount Monadnock* (Boston: Houghton Mifflin 1964)
> *Poems of Night* (London: Rapp & Carroll 1968)
> *Book of Nightmares* (Boston: Houghton Mifflin 1971)

Denise Levertov

> *With Eyes at the Back of Our Heads* (New York: New Directions 1959)
> *O Taste and See: New Poems* (New York: New Directions 1964)
> *The Jacob's Ladder* (London: Cape 1965)
> *The Sorrow Dance* (London: Cape 1968)
> *A Tree Telling of Orpheus* (Los Angeles: Black Sparrow Press 1968)
> *Relearning the Alphabet* (London: Cape 1970)
> *To Stay Alive* (New York: New Directions 1971)
> *Footprints* (New York: New Directions 1972)
> *The Poet in the World* (New York: New Directions 1973)
> *The Freeing of the Dust* (New York: New Directions 1975)

Translations:

> *Selected Poems by Guilleric* (New York: New Directions 1969)

Robert Lowell

> *Lord Weary's Castle* (New York: Harcourt Brace 1946)

The Mills of the Kavanaughs (New York: Harcourt Brace 1951)

Life Studies (London: Faber & Faber 1959; New York: Farrar, Straus & Cudahy 1961)

Poems 1938–1949 (London: Faber & Faber 1960)

Imitations (New York: Farrar, Straus & Cudahy 1961; London: Faber & Faber 1962)

The Voyage, and Other Versions of Poems by Baudelaire (New York: Farrar, Straus & Giroux 1961; London: Faber & Faber 1968)

For the Union Dead (New York: Farrar, Straus & Giroux 1964)

Selected Poems (London: Faber & Faber 1965)

The Old Glory (New York: Noonday Press 1966; London: Faber & Faber 1966)

Near the Ocean (New York: Farrar, Straus & Giroux 1967)

Notebook, 1967–1968 (New York: Farrar, Straus & Giroux 1969)

The Dolphin (London: Faber & Faber 1973)

For Lizzie and Harriet (London: Faber & Faber 1973)

History (London: Faber & Faber 1973)

Michael McClure

Hymns to St Geryon, and other poems (San Francisco: Auerhahn 1959; London: Cape Goliard 1969)

Dark Brown (San Francisco: Auerhahn Press 1961; London: Cape Goliard 1969)

The New Book: A Book of Torture (New York: Grove Press 1961)

Ghost Tantras (San Francisco: City Lights 1967)

Star (New York: Grove Press 1970)

Gargoyle Cartoons; or the Charbroiled Chinchilla (New York: Delacorte Press 1971)

Rare Angel (Write with Raven's Blood) (Los Angeles: Black Sparrow Press 1974)

September Blackberries (New York: New Directions 1974)

Jaguar Skies (New York: New Directions 1975)

Man of Moderation: Two Poems (New York: F. Hallman 1975)

Marianne Moore

Complete Poems (London: Faber & Faber 1918, 1967)

Poems (London: Egoist Press 1921)

Selected Poems (New York: Macmillan 1935; London: Faber & Faber 1935, 1969)

What Are Years? (New York: Macmillan 1941)

Nevertheless (New York: Macmillan 1944)

Collected Poems (New York: Macmillan 1951; London: Faber & Faber 1951)

Like a Bulwark (New York: Viking 1956; London: Faber & Faber 1957)

O To Be a Dragon (New York: Viking 1959)
The Arctic Ox (London: Faber & Faber 1964)
Tell Me, Tell Me: Granite Steel and Other Topics (New York: Viking 1967)

Charles Olson

O'Ryan, 2, 4, 6, 8, 10 (San Francisco: White Rabbit Press 1958)
The Maximus Poems (New York: Jargon/Corinth Books 1960)
The Distances (New York: Grove Press 1961)
O'Ryan, 1, 2, 3, 4, 5, 6, 7, 8, 9, 10 (San Francisco: White Rabbit Press 1965)
Selected Writings, ed. Robert Creeley (New York: New Directions 1966)
In Cold Hell, In Thicket (San Francisco: Four Seasons Foundation 1967)
Archaeologist of Morning (London: Cape Goliard 1970)

Kenneth Patchen

Before the Brave (New York: Random House 1936)
The Dark Kingdom (New York: Ganis & Harris 1942)
An Astonished Eye Looks Out of the Air (Waldport, Oregon: United Press 1945)
Pictures of Life and Death (New York: John Feselberg 1946)
Sleepers Awake (New York: Padell 1946)
Cloth of the Tempest (New York: Padell 1948)
First Will and Testament (New York: Padell 1948)
Red Wine and Yellow Hair (New York: New Directions 1949)
See You in the Morning (London: Grey Walls Press 1949)
The Journal of Albion Moonlight (New York: New Directions 1950)
Hurrah for Anything (Highlands, NC: J. Williams 1957)
When We Were Here Together (New York: New Directions 1957)
Double Header: Poemscapes and a Letter to God (New York: New Directions 1958)
Out of the World (New York: New Directions 1958)
Poemscapes (Highland, NC: J. Williams 1958)
Selected Poems (New York: New Directions 1958)
Because It Is (New York: New Directions 1960)
Love Poems (San Francisco: City Lights 1960)
Hallelujah Anyway (New York: New Directions 1966)
But Even So (New York: New Directions 1968)
Collected Poems (New York: New Directions 1968)
Aflame and Afun of Walking Faces (New York: New Directions 1970)
Wonderings (New York: New Directions 1971)
In Quest of Candlelighters (New York: New Directions 1972)

Kenneth Rexroth

The Phoenix and the Tortoise (Norfolk, Conn.: New Directions 1944)
The Signature of All Things (New York: New Directions 1950)
Thirty Spanish Poems of Love and Exile (San Francisco: City Lights 1956)
In Defence of the Earth (London: Hutchinson 1959)
The Dragon and the Unicorn (Norfolk, Conn.: New Directions 1963)
The Homestead Called Damascus (New York: New Directions 1963)
Collected Shorter Poems (New York: New Directions 1967)
Collected Longer Poems (New York: New Directions 1968)
With Eye and Ear (New York: Herder & Herder 1970)
Sky, Sea, Birds, Trees, Earth, House, Beasts, Flowers (Santa Barbara, Calif.: Unicorn Press 1973)
New Poems (New York: New Directions 1974)
Translations:
100 Poems from the Chinese (New York: New Directions 1956)
100 Poems from the Japanese (New York: New Directions 1959)
Poems from the Greek Anthology (Michigan: University of Michigan Press 1962)
Selected Poems of Pierre Reverdy (New York: New Directions 1969)
Love and the Turning Year: 100 More Poems from the Chinese (New York: New Directions 1970)
The Orchid Boat: Women Poets of China, tr. and ed. Kenneth Rexroth and Ling Chung (New York: McGraw-Hill 1972)

Theodore Roethke

The Waking: Poems 1933–1953 (Garden City, NY: Doubleday 1953)
Words for the Wind (Garden City, NY: Doubleday 1957; London: Secker & Warburg 1957)
I Am! Says the Lamb (Garden City, NY: Doubleday 1961)
The Far Field (Garden City, NY: Doubleday 1964; London: Faber & Faber 1964)
Collected Poems (Garden City, NY: Doubleday 1966; London: Faber & Faber 1968)
Selected Poems (London: Faber & Faber 1960)

Anne Sexton

To Bedlam and Part Way Back (Boston: Houghton Mifflin 1960)
All My Pretty Ones (Boston: Houghton Mifflin 1962)
Selected Poems (London: Oxford UP 1964)
Live or Die (London: Oxford UP 1967)
Love Poems (London: Oxford UP 1969)
The Book of Folly (Boston: Houghton Mifflin 1972)

Transformations (London: Oxford UP 1972)
The Death Notebooks (Boston: Houghton Mifflin 1974)
The Awful Rowing Toward God (Boston: Houghton Mifflin 1975)

Charles Simic

What the Grass Says (San Francisco: Kayak 196?)
Somewhere Among Us A Stone Is Taking Notes (San Francisco: Kayak 1969)
Dismantling the Silence (New York: Braziller 1971; London: Cape 1971)
White [by] *Simic* (New York: New Rivers Press 1972)
Return to a Place Lit by a Glass of Milk (New York: Braziller 1974)

Philip Whalen

Like I Say (New York 1960)
On Bear's Head (New York: Harcourt, Brace 1969)
Severance Pay (San Francisco: Four Seasons 1970)

John Wieners

Ace of Pentacles (New York: Carr & Wilson 1964)
The Hotel Wentley Poems (San Francisco: Dave Haselwood 1965)
Nerves (London: Cape Goliard 1970)
Selected Poems (London: Cape 1972)

Richard Wilbur

'*The Beautiful Changes*', *and other poems* (New York: Harcourt, Brace 1947)
'*Ceremony*', *and other poems* (New York: Harcourt, Brace 1950)
Things of the World (New York: Harcourt, Brace 1956)
'*Advice to a Prophet*', *and other poems* (London: Faber & Faber 1962)
Walking to Sleep (London: Faber & Faber 1963)
Opposites (New York: Harcourt, Brace, Jovanovich 1973)

Index